Jefferson and the Gun-Men

How the West Was Almost Lost

Also by M. R. Montgomery

In Search of L.L. Bean

A Field Guide to Airplanes

Saying Goodbye

The Way of the Trout

Many Rivers to Cross

JEFFERSON
and the
GUN-MEN

How the West Was Almost Lost

M.R. Montgomery

Illustrations by Gerald Foster

THREE RIVERS PRESS
NEW YORK

Copyright © 2000 by M.R. Montgomery

Published by Three Rivers Press, New York, New York
Member of the Crown Publishing Group

Random House, Inc. New York, Toronto, London, Sydney, Auckland
www.randomhouse.com

THREE RIVERS PRESS is a registered trademark and the Three Rivers Press colophon is a trademark of Random House, Inc.

Originally published in hardcover by Crown Publishers in 2000.

Printed in the United States of America

Library of Congress Cataloging-in-Publication Data

Montgomery, M.R.
Jefferson and the gun-men: how the West was almost lost / by M.R. Montgomery.—1st ed.
1. West (U.S.)—Discovery and exploration. 2. Louisiana—Discovery and exploration.
3. West (U.S.)—History—To 1848. 4. Jefferson, Thomas, 1743–1826. 5. Lewis, Meriwether, 1774–1809. 6. Clark, William, 1770–1838. 7. Burr, Aaron, 1756–1836.
8. Wilkinson, James, 1757–1825. 9. Pike, Zebulon Montgomery, 1779–1813.
I. Title.
F592.M685   2000
978'01—dc21   99-046547

ISBN 0-609-80710-2

10 9 8 7 6 5 4 3 2 1

First Paperback Edition

Introduction

By way of foreword and caution to the readers:

Any new account of the acquisition and exploration of Louisiana, that last huge remnant of French North America, depends on several lifetimes of scholarship by various professional historians. For sheer labor, and utter brilliance, the prize must be shared by two men. Donald Jackson edited *The Letters of the Lewis and Clark Expedition with Related Documents, 1783–1854* in two volumes for the University of Illinois Press; the most recent edition is 1978. Jackson also produced the definitive edition of *The Journals of Zebulon M. Pike,* in two volumes, published by the University of Oklahoma Press in 1966. Gary E. Moulton, at the University of Nebraska, Lincoln, has given us nine volumes of the journals, daybooks, and associated papers of that most famous exploration in United States history, all under the general title of *The Journals of the Lewis & Clark Expedition.* Two more volumes are planned. All of these works, by both men, are on every page witness to thorough scholarship, considerable insight, and almost unbelievable endurance. "The task of writing history," a professor once remarked to a class of new graduate students at the University of Oregon, "requires first, and foremost, one particular attribute." He paused, and we held our breaths, waiting for enlightenment. "An iron butt."

Reading history, on the other hand, should be less taxing. This book has, I hope, jettisoned all intellectual baggage. It is entirely innocent of construction, deconstruction, reconstruction, and post- and pre-modernism. If it is politically correct, I am pleasantly surprised but take no credit for that outcome. Students are hereby warned not to rely on its quotations from the journals of Lewis and Clark for term papers at the collegiate level. While the quotations are brought to the reader as accurately as possible, they have also been translated into modern, conventional spelling and, when it does not change the meaning, into regular English grammar. The originals can be easily located in Moulton, *op. cit.* Persons who read term papers for a living (underpaid graduate students, for the most part) are inordinately fond of things like *op. cit.* and exactly quoted material, including wrong tenses and amusing (to them) misspellings. This is a form of sic *(sic)* humor. It has been my experience that you should not try to get these people to agree that conventional English makes quotations easier to read and understand. That is something akin to trying to teach a hog to whistle. It is impossible, and will only annoy the pig.

This book is organized on the sensible principle elucidated by the Red King as he instructed the White Rabbit on the proper way to give testimony. "Begin at the beginning," the King said, very gravely, "and go on till you come to the end, then stop."

M. R. Montgomery

Illustrations

Portraits

Maps

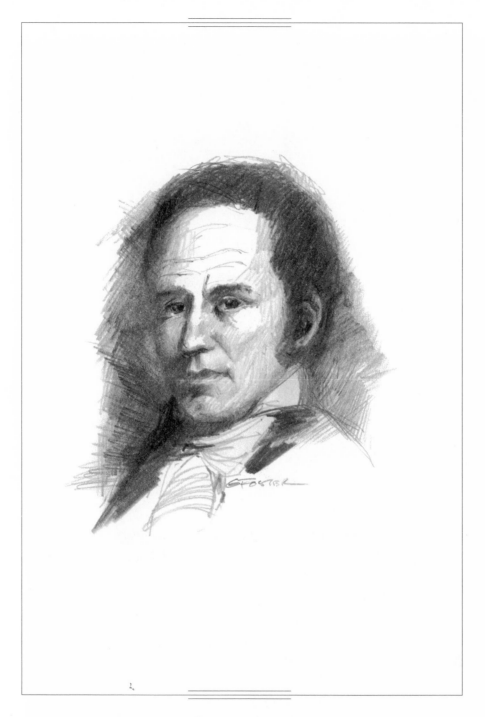

WILLIAM CLARK

ZEBULON PIKE

JAMES WILKINSON

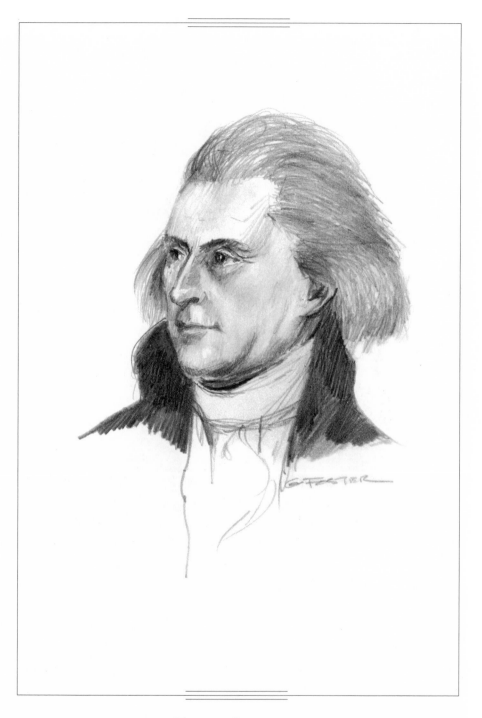

THOMAS JEFFERSON

Meriwether Lewis

AARON BURR

"I could tell you my adventures—beginning from this morning," said Alice a little timidly; *"but it's no use going back to yesterday because I was a different person then."*

"Explain all that," said the Mock Turtle.

"No, no! The adventures first," said the Gryphon in an impatient tone: *"explanations take such a dreadful time."*

—*Lewis Carroll,* Alice's Adventures in Wonderland

". . . we are all gun-men.*"*

—*Thomas Jefferson*

1

February 1803, Washington City

THOMAS JEFFERSON, third president of the United States, is writing a lengthy letter to William Henry Harrison, military governor of the Northwest Territory; that is, of the scarcely settled lands between the Mid-Atlantic states and the Mississippi River.

Jefferson is his own secretary, and he is almost certainly alone as he writes. The federal government of the United States is very small and highly personal. Jefferson will make a copy of this letter on an unsatisfactory machine called a letterpress that transfers a little of the ink from the original to a flimsy, almost transparent, sheet of paper. The third president is probably sitting in a pair of frayed trousers, wearing house slippers and a coat against the chill. He looks rather more like Bob Cratchit than Ebenezer Scrooge as he instructs Harrison on Indian policy and the role of the western country, across the Mississippi, in managing the Indian problem. We will get to the content of the letter in a moment, but if you are going to understand some of the history about to unfold, it is good to stop a moment and recognize that the entire Executive Office of the President consists of this middle-aged man, wearing casual clothes, alone in a rented house in Washington City.

Technically, Jefferson has a personal secretary. This is Captain Meriwether Lewis, U.S. Army, who is about to depart on an exploration of the country west of the Mississippi by ascending the Missouri River to its source and then proceeding down some western river to the Pacific Ocean. Lewis is probably unaware of the contents of the letter. He is a secretary in name only. Jefferson has brought him to Washington to prepare him for a more serious job than copying and filing letters. Lewis expects to lead a clandestine mission through a country that belongs to France, to Napoleon Bonaparte. The government funds for the expedition are a well-kept secret, the result of a concealed congressional vote. And Thomas Jefferson is keeping an important development hidden from the Congress: Two American envoys are about to begin negotiations to buy the island of New Orleans at the mouth of the Mississippi. Jefferson wants New Orleans so that trade down the Ohio and Mississippi Rivers can move freely to the sea from the still lightly settled American soil along the Ohio River and the eastern bank of the Mississippi. It is a few decades before railroads, and goods from Ohio and Kentucky and Mississippi must move on the rivers. The island of New Orleans, first in French, then Spanish, and now again in French hands, is a barrier to free passage.

Napoleon has his little secret, too. Shortly after reacquiring the Louisiana Territory for France (Napoleon is governing Spain with puppets and relatives), Napoleon wants to trade it in for cash. He's not only ready to sell New Orleans, he wants to dump the whole of Louisiana—that is, all of the vast country north of Spanish Mexico and south of British Canada and west of the Mississippi River as far as to the Continental Divide, to the very headwaters of all the western tributaries of the Mississippi. Napoleon is going to need money for more adventuring in Continental Europe, and he is bleeding whole armies into a failing attempt to hang on to France's Caribbean island colony of Santo Domingo (today's Haiti and Dominican Republic). But Jefferson has no idea that this Louisiana real estate deal is in the works. So, when we read Jefferson's secret addition to his otherwise official letter to Harrison, we must remember that America stops at the Mississippi, with or without the island of New Orleans.

Jefferson begins by telling Harrison that the nation's policy "is to live in perpetual peace with the Indians, to cultivate an affectionate attachment from them, by everything just and liberal which we can do for them within the bounds of reason." Having said that, Jefferson then instructs Harrison on how to get rid of every last independent Indian tribe between the Atlantic states and the Mississippi.

Harrison is to encourage a series of government trading posts selling at a discount (to undercut the few itinerant French-Canadian traders and the increasing number of British traders coming down from Canada). "We shall push our trading . . . and be glad to see them run in debt, because we observe that when these debts get beyond what the individuals can pay, they become willing to lop them off by a cession of lands. . . ."

Jefferson understands that some recalcitrant Indians may be unwilling to sell and "be foolhardy enough to take up the hatchet." In that case, Harrison is to seize "the whole country of that tribe" and drive them across the Mississippi. This would "be an example to others, and a furtherance of our final consolidation."

Jefferson is almost finished. As usual, the letter is in his own hand. And now he draws a firm line of emphasis under his last words. The contents of this letter, he reminds Harrison, "must be kept within your own breast, and especially *how improper to be understood by the Indians. For their interests and their tranquility it is best they should see only the present age of their history.*" So, from the very beginning, we see the Indian policy of the United States for what it is: all agreements and all promises are temporary, expedient, and faithless.

There will be times, in the next few years, when almost everyone involved in this business of Louisiana will be happier if they live only in the *future* age of their history. The wildest plots, the most grandiose dreams, will thrive as long as the actors move toward an imaginary future bliss while ignoring present realities. Only a few will even attempt to judge the practicality of their desired future. They are an odd mixture of schemers, dreamers, revolutionaries, blackguards, and braggarts. Before it is done, Jefferson, that most complicated and opaque personality, will have played more than one of those parts.

2

❧

April 1803, Harpers Ferry, Virginia

CAPTAIN MERIWETHER LEWIS is at this federal armory on the Potomac
River just forty miles upstream from Washington. It is located in
"Virginia." It will still be in Virginia when John Brown raids the arsenal in October 1859, hoping to raise a slave revolt in the South. West
Virginia, now the legal address of the historic armory, is a creature of
the Civil War, created in 1863 to carve a free state out of the old rebel-
lious dominion. Lewis is ordering rifles for his expedition up the
Missouri River, and by civilian standards they are simple and unre-
markable, a shorter version of the Kentucky "long rifle," and bored for
a heavy, 50-caliber round ball. For the United States government,
accustomed to issuing smooth-bore muskets, Lewis's rifles are so
unusual and fine that they get their own model number—1803.

Lewis acquires government-manufactured tomahawks and knives
to trade with the Indians. He orders gunpowder and lead that later will
be melted and poured into molds to make balls for the rifles. Perhaps
from his own invention, he has the gunpowder packaged in lead boxes.
One box of powder is enough to fire as many balls as the box, melted
down, will make. Lewis may earn a reputation as the luckiest explorer
in the history of the Western world, but he will certainly be the best
prepared.

The "Iron Canoe," as he styles it, is Lewis's pride and joy, and he
spends most of a month at Harpers Ferry perfecting the design and
supervising the manufacture of this watercraft. His orders are to
explore the Missouri River to its very headwaters. He will start in a
large wooden boat, or maybe two; he is still planning that part. And
he knows at some point he will need a smaller boat as he ascends, fol-

lowing his orders to the letter, until the wide Missouri has become a trickling spring on some distant mountainside.

An Iron Canoe, with wrought-iron ribs and covered with the hides of animals killed by some of the expedition's fifteen U.S. Army Model 1803 muzzle-loading rifles, is going to be the answer. Lewis writes Jefferson and proudly announces that his Iron Canoe, with only forty-four pounds of wrought-iron parts, will float 1,770 pounds of cargo and crew once they get the hides in place. It is the principle of Archimedes at work. There are no dimensions for the canoe that survive, but we can work it out. If the Iron Canoe displaces 1,770 pounds of water, that means it displaces thirty cubic feet of water. As a rough but reasonable estimate, working from the displacement figure, the magnificent Iron Canoe is about twenty feet long, averages three feet wide at the waterline, and will sink six inches or so into the Missouri when fully loaded and manned. It will be approximately the size of today's Maine summer camp "war canoes" and carry no more freight than a dozen juvenile campers' worth of weight.

Jefferson expected Lewis to stop by Harpers Ferry, place his orders, and move on to Philadelphia for a series of crash courses in medicine, botany, geology, and celestial navigation. But the Iron Canoe keeps him pinned down for an extra three weeks. He explains later that he has to stay to supervise the forging of the parts because no one there could understand the purpose of the work. They are excellent craftsmen at Harpers Ferry, but not very good at fashioning the improbable. It might help if Lewis could tell the workers that he needs this light framework so that it can be carried 2,000 miles to the headwaters of the Missouri River, but that, for several more weeks, is a secret. As far as Lewis knows at this point, his expedition will be in French territory. Meriwether Lewis has a stubborn streak, which is a very important asset to an explorer. The iron ribs are at last crafted to his high standards and packed in a waterproof canvas.

The next time Lewis sees the framework for the Iron Canoe is when it is unpacked at the Great Falls of the Missouri River in June 1805. That is the first time that Lieutenant William Clark, his co-commander of the expedition, hears about the Iron Canoe. Clark, as you will see, is an extremely practical human being and does not become less so when confronted with the Iron Canoe. Lewis is four years younger than Clark, and much more imaginative (and moodier). It shows in their faces: Clark is literally thick-skinned, his red-haired blond complexion is weather-beaten by his age of thirty-four. Lewis is thin-skinned, his cheekbones prominent; his aquiline nose and downturned mouth give him the look of a dour Scotch-Irish Presbyterian minister. Lewis once was Clark's junior in the army and he will soon ask his old commanding officer along for this journey because he knows Clark is steady as a rock. Clark will be ballast when the expedition reaches turbulent waters.

3

May 1803, Washington City

THOMAS JEFFERSON'S "present age of history," the one he recommended the Indians pay attention to, is turning topsy-turvy this springtime. His envoys report from Paris that a new America is aborning. Napoleon doesn't want to sell New Orleans for a few million dollars; he will only sell New Orleans if the United States buys Louisiana, all of it. The boundaries are vague, but it presumably includes all of the "high ground" of the Mississippi River and its tributaries. Louisiana's borders are at the headwaters, the line drawn by trickling sources of the great rivers scattered north and south along the Rocky Mountains and arcing east into Minnesota.

In February, when Meriwether Lewis began his preparations, exploring Louisiana was merely interesting. By May, it is still a mysterious landscape, but it is an American possession, and that intensifies the "philosophical" questions. Lewis and Clark will be exploring American territory and Jefferson wants new scientific discoveries to add to his country's glory. He has high hopes that his explorers will find great curiosities, *American* marvels in this terra incognita. He is thinking about the possibility of living woolly mammoths still surviving on those distant prairies. He desires to learn if horses, known in the modern world only as domesticated animals, truly run in wild herds on the Great Plains. It seems impossible. Of all the animals on a Virginia gentleman's estate, none is so difficult to breed, to rear, to manage as the horse. Like any farmer, Jefferson understands that a missing cow will turn up, sooner or later. A horse gone astray is as good as dead if left to its own resources.

Corresponding with William C. C. Claiborne, governor of Mississippi Territory, soon to be named governor of Louisiana, Jefferson writes as the proprietor, the trustee, of a land larger than the original United States of America and all their territories and possessions combined. We own a new world, but it is still a secret. He writes to Claiborne as if nothing more consequential had occurred than the long-anticipated acquisition of New Orleans.

Claiborne's first priority, Jefferson writes, is to continue to purchase Indian lands along the eastern shore of the Mississippi. The great river is to be fortified, to become an English Channel, an augmented natural barrier between us and them, whoever they may be. "I think it all important," Jefferson writes, "to press on the Indians, as steadily and strenuously as they can bear, the extension of our purchases on the Mississippi from the Yazoo" in Claiborne's territory, south toward New Orleans.

And then Jefferson lets slip, probably deliberately, a hint that the United States may do what it wishes with the land across the Mississippi. "I omitted to mention," while discussing land purchases from the southeastern tribes, "that I think it would be good policy in us to take by the hand those of them who have emigrated from ours to the other side of the Mississippi [he is being coy, not saying the

"French" side of the river], to furnish them generously with arms, ammunition, and other essentials, with a view to render a situation there desirable to those they have left behind."

This is his first idea of what in the world to do with the American west. He uses an odd word, a common word used oddly, to explain: By graciously oversupplying those who migrate across the great river, we can "toll them in this way across the Mississippi, and thus prepare in time an eligible retreat for the whole." Tolling is a way to hunt ducks. You put live, wing-clipped ducks out in front of the hunter's blind, and "toll" the free-flying birds to the guns.

Meriwether Lewis is in Philadelphia when this letter is sent. He is studying botany and geology, the better to find curiosities when he crosses the Mississippi and ascends the Missouri until it is nothing but a streamlet. It is never clear, from anyone's correspondence or Lewis's journals, if he understands, or ever will understand, that the land he is going to explore is, for the present age, intended to be nothing more than a vast dumping ground for eastern Indians.

4

June 1803, Philadelphia

MERIWETHER LEWIS, in the midst of his crash courses in botany, mineralogy, to which are added medicine and celestial navigation (this for the purposes of drawing an accurate map of the Missouri River and the Oregon country) writes his old acquaintance, William Clark, a former, now retired, army officer. He is more than Lewis's senior—in the Northwest Territory Indian wars, he was Lewis's commanding officer for six months. Lewis asks Clark to join him on the expedition: "My plan is to descend the Ohio in a keeled boat, thence up the Mississippi to the mouth of the Missouri, and up that river as far as its navigation is practicable with a keeled boat, there to prepare canoes of bark or raw-hides, and proceed to its source, and if practicable pass over to the waters of the Columbia or Oregon River and by descending it reach the Western Ocean." Lewis offers Clark a co-captaincy, an equal share in the leadership of the expedition. It will be the first, and the last, American military unit ever intended to be commanded by two equals. It defies all logic, and all tradition.

In fact, Clark is commissioned a second lieutenant, a reality hidden from the members of the expedition for the next three years. The official excuse is that giving Clark a captaincy when he comes out of retirement would upset regular army officers patiently awaiting their own promotion. Somehow, it works. It is the first of several enormous strokes of luck that Lewis and Clark get away with this masquerade. The enlisted men never know the truth and live in equal fear and equal admiration of the "two captains."

Lewis has a written order allowing him to pluck twelve enlisted men from army posts along the Ohio and Mississippi. He asks Clark, who is living on the frontier in the Indiana Territory, to find as many more civilians—vigorous, woods-wise, bachelor bravehearts—and authorizes him to hire them on as members of this corps of discovery.

"Thus my friend," Lewis writes, "you have a summary view of the plan, the means and the objects of this expedition. If there is anything . . . which would induce you to participate with me in its fatigues, its dangers and its honors, believe me there is no man on earth with whom I should feel equal pleasure in sharing them as with yourself."

They are an odd couple. Lewis is a bit aloof, and suffers fools badly. Clark is moderately gregarious with anyone—Indians, French-Canadians, mixed bloods, women, children—and shows occasional signs of a sense of humor, a trait rarely perceptible in Meriwether Lewis. There is another difference. Clark is matter-of-fact, persistent, and almost serene. Meriwether Lewis has moods.

One more difference between them survives to this day in their journals. We will dispense with it now and not bring it up again. Meriwether Lewis could spell. Most of the differences between his orthography and modern English prose are the results of haste, of contemporary standards that differ from ours (the possessive "its" he naturally spells "it's"), and more rarely, ignorance. William Clark would have trouble spelling "fir tree" if you didn't spot him the vowels. He found writing painful, and for most of the voyage west and back would limit himself to copying Lewis's journal notes into a second volume. When Lewis, for whatever reasons, does not keep a daily journal, poor Clark does his best.

Now he writes back to Lewis that he would "chearfully join you in an 'official Charrector' " even though the enterprise is "fraited with many difeculties." From now on we will correct everyone's spelling. Otherwise, dear reader, you could get the impression that William Clark is a buffoon, and that would be a dreadful mistake.

5

Summer 1803, In Philadelphia and on the

Southern Frontier of the United States

THREE CHARACTERS HOVER on the edge of this story, waiting to move onstage in starring roles. One of them is the Vice President of the United States, Aaron Burr. He is spending the summer of 1803 in Philadelphia. While Meriwether Lewis is studying basic sciences, anticipating his expedition, Burr is engaged in his two favorite pastimes: writing letters to his daughter, Theodosia, and fornicating. This summer, it is with a woman named Celeste, otherwise unidentified. Burr, a widower, has an insatiable craving for the comforts of female flesh, the pleasures of which he describes, in good humor and good taste, to Theodosia, his "Dear Theo."

Burr is a brilliant, charismatic man who is thoroughly disliked by Thomas Jefferson, who has the best of reasons. For the rest of Burr's enemies, including George Washington and Alexander Hamilton, the causes are more complex. Burr has offended Washington's sensibilities ever since they first met in Cambridge, Massachusetts, in 1776. Burr asked for a commission, and Washington (and his aide, Hamilton) found nothing to recommend the short, downy-cheeked Princeton graduate. Burr does become an officer, but only after trailing along as a civilian on the assault of Quebec. After the war, Hamilton comes to regard him with undisguised loathing. Burr has two great faults. He has no center of gravity politically. In an age of ideology and political passion, Burr sees politics as a means to his personal ends. He is very modern, and his world is not. Worse, he adores the company of women, including the few with whom he has spent time without proceeding to sexual relations. He is a woman's man in an age of men's men.

Jefferson's reason for despising Burr is simple. They ran as a ticket for the presidency and vice presidency in 1800. Quite naturally, they won the same number of electoral votes. It occurred to Burr that because they had jointly defeated John Adams, a Federalist, there was no legal reason why he could not be elected president. All he need do is add but a few Federalist votes to those of his Republican electors and he would outpoll Jefferson in the electoral college. ("Republican" will evolve, by the time of Andrew Jackson, into the parent of today's Democratic party; the Federalists will simply self-destruct.) This is the only time such an upstart idea is attempted. It ends as a possibility with the Twelfth Amendment to the Constitution, which requires electors to declare for a presidential and vice-presidential candidate on the ballot. The amendment passes in fourteen of the seventeen state legislatures in 1804, but not in Delaware, Connecticut, or Massachusetts. It was from those latter two New England hotbeds of anti-Republicanism that Burr had hoped to gain a Federalist elector or two and become president.

Burr does retain a small and loyal following of New York City Republicans. There is always room in politics for the charming rascal. Burr wants to be the emperor of his own realm, and when he is not making the two-backed beast with Celeste, he spends the summer mulling a multitude of schemes to acquire power. He was almost the third president of the United States, and power is even a greater seducer than Celeste. Burr is quite short, by the way. This may have something to do with the lengths to which he will go to acquire his own realm.

Down in southern Illinois, an overweight, florid, impressive-looking man named General James Wilkinson commands the U.S. Army posts scattered along the southern frontier of the United States territories. He is forty-six years old, and the personal hero of one member of his command, a Lieutenant Zebulon Montgomery Pike, who has just turned twenty-four years of age.

By an odd coincidence, Wilkinson is the quite victorious political and professional enemy of George Rodgers Clark, noted explorer and Indian Wars veteran. William Clark is George Rodgers's baby brother. Burr and Wilkinson are both veterans of the northern battles of the American Revolution, serving under Generals Gates and Arnold. They both have jaundiced views of George Washington. Wilkinson is an experienced traitor, Aaron Burr is seriously considering becoming one.

Wilkinson has been in the pay of Spain, possessors of Louisiana from 1787 until 1803, when Napoleon regained it merely for the purpose of selling it the United States. Wilkinson trades Spain military intelligence and blarney for dollars. The Spanish regard him as a bit of a fool and a liar, but he is their fool, their liar, and he is paid regularly.

Zebulon Montgomery Pike has admired Wilkinson since little Zebulon M. was an army brat living on a post commanded by the imposing general. The general is Pike's ideal, the very model of a military man. Pike is an extremely enthusiastic young man, set on making something of himself. He is, to use the word in its most neutral sense, naive. In his quest for glory, Pike's greatest asset will be his truly astonishing vigor.

It will be a year or two before these three men become involved in the exploration of Louisiana. Wilkinson will try to milk it for more gold. Burr, with the promised aid of Wilkinson, will attempt seizing it outright. The last, Pike, will follow their orders with all his considerable enthusiasm.

6

August 1803, Monticello

THOMAS JEFFERSON is home from the capital, escaping the dread heat and disease of that swampland in summertime. The nation's capital is not only miasmal, it is malarial, and even the inured, annually reinfected, are affected with each summer's plague.

Monticello is but a hint of what it will become. Older parts of the building, never completed or properly closed in to the weather, are being torn down. They are victims of neglect, orphans of his political campaigns and official duties. New work is going up in their place and the would-be mansion is all noise and dust in the daytime. All that is truly finished is an airy space encompassing Jefferson's bedroom, library, and study, a sort of studio apartment of the mind at the east end of the south wing of the house. Here he works and sleeps, rousted each morning by the light in the dawn-admiring windows.

The public announcement of the acquisition of Louisiana, on July 4, has alarmed and amused the Federalists. Paying 15 million Yankee dollars for a howling wilderness full of Indians is either folly or a southern plot to extend the power of the southern states by annexing more land to be filled up with slave-drivers, unruly frontiersmen, and Republican politicians. It sounds like a great deal of money, at a time when the entire federal debt totaled only $77 million, but in today's dollars, it's only about $166 million out of a federal debt of $5 *trillion*. The existing west, on the borders of the Mississippi, is already staunchly Republican (by which we would mean today Democratic), anti-Federalist, and developing its own culture—as a society it is a bit boastful, even swaggering. Jefferson is writing to John Breckenridge, an ally and a senator from Tennessee:

> *"Objections are raising . . . against the vast extent of our boundaries. . . . These federalists see in this acquisition the formation of a new confederacy, embracing all the waters of the Mississippi, on both sides of it, and a separation of its eastern waters from us. . . .*
>
> *"If it should become the great interest of those nations [the states and territories beyond the Allegheny Mountains] to separate from this [the original thirteen states], if their happiness should depend on it so strongly as to induce them to go through that convulsion why should the Atlantic States dread it?*
>
> *"We think we see their happiness in their union [with us], and we wish it. But events may prove it otherwise; and if they see their interest in separation, why should we take side with our Atlantic rather than our Mississippi descendants? It is the elder and the younger son differing. God bless them both, and keep them in union, if it be for their good, but separate them, if [it] be better. . . .*
>
> *"But above that, the best use we can make of the country for some time, will be to give establishments in it to the Indians [now living] on the east side of the Mississippi, in exchange for their present country. . . . When we shall be full on this side, we may lay off a range of states on the western bank from the head to mouth, and so, range after range, advancing compactly as we multiply."*

This is a slight change. No longer is the Mississippi a permanent, defensible, watery border, a protective moat between America and the wilderness. It is a temporary thing, and Jefferson now sees orderly states, tier upon tier, moving west across the continent. Once again, the Indians will be mere temporary residents, living, as Jefferson says, "in this present age."

7

September 1804, On the Ohio River

MERIWETHER LEWIS is under way at last, away from Pittsburgh, Pennsylvania, headed for the West. He is in his newly built, large wooden boat, with a hired crew of rivermen. The Ohio River, from Pittsburgh to the Mississippi River at Cairo, Illinois, runs so low in the end-of-summer drought that Lewis's boat cannot pass over the "ripples," as they are called. This is an annual problem, and along the river a steady trade in dragging loaded boats across the shallow riffles and exposed bedrock ledges occupies local farmers.

One must assume that Lewis spoke with a southern accent. He certainly notices the "Yankee speech" of the local residents, a voice he associates with greed. A stuck boat, of course, is a minor windfall to a subsistence farmer with a few pair of oxen and a rope. Greedy "Yankee farmers" and cheerless "Yankee settlements" annoy Captain Lewis no end. In silent condemnation, he underlines the word *Yankee* on occasion.

It is not entirely his fault that he is descending the river in a time of predictable difficulty. Yes, he is paying for spending too long at the Harpers Ferry arsenal, perfecting his Iron Canoe. But the problem increases in Pittsburgh, where the only boat builder capable of designing and building the great keeled boat for the expedition is an alcoholic who has trouble getting started until noon, when the brain fog clears.

It is an excellent boat, and it survives days of being dragged along the bottom, innumerable bumps against rocks and gravel bars. Days go by when the crew is lucky to make a mile, digging out gravel in front of the boat, prying it along, walking it back and forth in search of sufficient water to float it down.

Rank has its privileges. At Burffington's Island, lying between Virginia (now West Virginia) and Ohio, while the men were "getting the boat through this long ripple I went on shore and shot some squirrels. My men were very much fatigued with this day's labor," he writes in his journal, "however, I continued on until dark." As usual, given a choice, Lewis camps that night on the Virginia shore; he has no desire to camp on the Yankee, Ohio, bank.

His orders, once the expedition began, require him to take account of the natural history of the west. He practices on the way down the Ohio, as he encounters a peculiar migration of squirrels. Both banks, except for scattered farms, are solid woods, but for some reason the Ohio squirrels are swimming to Virginia, from the west bank to the east, which, as the river slants across mid-America, gives the squirrels a generally southerly direction. Lewis is mystified. Are they starving? After checking the woods on both shores and finding acorns and other nuts equally abundant, he gives up worrying about the cause and starts foraging himself:

"I made my dog take as many each day as I had occasion for, they were fat and I thought when fried a pleasant food. They swim very light on the water make pretty good speed. My dog was of the Newfoundland breed, very active, strong and docile. He would take the squirrels in the water, kill them, and swimming, bring them in his mouth to the boat." This is Seaman, Lewis's large, well-trained black dog. He is useful, in the next few years, because he can amuse and amaze the Indians with his obedience to command.

When he reaches Kentucky, Lewis picks up Clark, and several strong young men, Kentucky woodsmen, whom Clark enlists in the

Corps of Discovery. Clark brings his personal companion, York, who has been Clark's slave since they both were children. York is huge, agile, and self-reliant. Like Lewis's dog, York will sometimes be encouraged to amuse and astound the Indians. He has some rare talents, this York. Among other things, he is an excellent swimmer, unafraid of the water.

8

~~~

November 1803, Washington

THE RELATIONS BETWEEN the United States and Great Britain are somewhere between cool and belligerent. Britain is fighting, with only temporary truces, a decade-long war against France, an empire that stretches from the Mediterranean Sea to the Baltic, and has allies east to the borders of Russia. Britain continues its embargo on any cargo headed for France; America insists on free passage—"neutral ships carry neutral goods" is the popular expression. Britain not only takes "contraband" intended for Napoleon's empire, but insists on taking British subjects off American vessels, pressing them into service aboard his majesty's warships. Britain even denies the right of its citizens to change nationality by emigrating: born British, die British. England is a small country, and desperate for seamen. With hems and haws and starts and stops, this inevitable clash over trade and freedom will become the War of 1812.

President Jefferson has no intention of warring with Britain, and even less intention of treating Britain with deference. He has little opportunity to plague the government of Britain, and no desire to challenge it. But he has his ways of showing his disgruntlement.

Just arrived in Washington is the new British ambassador, Anthony Merry. He is a pretentious, small, and little-experienced civil servant, accompanied by a wife who is, if it is possible, even more self-impressed. Thomas Jefferson, after years as ambassador and secretary of state, is acutely aware of the rules and customs of diplomacy. He agrees to an appointment to receive Anthony Merry and accept his credentials as minister from the Court of St. James.

Mr. Merry dresses for the occasion. This is not easy. After putting on whatever sort of underwear that pleases him, Merry dons the appropriate uniform. He begins with a pair of white silk hose, and then pulls on a pair of white breeches which come to just below his kneecaps. They are fastened with large gilt buckles on the outside of each knee joint.

He puts on a white collarless shirt, which will soon be covered up entirely. His jacket is single-breasted, with a short standing collar. The opening of the jacket barely meets in front, where it is held together with nine gold buttons that link the embroidered edges of the jacket. There are two similar buttons at the rear of the jacket, pinching it in to his waist. Each of the two tails of the jacket have two more buttons at the bottom of their skirts. The buttons bear the British Royal Crest. The jacket has gilt embroidery completely covering the face, plus a four-inch wide band across the bottom and around the cuffs. The material underneath the embroidery on the cuffs and collar is blue, the rest of the jacket is red. His shoes are black patent leather with a large gilt buckle across the arch. He is carrying a cocked hat of black beaver felt adorned with a black silk cockade, gold bullion (not mere gilt) braid, and a brim bordered with black ostrich plumes. He wears a regulation dress sword in a black scabbard on a white sword belt. The last touch is a pair of white gloves.

Thus buffed, powdered, and starched, he makes his way to Jefferson's rented Washington home. A Negro slave shows him to the parlor. The president of the United States is waiting. Jefferson is sprawled comfortably on a couch and does not rise. The envoy of His Royal Highness George III is greeted by a man wearing scuffed slippers, stockings none too clean, corduroy trousers ungathered at the knee, and the president's "small clothes," his underwear, no cleaner than his stockings, are visible under a common-looking, well-worn, unbuttoned wool jacket. It is a magnificent unspoken insult.

When Stratford Canning, a famous British diplomat of the mid-century, arrives in Washington a dozen years later, members of the staff recall a detail that either did not occur or that Merry does not include in his dispatch to London. Jefferson, Canning is told, would listen to Merry make his introduction, and then flip one of the slippers in the air and catch it again, dexterously, on his toe.

And Jefferson is not finished tweaking the British lion's nose. Just three days later, he gathers the envoys of all the great powers, and their wives, to a gala dinner at his lodgings. The ministers of Spain and France, combatants against England, and Mr. and Mrs. Merry, upholding the dignity of Britain, avoid one another during the stand-up reception and await the opportunity to go in to dinner. Mr. Merry expects, if not the place of honor at the table, at least some comfortable distance from Napoleonic France and its puppet government of Bourbon Spain.

But Jefferson is not about to ease his misery. Dinner is announced, and the guests are left to their own devices to find their way to the table and then to find a place to sit. Jefferson remarks later that it is a "democratic custom," which he calls, "pell mell." Since Mr. Jefferson's other guests include humbler persons, far removed from diplomatic protocol, and since Mr. Jefferson serves marvelous food and classic French wines, Mr. and Mrs. Merry are almost trampled by the general rush toward the dinner table.

Mr. Merry is not amused. His dispatches home recount each slight in detail. He prays that his superiors, even the King himself, will feel the sting of Jefferson's deliberate insult.

In just six months, Anthony Merry will be having dinner with a much more sophisticated, genteel, well-mannered American politician. Merry will dine with Aaron Burr, and they will discuss a remarkable plan to rub Mr. Jefferson's nose in his own free and democratic customs.

9

March 1804, New Orleans

JAMES WILKINSON, commanding general of the United States Army, is corresponding with several Spanish officials. Spain owns East and West Florida, that is, Florida as we know it, plus the Gulf Coast west almost to the Mississippi River. Spain still possesses Old Mexico, New Mexico (which then includes Texas and Arizona), and California. The border between colonial Spain and the new American Louisiana is vague. There are conflicting claims. These will have to be negotiated someday, and if such negotiation fails, there will be a small war, followed by more diplomacy. There is no hurry; the border lies in a zone variously occupied by a few traders, large numbers of indifferently hostile Indians, and scattered settlements of dirt-poor subsistence farmers.

By Wilkinson's calculations, Spain owes him $20,000. After all, he expostulates to the Marquis of Casa Calvo, the former governor of Louisiana during its Spanish colonial days, you people haven't paid my bill for being your spy since 1793! What is more, when Spain and the United States come to blows, as he hints they must, over the border, Wilkinson will have to resign his generalship of the American army. The money, he explains, "will indemnify me for the eventual loss of the office which I hold, and which probably it will seem necessary for me to abandon in case of hostilities."

In addition to the straightforward bribe, Wilkinson wants a predictable and steady source of income. He would like a monopoly on the export of flour from New Orleans to Havana: exclusive rights for 16,000 barrels a year for the next four years. The benefit for Spain in this peculiar, four-year transaction is this: Wilkinson will use the money to purchase political offices and surround Jefferson, who has four years remaining in his second term, with "a corps of auxiliaries . . . made up of persons I know, and whose influence will be of irresistible weight." After the end of the Jefferson administration, Wilkinson will be content with a guarantee of a mere 5,000 barrels a year.

The Spaniards agree, after more negotiations, to a one-time payment of 12,000 gold pesos for the arrears, and $4,000 a year in return for current information. Wilkinson is pleased and offers his first memorandum of advice: Spain must fortify the borders of Florida and Texas, and try to regain the west bank of the Mississippi at New Orleans, this to stop Americans from moving toward the interior of Old Mexico and its still-valuable gold and silver mines.

10

May 1804, St. Charles, Missouri Territory

THE OLD FRENCH settlement of St. Louis lies on the west bank of the Mississippi River just a few miles downstream from where the Missouri River, the river to the west, pours into the greater flood. Since October, William Clark and twenty-two young men, the enlisted and volunteer Corps of Discovery, have been camped on the east bank of the Mississippi in quickly built log huts. They are there in a foggy bottom woodland for two reasons. St. Louis, when they arrive, is still foreign country. Even after it became United States territory in December 1803, it had been necessary to keep the young men a considerable distance from civilization. They are a rough crowd, and Clark would have enough trouble melding them into a unified whole without the distractions of women and whisky within walking distance.

As isolated as they are, by one means or another—pretending to go hunting, offering to bring in supplies, escorting the occasional government contractor arriving with food and materials—at least half of them manage to get blind drunk and thoroughly disobedient at one time or another in that winter. Lieutenant Clark, from his days in the Indian Wars of the old Northwest Territory, is experienced with the behavior of enlisted men on the frontier. He is a mild punisher. A few days confinement to camp, an occasional whipping, and discipline is restored.

Captain Lewis is gone nearly the entire winter. He hobnobs in St. Louis, spending weeks at no more difficult tasks than hiring some French rivermen to accompany the corps upriver, or purchasing extra trade goods for the journey. Clark, poor, patient William Clark, spends the winter in a chilly cabin, tries to bring some discipline to the Corps, and suffers for most of January and February with some inexplicable, debilitating illness. He never complains. While Lewis spends the last few days in St. Louis, Clark organizes the men, launches the great boat built in Pittsburgh, with its paired twenty oars, and the two smaller rowboats constructed that winter (the red and white pirogues of the expedition's narrative), and heads up the Mississippi, then up the Missouri to the frontier village of St. Charles, waiting for Meriwether Lewis.

St. Charles is a tiny town, perhaps four hundred inhabitants, all French. The men would like to go to town. The town would like to hold a going-away ball for the Corps of Discovery. Clark is understandably nervous. His orders to the enlisted men are summarized by Sergeant Ordway: "Note: the commanding officer is full assured that every man of his detachment will have a true respect for their own dignity and not make it necessary to leave St. Charles for a more retired situation."

The ball is not an unqualified success. Not everyone is given leave, the three boats and the camp must be guarded. Enlisted men William Werner and Hugh Hall are court-martialed for going absent without leave and gate-crashing the ball. Private John Collins, who already holds and will not relinquish the expedition record for punishments, is AWOL, and also is charged with "behaving in an unbecoming manner at the ball last night and thirdly, for speaking in a language last night after his return tending to bring into disrespect the orders of the commanding officers." Collins gets 100 lashes on his bare back, Werner and Hall get 25, remitted on their future good behavior. There is not a great deal of whipping on the expedition, just enough to bring tears to the eyes of a few miscreants, and on one occasion, to astonish and appall the Indians. The tribes routinely see some ferocious things, but they are quite unfamiliar with something as horrid as a public whipping.

11

May 1804, Manhattan Island

GENERAL-IN-CHIEF of the United States Army James Wilkinson—to give that portly gentleman his full title—while traveling through New York City from New Orleans, stops to rekindle his friendship with Aaron Burr, vice president of the United States and recently defeated candidate for the governorship of New York. It is an odd couple, of which Wilkinson is clearly, by default, the more successful, more reputable half. Among other things, he is the commissioner who has just received the Territory of Louisiana into the United States.

Burr is almost an object of pity, except for the majority of New Yorkers, for whom he is an object of ridicule. During the campaign for governor in the fall of 1803, Burr's implacable foe, General Alexander Hamilton, the great federalist author, statesman, and closest ally of George Washington, was a major opponent, working behind the scenes to remind the citizens that Burr is simply unreliable. The polar opposition of the two men began as long ago as 1776, when Washington and Hamilton refused to give Burr a commission in the new

Continental Army forming in Cambridge, Massachusetts. Hamilton is the leader of the Federalist Party, Burr, the Republican faction. Hamilton favors a single central bank, Burr is angling to charter a private one. Hamilton, though illegitimate and an immigrant, has all the airs of a gentleman; Burr, son of the president of Princeton College, puts on the cloak of the common man. Hamilton is austere and despises the common man; Burr is gregarious and loves politicking in lower Manhattan's liveliest saloons and bordellos. Hamilton's animadversions on Burr's public character would be hard enough to suffer, but Hamilton cannot stop there, according to a private letter that found its way quickly into the newspapers. (Postmasters, all political appointees, regularly scanned the letters entrusted to them and sent copies off to the newspapers of their political party.) Hamilton's remarks about Burr ("a dangerous man, and one who ought not to be trusted with the reins of government") are made worse by the letter writer with these words: "I could detail to you a still more despicable opinion which General Hamilton has expressed of Mr. Burr." The substance of the despicable opinion is not difficult for the politically adept reader. Burr's insatiable affection (it is much more than a mere appetite) for female flesh is notorious, and his most scurrilous opponents will hint at incest with his lovely daughter, Theodosia.

Wilkinson meets Burr in secrecy at the colonel's secluded country estate, Richmond Hill, with its distant views of the village of Greenwich to the north and the bustle of New York City to the south below Wall Street. (Richmond Hill is still there but is now surrounded by the city. It is a park in SoHo, just a block south of Houston Street.)

Wilkinson has an offer. Burr is the perfect vessel to receive it. Together they will raise a volunteer army in the west and, using New Orleans as a base, and engaging Great Britain as an ally, take the west and all of Mexico. There is no record, not a whit, of that meeting at Richmond Hill, and very little record of the entire "Burr plot," or more properly, the "Wilkinson plot," to steal the west.

Our best information comes from the British minister to Washington, Anthony Merry, the same aggrieved little man who got all dressed up to present his credentials to Jefferson in January 1804. A confidant of Burr approaches Merry in Philadelphia a few weeks after Wilkinson leaves Richmond Hill.

"I have just received an offer from Mr. Burr," Merry writes to his home office, "the actual Vice-President of the United States, to lend his assistance to his Majesty's government in any manner in which they may think fit to employ him, particularly in endeavoring to effect a separation of the western part of the United States from that which lies between the Atlantic and the mountains, in its whole extent."

Anthony Merry is as aware as anyone of Burr's reputation for fornication, which he politely describes as "the profligacy of Mr. Burr's character." But Burr has the potential to become a traitor, Merry adds: "His great ambition and spirit of revenge against the present Administration may possibly induce him to exert the talents and activity which he possesses with fidelity to his employers."

For many reasons, the British never cooperate with Burr. He is on his own, but Wilkinson has changed Burr's life with a single night's hint of a western empire waiting to be won. Burr begins to imagine a new life, far from Thomas Jefferson, Alexander Hamilton, and equally far from the small army of malcontents and office-seekers that make up his only political strength in New York. Campaigning for votes has begun to disgust him, as it usually does when one loses an election. Democracy is a joke. He begins to imagine another role. Burr as Emperor of the West, an American Napoleon whose sway runs from the Great Lakes to the Isthmus of Darién. But first, he must deal with Hamilton. Emperors must be admired above all men, and all men must fear them. As long as General Hamilton arrogantly spreads his "despicable opinion" of Aaron Burr, Hamilton is a threat to empire. Before conquering the west, Burr must humiliate Hamilton, extract a fulsome apology from him, rub his nose in his own words.

And Wilkinson? He takes advantage of his proximity to Washington City to communicate with the government of Spain through that empire's ambassador. He has added the grand office of Governor of the Territory of Louisiana, and he implies that he is now

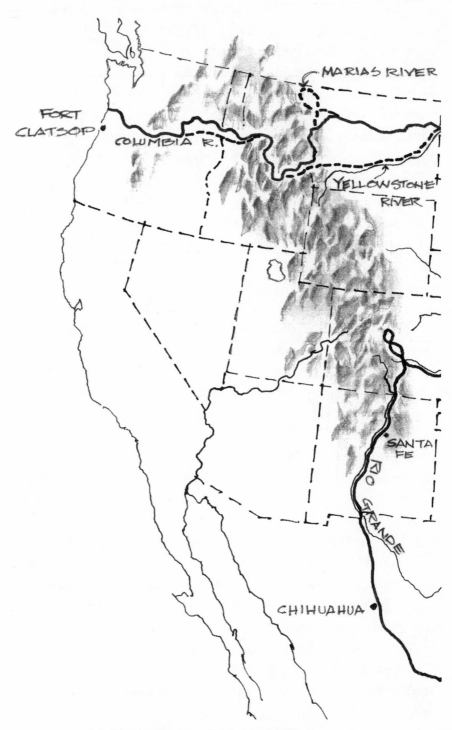

UPPER ROUTE: LEWIS AND CLARK,
MAY 1804 TO SEPTEMBER 1806.

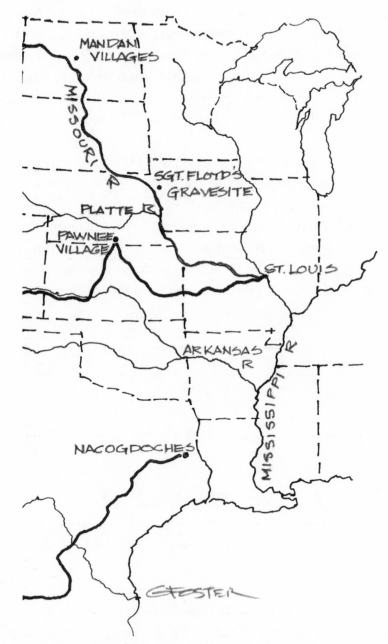

FIGHT

MANDAN VILLAGES

MISSOURI R

SGT. FLOYD'S GRAVESITE

PLATTE R

PAWNEE VILLAGE

ST. LOUIS

ARKANSAS R

MISSISSIPPI R

NACOGDOCHES

G FOSTER

LOWER ROUTE: ZEBULON M. PIKE, THE WESTERN EXPEDITION,
JULY 1806 TO MAY 1807

worth more. He has one piece of intelligence to offer, a hint of what is to come if he is treated well. There is an expedition to explore Louisiana leaving St. Louis this very month, under Captains Lewis and Clark. Immediately, the Spanish should send out a force to capture them, or turn them back. Wilkinson says they will be exploring the western tributaries of the Mississippi and the Missouri, thus encroaching on New Mexico (and its eastern region, Texas). It is impossible to tell if he is lying or misinformed. Lewis is under orders to stay off the plains, away from the upper reaches of the Platte, the Kansas, Arkansas, or Red Rivers, the ones that would bring him close to New Mexico.

Starting late that spring, several hundred horsemen—Spanish cavalry and local militia—will scour the plains from the Arkansas River to the Platte River, looking for the Corps of Discovery. The corps, of course, is safely out of sight, ascending the main Missouri. Their voyage begins with such inadvertent good luck as this: the Missouri is late breaking up and stays long in flood. The corps does not pass by the mouth of the Platte until July 21, more than a month after the Spanish have returned to New Mexico.

12

June 1804, The Missouri River

MERIWETHER LEWIS is in one of his funks, and the Journals of Lewis and Clark as they start up the Missouri are in fact the journal of Clark, who cannot spell, as you know, a fact we will ignore as you also know. The three boats, the great lead boat with twenty oars and the two small pirogues (think of them as dories) with six men in each, are working upstream against a Missouri in near-flood and against contrary winds. The Corps of Discovery is learning how to work together.

The most dangerous object in the water is what the boatmen call a "sawyer." This is a log, usually a huge cottonwood tree, with the base end sunk and fixed in the Missouri's mud and the top end bobbing up and down in the current, oscillating. The motion is vertical, like a two-man saw in a sawyer's pit, where one man is underneath and another man on top of the log that lies across the pit. Sometimes the river sawyer is completely submerged, but rears up high enough to catch the keel of the boat. On the fourteenth of June, they spy a huge sawyer just as the boat comes up upon it: "The boat struck and turned," Clark laboriously inks in his journal that night, "she was near oversetting. We saved her by some extraordinary exertions of our party (ever ready to encounter any fatigue for the promotion of the enterprise)." Time and again, members of the party will leap into the water, scramble ashore with lengths of rope to steady and move the boat ahead. Most of them cannot swim a stroke.

One member of the party takes his place within the first few weeks, peer among peers, perhaps the single most valuable member of the Corps of Discovery. He is George Drouillard, son of a mixed blood French-Canadian trapper and a Shawnee mother. He has remarkable talents: a great game tracker and shot (he will almost single-handedly feed the corps for the next two years) and the possessor of a secret talent still unknown to the captains. He is fluent in the lingua franca of the west; he knows sign language. He may also have a sense of humor. This is Clark's account:

"G. Drouillard tells of a remarkable snake inhabiting a small lake 5 miles below which gobbles like a turkey and may be heard several miles. This snake is of immense size. Drouillard gives the following account. . . . Passed a small lake in which there were many deer feeding, he heard in this pond a snake making gobbling noises like a turkey. He fired his gun and the noise was increased." It is that last detail in Drouillard's yarn that gives it the true tall tale cachet.

Drouillard, gobbling snakes aside, makes himself too valuable as a scout and hunter to be assigned to routine duties like guarding the camps or rowing the boats. For the rest of the expedition, including the winter camps, he will be a freelance, scouting on the point, hunting for game, translating at meetings with the Indians.

It is not a particularly happy crew. For some inexplicable reason, from the day they start up the Missouri almost every man is afflicted with dysentery, and worse, boils. Clark spends hours over the next month lancing boils and applying poultices. Lewis has taken the medical training but Clark, for the next two years, will do most of the doctoring. One of the healthiest men on the entire trek is York, Clark's black manservant. But Clark has to doctor him: On June 20, one of the men, never identified, throws a fistful of sand in York's eyes. Clark believes York "is near losing" the eye. Among other attributes, York is the tallest, strongest, most agile man in the entire party. But he learns his place, the eye heals, and that is the end of it.

John Collins, meanwhile, continues his position as the least ept and most punished of all the company. On June 29, Clark notes that "after making some arrangements and inflicting a little punishment to two men, we set out at half past four o'clock and proceeded on, and nearly got whacked by a sawyer." The punishment is at 3:30 P.M. Collins is charged with "getting drunk on his post this morning out of whisky put under his charge as a sentinel, and for suffering Hugh Hall to draw whisky out of the said barrel intended for the party." That is, he didn't steal "trade" whisky, but the men's rationed whisky.

It is, Clark notes dryly, a punishment (100 lashes on his bare back for Collins, and 50 lashes for Hall) "agreeable to the sentences of a court-martial of the party who we have always found very ready to punish such crimes." It becomes clear, by the way, that the Corps of Discovery is considerably more democratic than the regular army. Courts-martial are tried by the junior enlisted men, with the sergeants and the two officers merely supervising. A hundred lashes sounds like enough to kill a man, but the army cat-o-nine tails is a mild weapon compared to the navy's much heavier, deadlier whip. Still, it has enough heft to bring men to tears, including some Indians, a few months later.

13

❧

June 1804, Manhattan

AARON BURR is now forcing a duel on Alexander Hamilton. It is the culmination of years of resentment. The bitterness goes back to the American Revolution when Burr could feel the palpable contempt of General Hamilton toward him and the icy distance of Washington. It continues through twenty years of postwar politicking. Burr demands an apology, else there must be a duel.

It is odd that they should be such rivals and enemies, and it is entirely personal. In fact, they both despise democracy and the common man it celebrates. The difference is that Burr chooses to manipulate the voters, while Hamilton refrains from seeking any public office. Burr would be the Emperor of Mexico and all of western America. Hamilton, barred by his foreign birth from what he certainly regarded as his due—the presidency of the United States—chooses the life of senior statesmanship and the amassing of wealth. They have so much in common, except style, that their mutual distaste evolves into hatred, a not uncommon result between peers. The pro-Hamilton Federalist press reports that Burr practices daily with dueling pistols, aiming deadly shots at the presumed innards of life-size targets. This is highly unlikely. Burr has already been involved in one duel with pistols and has only managed to wound his opponent's overcoat.

Hamilton's behavior is puzzling. He seems indecisive, he offers a noncommittal response to Burr's demand for an apology. He seems almost paralyzed by Burr's challenge. Hamilton's associates try to negotiate for him. One suggests to Burr that Hamilton, if asked politely precisely what his "despicable opinion" of Burr actually is, will publicly say that his remarks were "on the political principles and views of

Col. Burr and the results that might be expected from them in the event of his election as governor, without reference to any particular instance of past conduct, or to private character." You can feel the condescension—no "particular instance" will be cited, Burr's "private character" will have a veil drawn over it.

If Aaron Burr has one quality, it is self-confidence. If Hamilton cannot write a proper apology, Burr will do it for him. He composes a complete statement of guilt for Hamilton to sign. It is actually rather mild and compromising. All Hamilton has to do is acknowledge that the "language I may have employed in the warmth of political discourse has been represented in a latitude entirely foreign from my sentiments or my wishes." This is not much different than what Hamilton has promised to do, only adding that his words, which he *may have* spoken, are being taken out of context. Except for one thing: Hamilton has to imply that he holds no "despicable opinion," that such a thought is "entirely foreign from" his "sentiments or wishes." This he cannot do. There is nothing else to be done but have, as it is called then, an interview. Dueling is illegal, but an interview with pistols may possibly escape the notice of the law.

14

July 4, 1804, The Missouri River

Above the Twin Kansas Cities

MERIWETHER LEWIS continues to ride along in a blue funk, and William Clark is in charge of the Corps of Discovery. He finds writing itself a painful act, and when Lewis is well and writing his journal, Clark will do little more than make a fair copy of Lewis's work. But this is Independence Day, and Clark cannot let it pass without commenting that the land beside the river is "one of the most beautiful plains I ever saw, open and beautifully diversified with hills and valleys."

The summer of 1804 is a good one, and the big bluestem grass on the benches above the river, Clark thinks, is "well calculated for the sweetest and most nourishing hay." It is an Eden, "interspersed with copses of trees, spreading their lofty branches over pools, springs, or brooks of fine water. Groups of shrubs covered with the most delicious fruit are to be seen in every direction, and nature appears to have exerted herself to beautify the scenery by the variety of flowers . . . raised above the grass which strikes and perfumes the sensation and amuses the mind."

Clark is working so hard at this unusual outpouring that he has to stop and cross out whole phrases. William Clark is not only moved to write, he is painfully *re*-writing. The beauty of the flowers, he continues, provokes the mind "into conjecturing the cause of so magnificent a scenery in a country situated, far removed from the civilized world, to be enjoyed by nothing but the buffalo, elk, deer and bear in which it abounds, and Savage Indians."

The captains of the Corps of Discovery will note many things in their journals, but besides this one make almost no references to beauty. The magnificence of mountains entirely escapes them, perhaps understandably, for mountains will become a horrid obstacle to their dream of finding a convenient connection between the waters, that short portage from the Missouri to some imagined River of the West that will carry them to the Pacific. Lewis, in particular, will note the aspects of the west most conducive to trade, or industry. They have already surveyed a lead mine and still have some hopes of finding that "mountain of salt" that Jefferson had promised to a skeptical Congress when he proposed adding the Louisiana country to the United States. Lewis, when he sees the landscape at all, most often remarks on the scientific curiosities or the potential for some metal to be extracted and brought home to the civilized world of the United States. Clark's July 4 journal entry is on a different level than anything that either one of them will write again.

Contrary to all their expectations, a land peopled with savages is beautiful. Beautiful enough for white men. The Fourth of July is celebrated properly. The bow gun, a swiveling blunderbuss intended to subdue any recalcitrant Indians, is fired at dawn and again at dusk. The men are given a double ration of whisky at the end of the day.

There is also a celebration in Manhattan that night. The Cincinnatis, that group of retired officers from the Revolutionary War, has its annual dinner. General Hamilton is there, Colonel Burr is there. They avoid each other's eye. Hamilton unbends a little, drinking and singing old campfire songs. Burr circulates nervously on the edge of the throng, and leaves early.

15

July 11, 1804, Weehawken, New Jersey

As DUELING IS illegal in New York, Alexander Hamilton and Aaron Burr agree to have their interview in New Jersey. The weapon (Hamilton's choice) is the pistol. A sword would have allowed a simple injury to settle the matter, a pistol is likelier to kill.

Aaron Burr has only one stipulation, that the hour be not too early. Hamilton, who seems almost disengaged from the event, has no particular requests. They both write wills. Hamilton's includes, although it is irrelevant, his assertion that he will not fire on the first exchange; he will "receive and throw away" his opportunity. If no wound is inflicted on him, he expects not to fire on the second exchange, "thus giving a double opportunity to Col. Burr to pause and reflect." Hamilton is acutely aware of the danger of dueling. One of his younger sons, Philip, is a little more than two years in an early grave. Philip is a victim of an outraged Republican whom he had slandered, much as his father has insulted Burr, and Philip dies after a duel at Weehawken, New Jersey, in October 1801.

Historians usually ponder why Hamilton chooses apparent martyrdom. It must be understood he cannot refuse the challenge. But has Philip's death made him abhor dueling so that his presence at the interview is merely fulfilling his gentleman's duty? Is Burr too contemptible to be actually dueled with, fit only to be ignored like an annoying gnat? The more serious, the more relevant, question is this: Why did Hamilton in effect commit suicide, letting Burr be the instrument?

He may simply be depressed, not from some chemical imbalance, but from the direction that the republic is taking. The acquisition of the Louisiana country adds, in his mind, more rabble (French and Spanish settlers) to an already unattractive population. Hamilton has even plotted with the New England Federalists to carve out a seceded nation-state. New York and New England would go it alone, and let the decadent south and the bumptious west depart in peace. Even this prospect has lost its charm to Hamilton. On the evening before his expected, possibly desired, death, Hamilton writes to one of the secessionists and remarks on his own "growing distaste for politics." He has come to disagree that secession is a solution to the problems "of our empire." That is a very odd word, *empire,* for America. It is seldom used in this era, except when accusing someone, usually President Jefferson, of malfeasance such as acquiring the Louisiana country. But it is the word that reveals Hamilton for what he has been and, though there are only a few hours left, what he always will be. He is a king-maker, a genius with no affection for anyone in the classes below the one to which he has aspired his entire life. He has made himself rich and genteel, and finds himself living in a country which merely envies wealth and increasingly seems to actually despise gentility.

The trouble with breaking up the empire, he writes the night before the duel, with dissolving the American nation, is not that it would be unpatriotic, but that it would encourage "our real disease which is *democracy,* the poison of which by a subdivision will only be the more concentrated in each part, and consequently the more virulent." This is not a terribly clear piece of prose, but one can forgive a man who expects to die momentarily.

The duel is simple enough. Burr takes the first and only shot. Hamilton's pistol may have fired, but if it does, it is apparently a reaction to having a lead slug the size of a child's marble smash through his liver, a part of the anatomy capable of exquisite pain. Hamilton is dead in a few days and Burr is in hiding, fleeing south and west from New York, accused of murder.

The effect of the duel on Burr is simple: He has no hope of a normal political career; all he has left is that improbable plan of Wilkinson's devising. Scoundrels are rarely elected to high office, but more than one has seized power. The duel also has an impact on Jefferson. He will be more cautious than ever, mistrusting all Federalists, and cleaving ever more strongly to men he perceives to be "true Republicans." General Wilkinson is one of Jefferson's truest Republicans, or so the president will always believe.

16

July 1804, Meeting the Osage Chiefs,

Washington City

THE DAY THAT Burr puts a bullet in Hamilton's liver, several Osage chiefs arrive in Washington. They are the first to come at Lewis and

Clark's invitation, and they are following a path typical of earlier visits by chiefs from the old Northwest Territory. Lewis and Clark and General Wilkinson have standing orders to bring as many chiefs as possible to Washington, to meet the Great Father face to face.

The chiefs are shown large cities, Philadelphia, New York, Boston, and then arrive at the capital once they are properly impressed with brick buildings, cobbled streets, and demonstrations of American firepower from cannon and musketry exhibitions.

These are the first Indians that Jefferson had taken a particular interest in, and he is as gracious as he will ever be in greeting them. They have had other fathers, French, then Spanish, but now, he explains, he is their Great Father.

This is a straight business deal: "You have furs and peltries which we want, and we have useful things which you want." Captain Lewis, he explains, is going to return with information on the Osage and their country, and "we shall hear what he has seen & learnt, & proceed to establish trading houses where our red brethren think best, & to exchange commodities with them."

With commerce out of the way, Jefferson proceeds to elaborate on the white man's claim for a natural right to take possession of land in America: "It is so long since our forefathers came from beyond the great water, that we have lost the memory of it, and seem to have grown out of this land, as you have done." And that makes him their true Great Father: "We are all now of one family, born in the same land, & bound to live as brothers; & the strangers [the French and the Spanish, he means] are gone from among us. The great Spirit has given you strength, and has given us strength; not that we might hurt one another, but to do each other all the good in our power."

It is his first oration to the western Indians. It will be the mellowest one he ever gives.

The Indians go home that fall to their camps along the Osage River, and they go very impressed, not so much with the United States, but with themselves. They have been treated lavishly, and are freighted down with small gifts, medals, uniforms, and American flags. They see themselves as very important Indians, and they swagger about the small army post in St. Louis on their way home. The commandant remarks that the Osage chiefs are all "puffed up with ideas of their great superiority to other nations."

Inflated egos are always a problem, and not just for Indians. Without one, Hamilton would be alive and Burr would be an honorable man practicing law in New York City.

17

August 1804, The Missouri River

MERIWETHER LEWIS continues sickly, William Clark remains the commander and the laborious chronicler of the voyage of exploration. Clark also continues doctoring the troops. The mysterious plague of boils rages unabated. He laconically notes that a lanced boil on a man's breast discharges a half-pint of pus. They are in Indian Country, and proceed cautiously. A few trusted men, including the remarkable George Drouillard, scout ahead and kill deer and elk by the half-dozen each day. The main body sticks to the river and the three boats. They camp on the sandbars and flats, and are much troubled by mosquitoes the size of houseflies and very "worrisome," Clark notes.

By pure coincidence, a few days after the duel at Weehawken, a private in the party has his name noted in the journal. This is Alexander Hamilton Willard, born in New Hampshire in 1778, when his namesake was a newly minted (and self-appointed) hero of the revolution against Britain. Willard is one of those characters who show up at all important events, a sort of hapless everyman with a few redeeming qualities set against a capacity, nearly a genius, for general ineptitude.

He, like any New England farmer's son, has some small acquaintance with carpentry, simple machinery, and blacksmithing. This makes him useful. And perhaps like any rural character, he is never quite clear on certain military and expeditionary rules. He is, in bowdlerized army slang, the company screw-up. On the night after General Alexander Hamilton is buried in New York, Alexander H. Willard, private, is discovered sound asleep at his guard post. This is a capital crime. Willard pleads guilty to lying down on his post, but denies sleeping on duty. A brief court martial convicts him of both offenses and decrees 100 lashes on his bare back, not quite enough to kill him. William Clark orders the sentence carried out over four days, 25 lashes at night, beginning at sunset. Considering the offense and the judgment, it is a merciful penalty.

A few days after the last whipping, Willard forgets his tomahawk at the previous night's campground and is sent back to get it. On the way back, tomahawk in hand, while fording a side stream, he loses his rifle. He cannot swim. Reubin Field, one of a pair of unusually vigorous and adept brothers in the corps, is sent back to retrieve the rifle. Alexander Hamilton Willard is one of those man-boys who is willing, but not very promising.

The first two weeks of August are busy times for Clark, as he meets with several chiefs from the local tribes—the Missouris and the flourishing Otoes. The meetings, which accomplish exactly nothing, give their name to Council Bluffs, Iowa, across the river from modern Omaha, Nebraska. Clark thinks Council Bluffs is highly promising for a future settlement. The air is good high above the river. There is clay for making bricks. Even the soil is amenable. The Indians are growing watermelons, he notes. Surrounded by savages, he sees a city on the plains.

Willard's adventure with the missing tomahawk has not gone unremarked by another soldier, Private Moses Reed. He admits to having left his knife at a previous camp. What he intends is to desert when he is sent back to recover the knife. One of the hired French-Canadian boatmen, known as La Liberté, takes another opportunity—an assignment to find the Otoe chiefs and bring them to a council—and also departs without leave. Reed and La Liberté are at large for a few days before being run to ground by a search party that includes one of the Fields brothers and the best plainsman in the party, Drouillard.

Reed is contrite. Clark is stern. The sentence is unusual. Reed is not to be flogged or hung. Desertion threatens the life of the whole expedition, and Clark decides on a gantlet. Reed will run by fourteen enlisted men, about half the corps, and each one will lash at him not less than nine times with a switch of their choice. He will run the gantlet four times. That is a little over five hundred blows. Reed survives.

He almost gets off without a whipping. Several Otoe and Missouri chiefs observe the trial and when they comprehend the punishment, beg, almost demand, that it be stopped. They cannot imagine how men could whip another unarmed helpless man. Kill him outright, that they understand. But, they tell the captains, not even a child is ever whipped. It is very bad for the spirit.

The negotiations with the Otoes and the Missouries go badly even without a whipping. Lewis and Clark intend to impose a peace among the tribes and to open the river to traders. The Indians are there to complain, in no particular order of priorities, about the behavior of the absent Indians, including the Omahas and the Sioux upriver, to get presents, and to drink. Days of negotiations turn into evenings of sullen and petty requests for more whiskey and more medals and more trade goods from the enormous keelboat. The Indians cannot imagine stinting; the captains own by far the largest and richest load of trade goods ever to come up the river from St. Louis.

The night that Moses Reed runs the gantlet four times is also Meriwether Lewis's birthday, and after parleying with the chiefs, passing out some medals, trade goods, and a few quarts of whisky, the Corps of Discovery celebrates Lewis's birthday with an extra four ounces of whisky per man, and dances until it is pitch dark just beyond the campfire's irregular light.

18

❧

The Last Week of September 1804, On the Missouri

THE CORPS OF DISCOVERY has a healthy appetite. Counting the extra hired boatmen who will return before winter sets it, there are forty in the party. Each man can eat four or five pounds of meat at a meal. Four elk, that is, at least a half-ton of meat on the hoof, can disappear in a day. They are just eating the good parts. Somewhere along the way (the journals leave out small details), they have acquired some horses, probably from the Omahas, and the hunters, foraging ahead of the three boats, are using horses to stalk game and transport the meat back to the river.

Their first encounter with the Sioux nation involves one of the hunter's horses. Near modern Yankton, South Dakota, John Colter, that day's designated hunter, leaves four elk carcasses by the river, and a few minutes later, comes down to the river to tell the captains that the Indians, the Sioux, have stolen his horse. This is to be expected; the Sioux are masters of the plains on both sides of the Missouri. A loose confederation of Lakota speakers will split up in a few decades into the famous warrior bands that gather at the Little Bighorn in 1876: the Brule (or Teton), Oglala, Miniconjou, Sans Arc, Two Kettle, and Hunkpapa. They extract a toll from anyone passing upriver, any traders headed for the Dakotas. Taking a horse is as routine to the Sioux as a hiker stopping to pick a wildflower.

Unfortunately, no one in the party speaks Lakota. The accounts in the journals of who says what to who probably exaggerate the amount of information that is passed back and forth. It is likely that most of the talking is sign language, and George Drouillard is the signer. When the boats find some Sioux down by the river, Clark makes a speech, so to speak, and announces that the corps is not afraid of any Indians. As for the horse, he lies, it is a gift from his Great Father to their Great Chief. So, if they know what's good for them, they'll return that horse, and quickly.

The next day's parley takes place on the big keelboat and begins with an ice-breaker, a "half a wine-glass" of whisky passed out to the chiefs. The Indians demand more. Failing to get it, some of them pretend to be drunk, and one of the chiefs plays drunk enough to deliberately crash into Captain Clark, who writes that the Indian plays at "affecting drunkenness as a cloak for his villainous intentions." A bitter argument breaks out over the presents, the usual collection of government medals, clothing, blankets, knives. Today, as they will every time they meet Indians, Lewis and Clark pick one as "First Chief" and give him the most goods. This understandably annoys the other "chiefs," who feel slighted. The debacle continues with the pretend-drunk chiefs unceremoniously rowed to shore and ordered out of the boat, with the warriors on the shore grabbing the anchor rope of the boat and refusing to let it go, with Clark drawing his sword, with Lewis, out in the center of the river in the keelboat pointing the cannon at the Indians. It ends quietly. The boat leaves with the men's rifles pointed at the Indians, the warriors on shore watch it go with arrows nocked in their tight-strung bows.

The Sioux, sober in the morning, decide to show their power in a more diplomatic manner. The next night, Lewis and Clark are invited to a feast followed by a dance. The Sioux women come "forward highly decorated with the scalps and trophies of war of their fathers husbands and relations and dance the war dance with great cheerfulness until" midnight. Lewis and Clark take their leave, not before turning down an offer of women, something that, they write in their journals, they never accept. In two days, they proceed on. The next night there is another war dance, another offer of young women. It is not all clear what the enlisted men are doing, except guarding the boats. The offers of women continue; the captains continue to abstain.

One of the Sioux chiefs, Black Bull (or Black Buffalo) is, the captains decide, the number one chief. He is offered a ride upriver on the keelboat and, to their surprise, he accepts.

As they work their way upriver, Sioux women trail the boats, offering to accompany the Corps of Discovery. It is possible to imagine this scene from the enlisted man's point of view. You are young, strong, sitting on a king's ransom of trade goods, and you cannot accept these offers, it is forbidden to bring women aboard the boats. What happens privately, in the Indian camps, is another matter. Clark thought them "cheerful fine looking women." Imagine how marvelous they look to a lonely young man.

The captains put Black Bull on the bank after a few days, although they wish he would come with them to the next Indian village and be, one supposes, a sort of character reference. Black Bull, frightened by the keelboat's encounter with a log, takes his parting gift of blanket, knife, and tobacco and rejoins the Sioux who are shadowing the boat. The captains tell him to keep his men away from the party. He assures them the river is safe. He explains—and the journals do not indicate that either captain got the irony—that it is safe because there are no more Sioux from this place on up. Lewis and Clark never quite figure out one thing: they can call someone a "first chief" but they cannot give him authority over his men. They hear his words—they are safe because they are past the Sioux—but they miss the point. Black Bull means that only the Sioux have the courage to attack an armed party. For the next several days they camp on mud bars and small islands in the river, fearful of the Indians. On the fifth of October, they agree that they are indeed above the Sioux. The men go to bed "refreshed with a glass of whisky." The stolen horse seems to have been forgotten in the meantime.

19

October 1804, On the Missouri at the Arikaras

THE CORPS, ALREADY elated to be shed of the unpredictable Sioux, are even more pleased when they encounter the Arikaras, just a few days upstream. This time it is not just the captains, with their endless, bumbling diplomacy who are happy, but the entire company. The Arikaras, whose name will be modified to "Rickarees" and shortened to "Rees" in the subsequent history and mythology of the opening of the west to immigration, are extremely hospitable from the first encounter.

The captains record no special precautions, extra guards, or fears of pilfering. No arrows are nocked, no bows or swords drawn. The Arikaras are a bit of a cultural hybrid, great horsemen of the plains and yet the women are excellent farmers. They dwell in substantial sod-covered pit houses. Industrious, home-loving, they appear at first meeting to be the most "civilized" of savages.

More important for the enlisted men, the Arikaras seem to regard sexual relations as a particularly welcoming equivalent of the American handshake, or perhaps the Japanese manner of bowing. Lewis and Clark are extremely reticent on the subject of sex. But more than half their discreet references to sex in three years' worth of journals are recorded in a few days among the Arikaras. Like the Sioux, Clark writes, "they think they cannot show a sufficient acknowledgment without giving to their guest handsome squaws and think they are despised if they are not received." On the third night in the Arikara village, Clark says, "they came up this evening and persisted in their civilities." The women, he notes, "are very fond of caressing our men."

One should not regard the Arikaras as some sort of orgiastic wife-swappers and daughter-deflowerers. Like many peoples, and especially cultures without real estate or durable personal property (and there-fore without inheritance), sex can be considerably more than mere pleasure or the first step in creating a kinship work force and a bio-logical retirement plan. Sex, given and taken, could be just another transaction: it might purchase goodwill, it might purchase trade goods. The two captains, perhaps to maintain their self-assumed importance as emissaries of the Great Father in Washington, apparently refuse all offers. The men are under no such constraints.

There is a third common practical use of intercourse, no less impor-tant than creating harmony or acquiring material things. Many of the Plains Indians regard the male's climax as a means of transmitting per-sonal power, ranging from wisdom to magic: "spirit" or "medicine" are the usual translations. Readers may recall the self-imposed celibacy of General Jack D. Ripper in the film *Dr. Strangelove*. He too believes in the magical powers of his "precious bodily fluids" and denies them to women. Just so, except they have no idea what is going on, are the men of the expedition seduced for their "medicine."

And what would the enlisted men's special powers be? In a world of scarcity, they are extraordinarily wealthy with their modest personal supplies of trade goods. More important, they are the guardians of by far the largest and richest boats the Arikaras have ever seen. With their military uniforms (the captains always begin a negotiating session with a bit of marching, salute with arms, and assorted close-order drills) and the inherent mystery of their collective mission (one or two whites at a time are all the Arikaras have ever seen), the enlisted men are surely mysterious and powerful enough to possess big medicine.

York, Clark's slave, is the most mysterious and powerful of them all. The Arikaras have never seen a black man, and this one is well over six feet tall, powerfully built but agile (one of his many tricks is walk-ing on his hands), and altogether awesome. York fairly glows in the attention paid him. Much to Clark's dismay, York does "not lose the opportunity to [display his] powers, strength, etc." With someone's help, likely George Drouillard's sign language and his own miming skill, York "made himself more terrible in their view than I wished him to do, telling them that before I caught him [he] was wild and lived on people, young children were very good eating." It is not mentioned in the journals, but after the expedition is over, Clark will tell a Philadelphia editor that York is peer among peers when it comes to transferring his medicine by intercourse. An Arikara man takes him to his lodge, introduces York to his wife, and then resolutely guards the door while the business is done. The guarding is a necessity; some of the enlisted men, apparently in good spirits of a bachelor-party sort, attempt to observe the activity.

If there is any best reason to understand that the Arikara are hardly debauched immoralists, it is their singular aversion to alcohol. They are hardly allergic to it, or unfamiliar with it. But they are shocked when the captains offer them whisky to create goodwill. To do that (and simultaneously refuse their women) is a great puzzlement to the Arikara chiefs. One of them tries to explain their distaste for alcohol, most particularly during negotiations, to Clark, who writes: "They say [that] we are no friends, or we would not give them what makes them fools."

In spite of the captains' gaffes, the Arikaras are interested in maintaining good relations with the Great Father in Washington. One of the chiefs will accompany the corps the few days upstream to the Mandan villages. Another one agrees to go downriver with the small returning party, and go on to Washington and meet the Great Father.

20

October 1804, Approaching the Mandan Settlement

THE CORPS DEPARTS the lower Arikara village with one of the chiefs, Piaheto, or Eagle's Feather. He has offered to introduce them to the next band of Arikaras upriver, and then to go on to the Mandan and Hidatsa villages and speak well of them to the chiefs of those nations.

Some of the Arikaras, on foot or horseback, follow the three boats upstream. Among them are women who by gesture or more formal sign language indicate their desire to be reunited with members of the Corps of Discovery, or, if the journals are true, to be united for the first time with either Captain Lewis or Captain Clark. The captains no doubt possess a superior "medicine." Understandably, the women are not allowed aboard any of the boats.

Perhaps that is what happens to Private John Newman. He is one of the quiet types, and carries an almost unblemished record since he joined the corps in the summer of 1803. He is not one of the handful of roisterers who steal whisky or can't stay awake on guard duty. But something snaps, and he makes what Lewis calls "repeated expressions of a highly criminal and mutinous nature." Unfortunately, we have no fuller explanation.

As in the past, there is a court-martial, and nine of his fellow soldiers convict him of uttering, in Clark's words, "mutinous expressions." He is sentenced to 75 lashes and "disbanded from the party." It is the first and last whiff of mutiny on the entire three-year expedition. One supposes that his intemperate language had everything to do with his forced separation from a nation of willing, handsome women.

It is a curiosity of the age, although not of the military system of justice, that mutinous expressions are punished so severely. There is no comparable crime in the civilian arena. Indeed, even calling for the dissolution of the United States or fomenting a revolution against its sovereignty is no crime. A Justice of the Supreme Court, Salmon P. Chase, will give a speech decrying the popular vote for office and other democratic practices as inimical to good government. Aaron Burr will try to raise an army and capture New Orleans before moving on to Mexico, and his defense will argue that there is no law against such behavior. General Wilkinson will declare martial law in the city of New Orleans and no one will question his right to usurp the civil authority of the United States. It is a very young country, still trying to work out what loyalty means, and even whether loyalty is required. But Private Newman is no private citizen, and the boats stop on an island in the Missouri for the public whipping he has earned.

"Halted on a sandbar," Clark writes that evening, "and had the punishment inflicted on him which caused the Indian chief to weep until the thing was explained to him." Eagle's Feather understands that discipline is necessary, and he certainly grasps the purpose of making an example, in front of all the men, of Newman. Eagle's Feather "observed that examples were necessary and that he himself had made" examples of disobedient and troublesome tribesmen. However, Eagle's Feather makes them examples by killing them. That makes sense, he tells Clark. But whipping? Like the Otoes and Missouris downstream, the Arikaras would not even whip a child.

The punishment either has a salutary effect on Newman or else he is a man of good character who, perhaps drunk, perhaps lovelorn, made a single mistake. He will, in the Mandan winter, make every effort to convince Lewis and Clark that he is reformed and fit to be a member of the corps when they start out in the spring of 1805. He exerts himself; he will suffer frostbite from hunting for buffalo in 40-below weather. The captains understand, even sympathize with him, but, as an example, he cannot be welcomed back. When the small return party goes down to St. Louis in the spring, he continues to be indispensable, foraging tirelessly, and when he is on the boat constantly alert and helpful. He is a very rare thing in the history of any event: Newman is a human being whose character is improved by a dose of brutal corporal punishment.

21

⸙

October to November 1804, at the Mandan Villages

WITH THE ARIKARA chief, the Corps of Discovery arrives at a complex of Indian towns in what is now central North Dakota, at a point easily located on an atlas. The Mandans and their coequals, the Hidatsa, whom the captains call the Minitarees, live just where the Missouri curves from its northerly direction and begins to flow more directly from the west. These villages are at the center of the Great Plains trading economy and are regularly visited by, and occasionally raided by, the Sioux and other Plains Indians. Traders from Canada, itinerants, and employees of the North West Company travel to the Mandan villages every fall. Into this rendezvous of the plains, the captains insert themselves and are greeted amicably. The Mandans and Hidatsa compete for their attention, each tribe hoping the expedition will build its winter camp close to their earth-lodge towns.

On the third day, October 28, women arrive with gifts of corn for everyone, plain dried corn boiled until it is soft. Clark writes that the corn was accompanied by other items, which, with his aversion to writing, he simply lists as "etc., etc." abbreviated, as is always his style, to "&c, &c." Dried pumpkin is almost surely on the menu. It is a Mandan specialty, a reliable preserved source of sweetening. What other commerce the women had with the men is not mentioned, except that Clark writes, "Our men very cheerful this evening." Two weeks later, the first outbreak of venereal disease among the corps is noted in the journal. The Mandan villages, visited by Europeans since 1738, suffer from all the usual ills of contact with foreigners.

On the next day, Lewis and Clark stage one of their patented Indian councils, with chiefs from the Mandan, Hidatsa, and Arikara

49

tribes. They propose a peace treaty, an alliance against the Sioux, and trade with the United States rather than with the British in Canada. The effect, even including the soporific effect of sequential translations from English to French to Mandan and Arikara, is hardly encouraging. The chiefs are variously restless, bored, and dismissive. Clark, observing Lewis's efforts, blames the failure on the tribes: "Those nations know nothing of regular councils, and know not how to proceed in them, they are restless &c."

The chiefs are given the usual gifts—clothing, knives, vermilion, blue beads, and very important silver Washington Medals. The medals are struck with that Great Father's image on the "heads" side and with plans for the Indians' future on the "tails" side: a woman works at a European-style loom, a man sows wheat; they are very civilized Indians on the medal.

Within a week of arriving at the Mandans', while the construction of their winter fort is under way, the captains make one of the most important decisions of their Mandan winter. A French-Canadian, Toussaint Charbonneau, a man of middle age who has lived with the Mandans for several years, offers himself as an interpreter. Unfortunately, English is not one of his languages. But the corps has two French speakers, the inimitable George Drouillard and the less prepossessing Private Pierre Cruzatte, half French and half Omaha. But Charbonneau's real asset is one of his two wives, a teen-age Shoshone woman named Sacagawea. She had been kidnapped from her Rocky Mountain home by a Hidatsa band from Knife River, kept in slavery at the Mandan-Hidatsa villages, and won by Charbonneau in some gambling exploit. One of the few things the captains know about the western tribes is that the Shoshone, or Snake Indians, live at the headwaters of the Missouri. They are the one tribe that the corps must inevitably meet, whose help the corps will undoubtedly need. Sacagawea, already visibly pregnant, will join the Corps of Discovery with her husband.

Charbonneau is a man unloved by historians. He has character flaws, including a dislike of discipline (when offering his services, he demands to be exempt from such chores as guard duty and rowing the keelboat) and one particularly unhelpful neurosis: Charbonneau is frightened to death of drowning, a certain disability on a thousand-mile boat trip. His bride is more sympathetic, and his child, a little boy born in the Mandan winter and known to the corps and the captains as "Pompey," is utterly charming. Charbonneau is at best a figure of fun to Lewis and a tolerable companion to Clark. There will be times in the next two years when Charbonneau is of enormous service, if inadvertently, to the expedition. Even then, as you will see, he is a great irritant to Lewis and a puzzlement to Clark. This is one reason that historians should be more fond of Toussaint Charbonneau. By simply being his bumbling self, he provides an insight into the character of Lewis (judgmental, demanding, quick to anger) and the character of Clark (more tolerant, more affectionate, more realistic about human nature).

22

1804–1805, Aaron Burr in Winter

THE VICE PRESIDENT of the United States, under indictment for murder in New Jersey (where he shot Hamilton) and in New York (Hamilton's residence) heads south in the early fall. His daughter, Theodosia, lives in the Carolinas with her husband, and the south is also a comfortable venue for a notorious duelist. That he is a Yankee-killer (Hamilton is not only from the north, but allied with all the mercantile and financial instruments that are anathema to the plantation south) is part of it; the rest comes from the historic southern fondness for dueling as the solution to arguments.

But Burr is headed much farther south than his son-in-law's plantation. It is all perfectly mysterious then, and still is, for Aaron Burr conceals his motives more than any other protagonist in the history of the United States. This we know: Carrying a letter of introduction from the Spanish ambassador, he heads for Florida in September. As far as we know, he gets no farther south than the St. John's River, just a few dozen miles south of the Georgia border and short of his goal of St. Augustine, capital of the Floridas.

Yet he writes Theodosia that the trip was successful and he was met with welcome wherever he went in Spanish Florida. The letter makes no sense, except as a bit of harmless bluster to make his daughter think his life is going well. It is difficult to imagine the purpose of the trip. It may have been to assess the sentiment of the settlers along Florida's coast, should he need help and a safe port on an expedition against Mexico. It may have been mere idle curiosity, for until the Senate reconvenes, the vice president of the United States has nothing to do.

When Burr returns to Washington City just before Christmas, he is greeted almost warmly by the Republicans. He dines with Jefferson. Secretary of State Madison gives him a carriage ride to a social event at the French embassy. The Federalists are outraged, and believe he is so well received precisely because he is the murderer of Hamilton, the hero of their quirky, often antidemocratic faction. The Republicans are treating Burr rather more nicely than you would expect, given that he is the man who tried to steal the election of 1800 and become president.

There is a reason the Republicans cosset Burr, and it has nothing to do with Hamilton. An impeachment trial is scheduled, and Burr, as presiding officer of the Senate, will be the approximate equivalent to a judge in a courtroom, ruling on procedures and the admissibility of evidence and controlling the behavior of the defendant and the attorneys for both sides. The defendant is a Supreme Court Justice, Salmon P. Chase. His crime, his "high crime" or "high misdemeanor" is an odd one for a citizen of the United States. Judge Chase believes that democracy is a terrible political system. He is opposed to giving the vote to all citizens (some states still have property requirements for the franchise, and of course women may not vote anywhere). He says in public that universal suffrage is the first step to "mobocracy."

In short, the Justice is opposed to the America of Thomas Jefferson, with its goal of a free franchise and popularly elected officials. The Justice is for the oligarchy of the rich and wise, as was Alexander Hamilton. The Justice has nothing but contempt for the ballot box.

In the history of the United States, the trial of Justice Chase is regarded as a landmark in the confirmation of the separation of powers and the independence of the judiciary. It is quite another matter to Republicans and Federalists in the early winter of 1805. It is a political struggle between the Republicans and its strong, elected central government and the Federalists who desire a weak government dominated by commercial interests. In a mere fifty-six years, when the Civil War begins, the Republicans will have somehow evolved into southern states-rights Democrats and secessionists, and the heirs of the Federalists, the first party to propose secession, will be northern Republicans and Unionists. But that is in the future. It is better to concentrate on the history Burr is living now.

In early January, Justice Chase appears before the Senate. He is nearly a foot taller than the petite presiding officer, but Burr immediately cuts him down to size. A chair has been set out for the Justice's use. Burr orders it removed, and is heard to say, "Let the judge take care to find a seat for himself." Indeed, the elderly Justice is obliged to ask for a chair and Burr, ungraciously, "permits" one to be brought. Burr, a contemporary alleges, is modeling himself and his "courtroom" after the House of Lords in Britain. Burr is credited with saying, "In Great Britain, when an officer is impeached and appears before the House of Lords—instead of having a chair, the accused falls on his knees and rises not until the Lord Chancellor directs him." That is one example of the mood, the self-image, of Aaron Burr in the winter of 1804–1805. Here is another. He circulates a list of rules for the senators and the audience that go right down to such precise prohibitions as not to eat apples or cakes at one's desk or to walk between the defen-

dant and officers of the court. A Federalist senator suggests that Burr
is being a schoolmaster, and only lacks a birch whip to make the resem-
blance perfect. And, when Justice Chase is given a month to prepare
his defense and return in the first week in February, Burr spends the
month of January refinishing the interior of the Senate Chamber.
Carpenters work cheek by jowl installing rich paneling. There are new
drapes, new benches, new railings, and theatrical stadium-style seats
for the members of the House of Representatives and guest observers.
Burr, in a single frenzied month, creates, temporarily, the most beautiful, elegant meeting room in North America.

In this rehabilitated splendor, Burr conducts the trial in such a fair
and rigorous manner that neither Republicans, who will fail to oust
Justice Chase, nor the victorious Federalists, will find it in their hearts
to criticize the vice president. Immediately, when the Senate reconvenes
after the trial, Burr, speaking without notes, makes a moving and
apparently heartfelt speech of resignation. He is, of course, a lame
duck. After his attempt to steal the election of 1800 from Jefferson,
there was no possibility of Burr running for a second term. In a few
weeks, the newly elected vice president of the United States (a New
York Democratic-Republican and amiable nonentity, George Clinton)
will be the presiding officer, so the resignation is, well, gratuitous at
best, self-serving, and theatrical. Readers may find it improbable, even
ludicrous, that a man sought for murder in two states could preside
over a trial in the Senate. But it is perfectly acceptable in 1804 and
1805. It is a young nation of heavily armed citizens and the "frontier"
is just a few hundred miles west or south of Washington City.

In the next two years, Burr will attempt to raise an army in the
west, apparently both to invade Spanish Mexico and to separate the
trans-Appalachian states from the Union. He dreams of an hereditary
monarchy, and Theodosia will be his successor. This future is not at all
inconsistent with his last weeks in the legitimate government of the
United States. He is an autocratic presiding judge working in a new
and glorious Senate courtroom modeled after Westminster Hall in
London. Within the limits of the institutions of Congress, Burr, to the

greatest extent he can grasp, rules like an autocrat in a sumptuous palace. He is not contradictory, this Burr; he is all of a piece in the winter of 1804–1805.

23

❧

November 30 – December 1, 1804,

A Mandan War Party

ON THE LAST day of November, William Clark learns that his Mandan hosts have suffered a grievous wound from a roving band of Sioux and Arikara warriors. A Mandan hunting party, he is told, has lost one young man to Sioux arrows and nine horses are missing. Clark is aroused. The Arikaras promised peace, and now this. The Sioux he remembers vividly: the tribe that threatened his men, tried to commandeer his boats, and scorned his offer of negotiations.

Clark is the steadiest, least emotional, of men. But this is, even at this long remove, an understandable moment of elation. He can imagine himself as the commanding officer of a crusade against the obnoxious Sioux, a vengeful captain dispensing swift and terrible judgment.

Clark takes twenty-three men, leaving a handful to defend Fort Mandan, arms them, and marches toward the nearest Mandan village. He writes that night that he is "determined to collect the warriors of the different villages and meet the Sioux." The Mandan, seeing his approach, are appalled. "The village not expecting such strong aid in so short a time was much surprised and a little alarmed of the formidable appearance of my party." The Mandans were not expecting aid of any kind. They weren't planning to do anything.

The chiefs, Clark notes, meet him before he can approach the village. "I told the nation the cause of coming &c. was to assist in chastising the enemies of my dutiful children." The latter phrase is an odd expression for Clark, as he usually makes a clear distinction between the Great Father and himself, but in the heat of outrage at the Sioux he stands as the very embodiment of the Great Father in Washington. His dutiful children have their doubts.

"The Sioux who spilt our blood is gone home," one of the chiefs explains, and "the snow is deep and it is cold, our horses cannot travel through the plains in pursuit." If, when spring comes, Clark is still so interested, well, "we will assemble all the warriors and brave men in all the villages and go with you."

Failing to arouse the Mandans' ire, Clark tries another tack. The fact that the Arikaras joined with the Sioux must not be countenanced, he says. The Sioux control the flow of goods, particularly guns and powder, to the Arikaras, and if those tribes join together, the Mandans will be cut off from trading with the St. Louis companies. Trade north, across the plains to Canada, is no safer. The Mandans must kowtow to the Assiniboines and Crees, Canadian tribes, or else those tribes will not allow the Canadian traders to come south to the Mandans. The Mandans listen, but remain uninterested in swift retaliation.

Clark is stuck there, out in the snow, his once-eager men now stamping their feet for the illusion of warmth as the parley goes on. He will not go back to Fort Mandan without some sign from the chiefs that they appreciate his good intentions. He reminds them again that they are at the mercy of hostile, insulting tribes for their trade goods. This must, he tells them, "distress you very much." Well, the solution is simple. Your Great American Father will supply you with guns and powder and shot. When you have "all of those articles, you will not suffer any nation to insult you."

One supposes it sounds agreeable to the chiefs. They have almost nothing to trade for guns and ammunition. The St. Louis traders are not going to haul back boatloads of dried corn and pumpkins. The Mandans exchange their food for more tradable items, buffalo hides and especially furs, brought by the far-ranging Sioux and the Arikaras and even by their cousins, the nearby Hidatsa. If Clark is promising to keep them at the center of the Great Plains trading economy, they are pleasantly surprised and a little mystified about how he is going to do it. But he sounds as if he is promising them both armed protection and a supply of firearms. They take him at his word, and say "now they would wipe away their tears" for the dead warrior. They would "rejoice in their Father's protection and cry no more."

Clark marches his men back to the palisaded Fort Mandan. They stagger home with difficulty in the chill wind and the slippery cold snow. "I gave a dram of rum to the party," Clark writes that night.

24

January, 1805, A Mandan Winter

RELATIONS BETWEEN the corps and the Mandans and the Hidatsas settle into a routine. They hunt together occasionally, although the few elk, deer, and buffalo that stay near the villages are thin, in poor condition, without the life-sustaining fat that everyone desires. It is possible to starve to death with a full belly of lean meat. For carbohydrates, the corps is increasingly dependent on the Mandans and their store of dried corn.

The trade begins almost by accident, casually. John Shields, the expedition's blacksmith, and Alexander Hamilton Willard, he who took a hundred lashes for sleeping on duty, make some small repairs of the Mandans' few iron hoes. They find that any small article—a knife, an awl, a new hoe blade—can be swapped for dried corn by the double-digit gallons. By the end of the month, with the captains' blessing, they are turning out tomahawk blades and cutting up some old sheet iron from a burned-out stove into the raw material for making arrowheads and hide scrapers. Lewis, who has not really planned for a long winter with such scarce hunting, remarks in his journal that "it would have been difficult to have devised any other method to have procured corn from the natives." The Hidatsa are particularly eager to have the tomahawk heads made to their specifications, creating a blade they think is much superior to the classic "trade" tomahawk. For decades, governments and individuals have traded heavy steel tomahawks with all the tribes.

The Hidatsa pattern is a thin blade with several holes punched through it, creating a much lighter weapon than the hatchetlike trade tomahawks. The Hidatsas are critical informants in this winter at Fort Mandan and the corps needs their knowledge as much as they need the Mandans' corn. It is the Hidatsas that regularly go by horseback across the plains to the Snake Indian country at the headwaters of the Missouri. Toward the end of the month, the Hidatsas give Lewis and Clark a rather accurate map to the Great Falls of the Missouri and on up to the Snake country at the westward headwaters of the Missouri. Then they announce that they will be leaving, as soon as the snow is gone, riding west to the Snake country where they will make war, kill some braves, steal some horses and young women; in short, do what men ought to do in a Rocky Mountain springtime.

Lewis and Clark are appalled. They are planning on meeting the Snake Indians at the headwaters of the Missouri and to trade for horses to make the portage over the divide to the great Oregon River of the West, the Columbia. They still believe in the power of rational discussion: "We advised him [the Hidatsa chief] to look back at the number of nations who had been destroyed by war and reflect upon what he was about to do." They also mention that the Great Father will be extremely displeased if he hears about the Hidatsa making war. It seems to work. "This chief said that he would advise all his nation to stay at home until we saw the Snake Indians and knew if they would be friendly."

The events of the coming summer imply that the chief is lying, perhaps to make Lewis and Clark comfortable, or he is simply unable, when the snow melts, to convince his tribe of the benefits of peace. The other possibility is that what Lewis tells him is so absurd (no war?) that he cannot understand what Lewis is up to and merely agrees to change the subject. By the time the corps departs the Mandans that spring, a large raiding party of Hidatsa warriors will be halfway to Snake country. When the corps reaches across the divide that fall, they will find some of their Hidatsa-style tomahawks in the possession of the western tribes.

Besides the material magic of the blacksmiths and their charcoal forge (the natives make their metal arrow points and scrapers with simple Neolithic methods, shaping and sharpening the metal with abrasive rocks), the corps has a kind of collective spiritual magic, some of that mystery that usually translates as "medicine." The Indians are quite fond of watching the men dance to fiddler's tunes. One supposes the dance is something like line or clog dancing. The captains are able to see the "medicine" in Indian dances; why shouldn't the Indians see medicine in a hornpipe or a jig?

Medicine is well and good, but the question for the Mandans is how to acquire it from the whites. It is simple enough; they will get it in the same way they have always transferred the wisdom of the tribal elders to the younger generation. They will use sex. The Mandan buffalo dance ends with a ceremonial series of copulations between the young wives and the oldest men—men, Clark notes, who could hardly walk outside to participate. The old men are required to at least pretend to pass along their wisdom, to go through the motions. The members of the corps are regarded as, by definition, wise men. They arrive in this remarkable boat. They have bales of trade goods. They can make iron bend to their will. One of the enlisted men, Clark notes with some astonishment, is given four women at the buffalo dance. The medicine is transferred; the buffalo return.

Pierre-Antoine Tabeau, one of the French-Canadian traders who lives with the Mandans, will recall the corps years later. He tells a visitor who inquires about them that the explorers "were untiringly zealous in attracting the cow." Within a few weeks of the dance, Lewis and Clark are treating numbers of cases of venereal disease. But within a few weeks of the dance, more buffalo, animals in better condition, return to the Missouri River valley at the Mandan villages.

25

March–April 1805, Leaving the Mandans

AT LAST, with the ice out of the Missouri in an unusually warm and early spring after a bitter winter, the corps makes ready to move upstream to the headwaters of the Missouri. Lewis has acquired some rather accurate knowledge of the passage before them. Somehow he has managed to convey the idea of "navigable" to the Hidatsa, who own no boats and move west on horseback.

"The Indians in this neighborhood inform us that the Missouri is navigable nearly to its source, and that from a navigable part of the river, at a distance not exceeding half a day's march, there is a large river running from South to North, along the Western base of the Rocky Mountains; but as their war excursions have never extended far beyond this point, they can give no account of the discharge or source of this river. We believe this stream to be the principal South fork of the Columbia River, and if so, we shall probably find but little diffi-culty in passing to the ocean." The Hidatsa are correct, in the sense that from the headwaters of the Missouri it is a short horseback ride over the divide to the Snake River. Lewis and Clark will get a better idea of what "navigable" means to a Hidatsa in the coming months. The Hidatsa may have meant to describe the Clark Fork of the Columbia, which is a long day's ride over the Continental Divide from the Missouri near the Great Falls. Clark Fork runs due north for more than a hundred miles before looping around and heading south and west to the Pacific.

The Hidatsa landmark for the Great Falls, by the way, is an eagle's nest. For the corps, boating upstream in the Missouri River canyon, the falls themselves are the landmark. For the Indians, coming over the plains on horseback, the eagle's nest, high in the top of a towering cottonwood, would project above the canyon of the Missouri into their horizon.

The captains elicit almost no information on the plains between the Mandan-Hidatsa homeland and the Rockies. After all, their expedition is by boat. That is not so much a strategic plan, but a function of the geography they are trying to establish. The headwaters, the very watershed lines, of the Missouri mark their long-sought boundary. How fortunate they will be to be boatmen wherever possible. How difficult they will find it even to attempt to be horsemen on the Great Plains of the west. But that is all in the future. They leave the Mandans in good fettle, by boat.

"All the party in high spirits," Clark writes in his daybook, "but few nights pass without a dance. They are healthy enough except the venereal which is common with the Indians and has been communicated to many of our party at this place, those favors being easy acquired." Clark knows that Lewis is going to send his journals down to St. Louis in a day or two, and then on to Washington. Much as he dislikes writing, Clark sits down that night and rewrites his daybook comments into the official journal, leaving out the comments on sexually transmitted disease. This is what Thomas Jefferson will read: "They pass few nights without amusing themselves dancing, possessing perfect harmony and good understanding towards each other." Even bowdlerized, Clark must be telling the truth. There hasn't been a fistfight since they left St. Louis a year earlier. There won't be one in the next year and a half. Even in the most confined quarters with the least amusement, rainbound in Oregon for an entire winter, there isn't a hint of trouble.

Lewis knows that he was supposed to have done several things in the fall of 1804: send the extra men back to St. Louis, arrange for the first year's maps and journals to be forwarded to Washington, send Indian curiosities and animal, mineral, and vegetable specimens to Jefferson and in the president's name to the American Philosophical Society in Philadelphia. None of this was done. Lewis wanted to keep every able-bodied soldier and the hired boatmen in Fort Mandan for the winter. The natives seem friendly, but . . .

Lewis writes his mother in the spring. He says little about the journey ahead but wants her to know that the first year's exploration has been worthwhile: "This immense river, so far as we have ascended, waters one of the fairest portions of the globe, nor do I believe that there is in the universe a similar extent of country, equally fertile, well watered." Lewis is liable to a certain exaggeration, but in fact he has passed through the Great Plains that will become the states whose very names remind us of fertility: Kansas, Missouri, Iowa, Nebraska. He has not seen the hard country yet.

The big keelboat returns to St. Louis, carrying a few Arikara chiefs who agree to go see the Great Father. The corps pushes off in their two rowable boats (the red and white pirogues) and dugout cottonwood canoes. Clark counts them: twenty-six Americans plus Charbonneau and Sacagawea and their six-week-old son, Jean Baptiste Charbonneau, or Pompey. George Drouillard is noted as having been promoted from enlisted soldier to "translator and hunter." Oh, and Clark remembers to add York, "my servant."

They have counted everything during the long Mandan winter. They leave with provisions for four months and a mix of trade goods and presents for the chiefs. Fifteen military jackets, including nine artillery officer's dress coats, and some ninety medals are for chiefs. The seven bales of trade goods include twenty-two dozen butcher's knives, a hundred magnifying glasses to be used as burning lenses, almost four thousand assorted needles (needles will be the last trade goods they have, when things get hard), and ten small "bales" of tobacco. From time to time, they will count things like this. It is a military habit.

On April 8, 1805, they leave the Mandan villages. On virtually the same day, Aaron Burr arrives in Pittsburgh, Pennsylvania.

26

❦

April 1805, Burr on the Ohio River

AARON BURR, private citizen, moves west from Philadelphia and New York to the frontier town of Pittsburgh, where the three rivers that make up the Ohio join. Except by sea, sailing around Florida and into the Gulf of Mexico and then up the Mississippi delta to New Orleans, Pittsburgh is the only starting point for any voyage to the territories of Louisiana and Orleans.

Burr's co-conspirator, General Wilkinson, is the governor of Louisiana Territory, which amounts to the entire Louisiana Purchase north of the Thirty-third parallel. South of that line of latitude lies the Louisiana and Orleans Territories and the crucial city of New Orleans. The line is still there on maps of the United States, it is the border between Arkansas to the north and present-day Louisiana.

Almost two years earlier, in the fall of 1803, Meriwether Lewis left Pittsburgh in his keelboat and descended the river with difficulty in the low water of early autumn. Burr has no similar problems at the beginning of his exploration of the west. Anticipating the high waters of spring, he has acquired, apparently built to his specifications, a huge barge, 16 feet wide, 60 feet long, with a substantial house built on it that includes a kitchen, servants quarters, a sitting room, and two bedrooms. It even has glass windows, a luxury in the trans-Appalachian west.

It is a curious tour. He stops with visits to local politicians. He visits small army posts with the self-assurance of his former office, as though he were still a national leader. And everywhere he goes, there springs up behind him, like mushrooms after a rain, rumors of what he is planning to do. Burr will invade Mexico. Burr will take Baton Rouge as a base before invading Mexico. Burr will capture New Orleans and sail to Veracruz to invade Mexico. It is difficult to tell, at this distance, whether Aaron Burr has lost all semblance of discretion or whether he is deliberately letting the plot circulate as rumor in order to test the wind.

Heaven knows, it is no secret in Washington, although President Jefferson maintains an air of disinterest in Burr or rumors about Burr. The French ambassador, by no means the cleverest diplomat in Washington, is perfectly well-informed and writes to his home office that "Louisiana is going to be the seat of Mr. Burr's new intrigues; he is going there under the aegis of General Wilkinson." This is all very interesting reading in Paris, but Napoleon has no stake at all in what happens to Louisiana, or Mexico, or anything in the Americas. Haiti, where Napoleon's brother-in-law, General LeClerc, buried most of an army of 45,000 men, has declared its independence. France has nothing left in the Americas but French Guiana, and its only worth is as a place of exile and imprisonment (it is the home of the famous Devil's Island).

How odd it is. As Lewis and Clark and the trimmed-down corps of exploration head north and west up the Missouri River from the Mandan villages, Aaron Burr glides down the Ohio to the Mississippi and on to New Orleans. They are bound upriver to determine the extent of Louisiana, Burr is floating downriver with every intent of stealing it all. But not this spring. Burr is just testing the political waters and meeting with various junior officers at the army posts along the Mississippi and Ohio. He pretends to have a commission from the secretary of war to lead a mix of volunteers and regulars on to Mexico.

As long as his audience believes that he is a representative of the government in Washington, he succeeds in generating great enthusiasm for his Mexican adventure. It is always easy to believe the most outrageous things if they are exactly what the audience wants to hear.

General Andrew Jackson, like all the planters dependent on passing their produce through New Orleans for export, has learned to hate "the Don," as the Spanish government is called. The Don is one of those shorthand names that carries a curse within it, like "the Hun" in World War I, "the Jap" in World War II. Jackson likes the idea of whipping the Don so much that he requisitions an army squad to row Burr on to New Orleans. Later (Jackson is not a quick apprehender of complex ideas), the general realizes he has been duped by this diminutive, smooth-talking Princeton graduate and New York lawyer.

Burr, scion of a long line of New England preachers (Jonathan Edwards is his grandfather), even makes allies of the Roman Catholic clergy in New Orleans. Burr will liberate the oppressed peons, good Catholics all, from the ruthless hand of the Don. Before he leaves New Orleans, he can even count an order of teaching nuns among his cadre of swashbucklers. His energy is unquestioned; Burr seems electrified by the prospects. He makes his way back to Philadelphia and Washington on horseback, stopping along the way to preach the gospel of an American Mexico to everyone from innkeepers to the governor of Indiana.

27

April 1805, To the Yellowstone via Grizzly Country

THERE is one clear difference in the mental makeup of Lewis and Clark. With rare exceptions, Clark lives in the present, except when deliberate planning requires him to anticipate the future. Lewis does have the urge to imagine a world unborn. Lewis actually uses the word *future,* Clark, never.

This is Lewis, the eighth of April, 1805:

"We were now about to penetrate a country at least two thousand miles in width, on which the foot of civilized man had never trodden; the good or evil it had in store for us was for experiment yet to determine, and these little vessels contained every article by which we were to expect to subsist or defend ourselves." Clark could have written that, although in a few shorter declarative sentences. But Lewis continues:

> *However, as this, the state of mind in which we are, generally gives the coloring to events,* when the imagination is suffered to wander into futurity, *the picture which now presented itself to me was a most pleasing one. Entertaining as I do the most confident hope of succeeding in a voyage which had formed a darling project of mine for the last ten years, I could but esteem this moment of my departure as among the most happy of my life.*

For the next two weeks, they row and pole their way up the Missouri. The grazing animals are all lean and out of condition after the winter, their stores of fat long since metabolized. The best available meat is beaver. Lewis asserts: I "think it excellent, particularly the tail and liver." The beaver stores energy in its tail as fat, and converts fat to useful sugars in its liver. Lewis is ignorant of the metabolism of hydrocarbons, but his body tells him what to eat. The men of the expedition are absolutely dependent on cholesterol-saturated meat for their survival. Toward the end of the month they discover, quite by accident, that the nursing buffalo calves are fat and tasty. Until then, they assume it is the hunter's job to shoot the largest available animals.

And the largest animal they are all desirous of shooting is the "white bear," that is, a grizzly bear. This urge has nothing to do with food, it is what we call today "trophy hunting." Lewis finds it amusing, before he has seen one, that "when the Indians are about to go in quest of the white bear, they paint themselves and perform all those superstitious rites commonly observed when they are about to make war upon a neighboring nation."

Lewis, scouting on foot ahead of the boats, finds himself wandering in a kind of herbivore Eden. "The buffalo, elk and antelope are so gentle that we pass near them while feeding without appearing to excite any alarm among them, and when we attract their attention, they frequently approach us more nearly to discover what we are, and in some instances pursue us a considerable distance apparently with that view."

Clark, more to the point, notes on April 27 that "although the game of different kinds are in abundance, we kill nothing but what we can make use of." And two days later, they kill their first grizzly, which, though badly wounded, chases Lewis for 70 or 80 yards. He writes that night that "in the hands of skillful riflemen they are by no means as formidable or dangerous as they have been represented."

A few days later, Clark and Drouillard kill a very large bear, which chases them for hundreds of yards, even though it had been shot ten times, five lead balls passing through the lungs. This phenomenon is discussed by the men. "I find," Lewis remarks the day after this second grizzly dies, "that the curiosity of our party is pretty well satisfied with respect to this animal; the formidable appearance of the male bear killed on the 5th added to the difficulty with which they die even when shot through the vital parts, has staggered the resolution of several of them."

Lewis's mind travels more easily than Clark's. It will even, in the midst of a wilderness, return homeward. A creeping juniper attracts his attention, a plant that grows "so close as to perfectly conceal the earth. It is an evergreen; the leaf is much more delicate than the common cedar." He thinks "this plant would make very handsome edgings to the borders and walks of a garden. It is quite as handsome as box, and would be much more easily propagated."

And having imagination, Lewis finds himself an observer of his men and their more heedless mentality. At the mouth of the Yellowstone, they rest for a few days. "In order to add in some measure to the general pleasure which seemed to pervade our little community," Lewis writes, "we ordered a dram to be issued to each person; this soon produced the fiddle, and they spent the evening with much hilarity, singing & dancing, and *seemed* as perfectly to forget their past toils as they appeared regardless of those to come."

28

May 1805, Washington City

THOMAS JEFFERSON, who is still waiting for his first communication from Lewis and Clark, and who is steadfastly ignoring all hints and rumors about Aaron Burr's plans for the Louisiana country, writes to two of the better educated residents of Louisiana: William Dunbar, a Scot, and to a medical doctor, John Sibley, a transplanted New Englander. Dunbar is a man after Jefferson's heart: a planter, a scientist, a geographer (he is working on a system for calculating longitude without a chronometer), and an explorer. Sibley's travels through Louisiana west of the Mississippi are unique; he is one of the few explorers totally uninterested in personal gain; he is curious, not avaricious.

What Jefferson wants is their help, their very discreet help, in gathering information on the southwestern tributaries of the Mississippi and the Indians who live there. This is along the border with Spain's Mexican provinces. Jefferson certainly remembers, although he does not mention in his letters, forbidding Meriwether Lewis to explore this country in the fall of 1804. Lewis, while Clark ran the camp across the river from St. Louis, volunteered to make a quick survey toward the Rocky Mountains and perhaps as far as Santa Fe. Jefferson told him to stay close to base.

The southwestern corner of the Louisiana Purchase has ill-defined boundaries between France's Louisiana and Spain's Mexico and New Mexico. It is too delicate an area for the United States to survey officially; any military expedition, like that of Lewis and Clark, would amount to a preemptive claim on the land traversed. Jefferson is negotiating with the Spanish government to acquire the Floridas, and he is looking for inconspicuous private citizens to round out the map of the Louisiana Purchase without irritating the Don.

To William Dunbar, May 1805

> Your observations on the difficulty of transporting baggage from the head of the Red River to that of the Arkansas, with the dangers from the Osages residing on the last river, have determined me to confine the ensuing mission to the ascent of the Red River to its source [again, as always, to the watershed line which is the boundary of Louisiana Territory] and to descend the same river again.

Jefferson wants the expedition to appear purely "scientific," the same claim he makes for the Lewis and Clark party. The way to do this is to ask the Spanish consul in New Orleans for a passport to the perhaps disputed lands and to offer to take a few people along named by the consul as proof that the expedition "is merely scientific, and without any views to which Spain could take exception." Besides surveying, the main work is "conferences . . . with the Arkansas and Panis [Pawnees] . . . everything possible be done to attach them to us affectionately. In the present state of things between Spain and us, we should spare nothing to secure the friendship of the Indians within reach of her."

To Dr. John Sibley, May 1805

"You will receive," Jefferson adds almost as an afterthought to a long letter on philosophical matters, "from General Dearborn some important instructions with respect to the Indians. Nothing must be spared to convince them of the justice and liberality we are determined to use towards them, and to attach them to us indissolubly." Sibley is to work among the tribes on the Spanish border closest to New Orleans, into southwest Orleans (modern Louisiana) and what will become Texas.

But what Jefferson really cares most about is his special, near life-long project: to determine if the Indians have emigrated to America or whether they sprang up there independently of the rest of the human race. "Their vague and imperfect traditions can satisfy no man on that subject. I have long considered their languages as the only remaining monument of connection with other nations, or the want of it, to which we can now have access." Lewis and Clark are carrying printed forms with a standard vocabulary of ordinary objects and will try to get the native words for these commonplaces from every tribe they meet. That is what Jefferson wants Sibley to do as well: "I enclose for you a number of my blank vocabularies, to lessen your trouble as much as I can."

It is a wonderful time, this bare beginning of the nineteenth century. Jefferson sends out men who are at once explorers, diplomats, surveyors, and linguists. Thus does the Enlightenment cross the Mississippi and ascend the rivers of the west. Well, partially ascend: the Dunbar expedition is turned back by the Spanish when it attempts to survey the Red River. Our General Wilkinson has tipped off the governor of Mexico. The next attempt in that corner of Louisiana is two years off, and Wilkinson will have something to say about that trip.

29

May 1805, On the Missouri

As YOU KNOW, Meriwether Lewis is both curious and imaginative, and William Clark is practical and productive (he is doing the laborious business of making a map of the Missouri and its tributaries, while Lewis does the more intellectual work of locating their latitude and longitude by celestial observations). On April 22, while Lewis is scouting along the bank of the Missouri, a buffalo calf approaches him. "It attached itself to me and continued to follow close at my heels until I embarked and left it." On April 23, a buffalo calf follows Clark. He eats it for dinner.

The Corps of Discovery is probably just a little bit bored. Working the pirogues and canoes up the river is laborious, and buffalo are becoming scarcer in the broken country that surrounds the river on both banks. They haven't seen any evidence of Indians. For some of the men, the grizzly bears are the only entertainment, the only enemy.

William Bratton, one of the young men from Kentucky enlisted by Clark, is among the last victims of the plague of boils that accompanies the men up the river. One of his hands has a severe boil and he is excused from duty, either from rowing a boat or pulling a tow rope. He is allowed to go strolling along the Missouri (in a section now flooded by Fort Peck Dam). At midmorning, he returns to the boats, screaming. He's shot a grizzly, he tells them, and it has been chasing him for a half a mile right up to where the boats are stopped for a noon meal. Lewis and a few men trail the grizzly for a mile. The bear "was perfectly alive when we found him which could not have been less than two hours after he received the wound." Bratton, they discover, has shot the bear neatly through both lungs. "These bears being so hard to die," Lewis writes later that day, "rather intimidates us all; I must confess I do not like the gentleman and had rather fight two Indians than one bear."

The bears remain on Lewis's mind. He remarks that when carrying his rifle and armed with his espontoon, he feels "more than an equal match for a brown bear provided I get him open woods or near the water." The espontoon, a stylized spear or pike, is usually nothing but a ceremonial badge of office carried by artillery officers like Lewis. But he has modified his for the expedition. A crossbar at shoulder height turns the staff of the spear into a steady mount for his rifle. And he sharpens the usually blunt spearhead. Even so armed, he writes that I "feel myself a little diffident with respect to an attack in the open plains. I have therefore come to a resolution to act on the defensive only, should I meet these gentlemen in open country."

The enlisted men haven't given up on meeting the gentlemen. The next day, as Lewis recounts in the journal, "six men, all good hunters, snuck up on a grizzly, all shot him . . . including breaking his shoulder, the men unable to reload their guns took to flight, the bear pursued and had very nearly overtaken them before they reached the river." Two paddle away, another pair "throw themselves into the river although the bank was nearly twenty feet perpendicular; so enraged was this animal that he plunged into the river only a few feet behind." George Drouillard reloads while the bear is distracted and kills the animal with a brain shot.

Before the party reaches the mountains, where grizzlies are much less common than on the plains in those days, they will encounter bears more than a dozen times. No one, except for the bears, is hurt.

A year later, up in the Marias country, Lewis will have an opportunity to see if two Indians are as dangerous as one grizzly.

30

❦

May 1805, Aboard the White Pirogue

LEWIS AND CLARK put all their important papers—maps, journals, daybooks—aboard the white pirogue. It is their personal boat, and Pierre Cruzatte, who is the most experienced waterman in the Corps of Discovery, is its master. He is an odd little man, blind in one eye, nearsighted in the other. He plays excellent fiddle tunes and has attached himself to the captains. The other regular members of the crew of the white pirogue are Touissaint Charbonneau and Sacagawea, and Pompey, their toddler. There is usually another crewman, although his presence is rarely noted. York, Clark's slave, is usually near his master, although Clark does allow him some freedom to rove with the hunters.

Charbonneau has two assets and one talent. His assets are the Indian Woman, as Lewis and Clark usually call her in their journals, and the baby boy, who is a source of constant merriment for William Clark. Charbonneau's talent is cooking. While the enlisted men and the hired boatmen subsist almost exclusively on meat roasted over an open fire or on dried meat, or, on those rare occasions when the camp is set up for more than a day, on boiled meat, Lewis and Clark occasionally have real meals. Sacagawea may contribute some herbs or roots foraged from the riverside. York may swim out to an island and pick greens. But Charbonneau, well, he makes sausages.

From St. Louis to the Pacific Ocean and back, Lewis and Clark mention food regularly. It is abundant, or scarce. It is healthy (almost always), it is sickening (rarely). Lewis mentions exactly two recipes in two years. And the best is Charbonneau's *boudin blanc,* his white sausages: buffalo rump and suet, chopped; liver and kidneys, chopped very fine; a little flour, salt, pepper (the only spice mentioned in two years). Buffalo intestine rinsed in the river, briefly, is tied with a knot at one end and then forced full of the chopped stuffing. As it fills, the intestine turns inside out, wrapping itself up and around the stuffing, which puts the intestine's coating of fat on the inside of the sausage. Boil until done. Slice it thickly and fry it in bear grease. Describing the sausage is one of the longest single entries Lewis writes in two years of journals. It is also the only entry about Charbonneau that is not disdainful, critical, or irate. Charbonneau, as you will see, is utterly useless in times of crisis.

On the fifteenth of May, the white pirogue is sailing up the Missouri below the cliffs of the broken country near the mouth of the Judith River. A sudden change in wind direction, a "williwaw" sailors call them, strikes the sail sideways and swamps the pirogue, tipping it until the water rushes over the gunwales. Charbonneau is steering the boat, Cruzatte is up in the bow, looking ahead for snags, sandbars, and sawyers. Lewis describes the scene:

"Charbonneau, still crying to his God for mercy, had not yet recollected the rudder, nor could the repeated orders of the bowman, Cruzatte, bring him to recollection until he threatened to shoot him instantly if he did not take hold of the rudder and do his duty." Charbonneau finally takes the tiller and steers the swamped boat to shore. It is bailed and the goods dried and they proceed on. That night Lewis remarks on Sacagawea's remarkable contribution while her man is hysterical:

"The Indian woman, to whom I ascribe equal fortitude and resolution with any person onboard at the time of the accident, caught and preserved most of the light articles [including copies of the journals] which were washed overboard."

She is a remarkably calm woman in the face of disaster. A few days later, Charbonneau, Clark, Sacagawea, and Pompey are walking the high ground above the river near the Great Falls of the Missouri when a terrible hailstorm strikes with hail the size of pigeon eggs and larger. Clark, trying to be a sensible person, makes one of his few serious errors in judgment. He leads the party (he is very worried about the baby) to shelter in a dry ravine, where they crouch beneath the overhanging, undercut bank. There is a reason why dry ravines out west are carved so sharply from the earth, and a few minutes after they huddle under the bank, a great flood bears down on them. The storm has poured water down into the headwaters of their gulch, and it nearly sweeps them all to their death. Charbonneau prays, Clark holds on for dear life, and Sacagawea, clutching her baby in one arm, manages to save a few of the possessions being torn away by the flood. She saves Clark's compass. Unfortunately, she is unable to save one of his prized possessions: his umbrella.

William Clark has been carrying an umbrella since he left St. Louis. Fair enough, he is red-haired and fair-skinned and a parasol makes sense. It is not, however, how one imagines the first American explorer of Montana to look—carrying an umbrella on the grizzly-infested high plains.

31

Late May 1805, In Sight of the Rocky Mountains

THE GENERAL IMPRESSION of this voyage that most books give a reader is that somehow Lewis is an important leader and Clark is some sort of loyal adjutant. First, it should be noted that they are not inseparable, joined-at-the-hip comrades. Nor is Lewis, who could spell, any cleverer than Clark, who couldn't. Nor do they always agree. They never disagree in front of the men, and as near as we can tell from the journals, they never even argue with each other in private. You have to read into the evidence, you have to think about the few words we have.

One of the ways to wonder about all this is to look at the nature of the journals when they are being written under these circumstances:

First, Lewis is not in one of his moods and is writing a daily journal. Second, Clark has time to copy it, either at the same time (which is usual) or during the long winter on the west coast. Most days, Clark simply copies Lewis's journal entries. He is making a duplicate copy in case something happens to the original (say, Charbonneau upsets the pirogue and the Indian woman doesn't rescue the paperwork). Where Lewis writes in the first person, Clark will copy and change it to the third person.

The following entry by Lewis does get copied, almost word for word, but not at the time. Clark will copy it in Oregon, in that long, wet winter with little else to do.

Lewis ascends a hill near the Missouri upstream in the vicinity of Havre, Montana, and gets his first clear view of the Rocky Mountains:

> *. . . from this point I beheld the Rocky Mountains for the first time. I could only discover a few of the most elevated points . . . these points were covered with snow and the sun shone on it in such a manner as to give me the most plain and satisfactory view. While I viewed these mountains I felt a secret pleasure in finding myself so near the head of the heretofore conceived boundless Missouri; but when I reflected on the difficulties which this snowy barrier would most probably throw in my way to the Pacific, and the sufferings and hardships of myself and party in them, it in some measure counter balanced the joy I had felt in the first moments in which I gazed upon them; but I have always held it a crime to anticipate evils. I will believe it a good comfortable road until I am compelled to believe differently.*

Clark's entry for the day, written on the spot, repeats none of these philosophical and psychological thoughts. He does not mention the possibility of either hardships or "a good comfortable road." His journal entry for the same day is therefore shorter than usual, even for him.

> *Game scarce. This country may with propriety I think be termed the Deserts of America, as I do not conceive any part can ever be settled, as it is deficient in water, timber, and too steep to be tilled.*

Besides not bothering to copy everything, Clark has another way of dealing with disagreements. He finds something interesting and useful to do in a different place than where Lewis is working (or, for that matter, thinking). Clark is going to do that within a few weeks, at the Great Falls of the Missouri.

32

June 1805, At the Great Falls of the Missouri

AFTER FIRST IMPRESSIONS are finished, one of the most important things about the Great Falls is that the countryside is infested with grizzly bears. This does not become clear to the Corps of Discovery for a few days. One of the attractions of the Missouri below and between the several falls is that drowned buffalo are plentiful, and grizzlies, like all bears, would just as soon eat ripe meat as fresh food. It takes a few days before anyone notices that the smell of rotting flesh and the rumblings of grizzlies are part of the ambiance.

Lewis, reaching the long-sought-for falls, is provoked to one of his occasional pieces of descriptive prose. He is at the first fall, the most downriver of the four cascades, and the highest. He guesses it is eighty feet. A few days later, Clark will scramble down with a transit and fix its height at almost exactly one hundred feet. Clark will almost drown, a fact which he notes briefly in his daybook.

Lewis works his way to the bottom of the falls for the view, to "gaze on this sublimely grand spectacle." It is a bright clear day, and "from the reflection of the sun on the spray or mist which arises from these falls there is a beautiful rainbow produced which adds not a little to the beauty of the majestically grand scenery." He considers crossing out these words. They seem at once overblown and understated, but then he "reflected that I could not perhaps succeed better than penning the first impressions of the mind. . . . I hope still to give the world some faint idea of an object which at this moment fills me with such pleasure and astonishment, which of its kind I will venture to assert is second to but one [Niagara Falls] in the known world."

He discovers in a few days that the next cascade upstream is lower but carries across the full width of the river and drops in a single arc, an "unbroken smooth sheet . . . at length I determined between these two great rivals for glory that this [one] was pleasingly beautiful while the other was sublimely grand."

Shortly after making this aesthetic distinction, Lewis shoots a buffalo, and while waiting for the animal to succumb, and having neglected to reload his rifle, finds himself being charged by a grizzly bear at the foot of the pleasingly beautiful falls.

"The idea struck me to get into the water to such depth that I could stand. He would be obliged to swim, and that I could in that situation defend myself with my espontoon." The bear, for some reason, turns and runs as Lewis wades into the Missouri. It is one of several odd moments during the day: "The cause of his alarm still remains with me mysterious and unaccountable."

Later in the day he spies a large striped animal and believes it is a tiger of some kind. And a while later he is charged by a bull buffalo. He is planning to sleep out all night (Lewis is the only deliberate loner in the Corps of Discovery) but decides to return to the main camp. Mysterious bears and tigers and buffaloes are too much for him: "I did not think it prudent to remain all night at this place which really from the succession of curious adventures wore the impression on my mind of enchantment; at sometimes for a moment I thought it might be a dream." Walking back, he occasionally stepped on prickly pear cactuses in the dark "which pierced my feet very severely once in a while [and] convinced me that I was really awake."

When he returns to the rest of the party there is another dose of reality to deal with. Sacagawea, who is ill and has been for over a week, is much worse. Clark fears she might die.

33

꧁ ꧂

Mid-June 1805, Near Death at the Great Falls

THE CORPS OF DISCOVERY appears to lose a sense of purpose, of forward motion, at the Great Falls of the Missouri. There are several reasons; all human behavior has multiple causes. Their plan, since before they left St. Louis, is unchanged in its particulars. They will ascend the Missouri to its headwater, to its farthest extent, that is the geopolitical purpose of the expedition. Then they will descend the River of the West, the Columbia, sometimes called the Oregon River, to the Pacific Ocean.

But they have been told, and the captains do believe, that the shortest route to a tributary of the Columbia is from the Great Falls due west across the Rocky Mountains. The Mandans have explained it to them. Lewis sends out some of his reliable men, Drouillard among them, to explore the Sun River, which comes down out of the Rockies to near the Great Falls. One suspects that if they had found an easy route across the mountains, the captains would be sorely tempted to take it and leave the exploration of the upper Missouri for another time.

There are three reasons they decide to press on up the Missouri. First, to establish its extent, which will mark the western border of the

United States. Second, Lewis, trained in the geographical thinking of his time, believes that all the great rivers of the west, the Missouri, the Columbia, the Colorado, and the Rio Grande, arise from the same high ground, perhaps even from the same lake. This is an example of the symmetrical philosophizing of the Enlightenment, which supposes certain immutable laws of geography. The third reason is simply that they expect to meet a band of Indians, the Snakes or Shoshones, who live on both sides of the Continental Divide, on the headwaters of the Missouri and the Columbia. They are a horse people who can assist the corps if it becomes necessary, absent the universal lake, in portaging across the Great Divide.

This was the reason they quickly agreed to bring the Shoshone woman, Sacagawea, with them all the way from the Mandans. It is part of the reason they hired her husband, the ineffable Charbonneau, as an interpreter. Sacagawea will talk to her kin, and then to Charbonneau in Mandan, a second language for both of them. Charbonneau will translate it into French, Cruzatte will translate to English. It is a great gamble: success depends on an Indian woman, an unstable mixed-race frontiersman whose only visible talent is making buffalo sausages, a cheerful, nearsighted, fiddle-playing illiterate French-Canadian, and most of all, on the goodwill of a tribe of Indians who have almost no contact with other tribes, let alone with Europeans. The Corps of Discovery will be as unfamiliar as Martians. This is no mere metaphor. They will say to the first Snake Indians they meet: "Take us to your leader."

And Sacagawea is near death. Feverish, in pain, unable to eat. What she has is a severe flare-up of a chronic pelvic inflammatory disease acquired at the hands of her captors, the Mandans, or her husband, Charbonneau, or likely all of them.

Lewis, returning to the Great Falls from a brief exploratory trip finds "the Indian woman extremely ill and much reduced by her indisposition. This gave me some concern as well for the poor object herself . . . as from the consideration of her being our only dependence for a friendly negotiation with the Snake Indians on whom we depend for horses to assist in our portage from the Missouri to the Columbia River." Lewis is extremely circumspect: "She complains principally of the lower region of the abdomen."

Clark, on the other hand, is actually dealing with the problem. "Our woman sick and very low spirited." He settles on quinine as the medicine. "I gave her the bark & apply it externally to her region which revived her much." Clark has a good idea of the cause of her infection: "If she dies," he writes a few days later, "it will be the fault of her husband as I am now convinced."

Her illness adds to the question of what to do about sending a small party back to St. Louis. The captains were supposed to do that when they stopped at the Mandan villages in the fall of 1804, but they decided to keep every man through the Mandan winter, purely for self-defense. In the spring, when they did send back the extra men (and the magpie and the prairie dog) they promised Jefferson that maps and specimens would be sent back with a small party from the Great Falls.

In Clark's hand, but probably copied from a now-lost entry in Lewis's journal (so one assumes because it is tolerably well spelled in the original manuscript):

> Not having the Snake Indians or knowing in fact whether to calculate on their friendship or hostility, we have conceived our party sufficiently small, and therefore have concluded not to dispatch a canoe with a part of our men to St. Louis as have intended early in the spring. We fear also that such a measure might also discourage those who would in such case remain, and might possibly hazard the fate of the expedition. We have never hinted to anyone of the party that we had such a scheme in contemplation, and all appear perfectly to have made up their minds, to succeed in the expedition or perish in the attempt. We all believe that we are about to enter on the most perilous and difficult part of our voyage, yet I see no one repining; all appear ready to meet those difficulties which await us with resolution and becoming fortitude.

All except Charbonneau, who claims his wife will be healthy if only they let him take her back to the Mandans. Clark, in his usual short-hand: "The Indian woman much worse this evening, she will not take any medicine, her husband petitions to return &c."

So, camped on a fearsome river, surrounded by grizzly bears, attacked by mosquitoes day and night, they carry on with, well, becoming fortitude.

34

Late June 1805,

The Bishop's Residence, New Orleans

WHILE THE CORPS OF DISCOVERY is camped at the Great Falls of the Missouri, Aaron Burr is in New Orleans. Picture this: a short, foppish, overdressed Anglo-Saxon descendant of New England Protestant ministers, who happens to be an atheist himself, presents his credentials to the bishop of New Orleans and to the abbess of the local nunnery. The clerics are Spanish citizens and have served in churches and schools in Old Mexico. Aaron Burr is there to enlist their aid in fomenting, he tells them, an uprising by the downtrodden peasants of Mexico against the oppressive Spanish governors. Picture this occurring in darkened rooms, screened against the fetid heat of a New Orleans summer.

According to Burr, they agree to help. So far, Burr has enlisted the help of two western governors, the head of the American army in the west (our acquaintance, Wilkinson) and Andrew Jackson, later to be the sixth president of the United States. He has emissaries in Britain, begging funds to support his campaign against Spain's North American colonies. He has hinted at an expedition against Mexico with everyone from tavern owners to army garrison commanders. There is hardly an adult American west of the Alleghenies who hasn't heard that Burr is up to something. Even Thomas Jefferson has been warned, but he does nothing.

If Jefferson looks back over his copies of his own correspondence on the subject of the American west, he will find this letter, written to the U.S. Senator from Tennessee just after the purchase of Louisiana:

August 12, 1803, To John Breckinridge, from Monticello

> *Objections are raising to the eastward against the vast extent of our boundaries, and propositions are made to exchange Louisiana, or a part of it, for the Floridas. These Federalists see in this acquisition the formation of a new confederacy, embracing all the waters of the Mississippi, on both sides of it, and a separation of its eastern waters from us. I place little reliance on them. We have seldom seen neighborhood produce affection among nations. The reverse is almost the universal truth. Besides, if it should become the great interest of those nations to separate from this, if their happiness should depend on it so strongly as to induce them to go through that convulsion, why should the Atlantic States dread it? But especially why should we, their present inhabitants, take side in such a question? . . . The future inhabitants of the Atlantic and Mississippi States will be our sons. We leave them in distinct but bordering establishments. We think we see their happiness in their union, and we wish it. Events may prove it otherwise; and if they see their interest in separation, why should we take side with out Atlantic rather than our western descendants? It is the elder and the younger son differing. God bless them both, and keep them in union, if it be for their good, but separate them, if it be better.*

He writes as much, and more succinctly, in early 1804:

To Joseph Priestly, January 29, 1804

> *Whether we remain in one confederacy, or form into Atlantic and Mississippi confederacies, I believe not very important to the happiness of either part. Those of the western confederacy will be as much our children and descendants as those of the eastern, and I feel myself as much identified with that country, in future time, as with this; and did I now foresee a separation at some future day, yet I should feel the duty and the desire to promote the western interests as zealously as the eastern, doing all the good for both portions of our future family which should fall within my power.*

So, Jefferson is in a quandary. Every intellectual instinct is to let nature take its course. But every emotional instinct is the opposite. He despises Aaron Burr, who tried to steal Jefferson's own presidency by fiddling with the electoral college votes. Not even killing Hamilton, whom Jefferson also disliked to the point of pure hatred, puts Burr in Jefferson's good graces. For the next year, Jefferson will vacillate between his deepest belief in self-government and his fervent wish that Aaron Burr be dismissed as the rogue he is.

35

June–July 1805, Meriwether Lewis, Inventor

ON A HOT SUNDAY MORNING, June 23, Lewis unpacks his invention, the Iron Canoe. It is a wrought-iron frame, ready to be bolted together and supplemented with wooden ribs, and then covered with animal hides. He has been carrying the iron frame since the spring of 1803, some 3,000 miles by river, down the Ohio, up the Mississippi to St. Louis, up the Missouri to the base of the Great Falls, and his men lug it up the steep, canyon-cut banks to the campground above the falls.

The pirogues, the heavy rowboats, are to be cached at the falls, picked up on the return trip, repaired and refloated back down to St. Louis. The Iron Canoe will carry their minimum supplies up the increasingly shallow Missouri, and then its main tributary, and then the canoe can be disassembled, portaged, reassembled, and paddled to the sea. It starts out well enough, this boat building.

Hides are no problem; the men cover it with twenty-eight elk hides and four buffalo hides, and sew it all together. (They are eating, Lewis notes, the equivalent of a buffalo a day, or two elk, or four deer.) Unfortunately, their needles make too-large holes, and the sinews and rawhide strips they use for thread cut into the soft, untanned hides. The boat, not even loaded, begins to fill with water the minute they set it in the river.

Clark begins to refer to it as "Lewis's project." It is the first time that they are not thinking as one. It begins to drive Clark a little crazy, watching the men waste their time. Lewis even has them searching for pine trees to make tar to caulk the sewn seams, and there are no pine trees within dozens of miles. He has them try to cook tar out of cottonwood and willow trees. None can be produced. The men speak of the boat with contempt, when Lewis cannot hear them.

Clark, for the first time on the expedition, deliberately separates himself from Lewis. He takes Charbonneau, Sacagawea, little Pompey, and goes off camping on the river. He wants to be out of sight, away from the boat.

There is an interruption in the boat building and Clark's camping trip. Saturday, June 29, a thunderstorm with hailstones the size of goose eggs strikes the camp and knocks down the men, "one of them three times, and most of them were bleeding freely and complained of being much bruised." Clark, returning to camp, "gave the part a dram [of whisky] to console them."

Lewis tries everything on his Iron Canoe. The men caulk it with bear grease. It leaks. He tries a mixture of buffalo tallow, bee's wax, and charcoal. It leaks. On July 8, more than two weeks into the boat-building program, he has the men paint it with two coats of ordinary paint they have brought for maintaining the pirogues. "This adds very much to her appearance," Lewis writes that night, "whether it will be effectual or not." It is not.

Lewis regards the Iron Canoe settling to the shallow bottom of the river's shore. "In every other respect," he notes, "the boat completely answers my most sanguine expectation."

He gives up on the ninth day of July. "I need not add," he writes in his journal that night, "that this circumstance mortified me not a little . . . but to make any further experiments in our present situation seemed to me madness . . . it is now too late to introduce a remedy and I bid adieu to my boat, and her expected services."

In two days, his men chop down and hollow out several cotton-wood tree canoes. Three days after Lewis gives up, three weeks after he begins his adventure in iron canoe building, leaving the grizzly-infested banks of the Great Falls of the Missouri at last, the Corps of Discovery paddles upstream. As Clark was fond of repeating in his journal entries: "We proceeded on."

36

July 1805, Lieutenant Pike Gets a Real Job

THE FIRST THING to remember about Lieutenant Zebulon Montgomery Pike is that he is a twenty-six-year-old who has one hero in life: General James Wilkinson. His explorations in the years from 1805 to

1807, overlapping the Lewis and Clark expedition, are done directly for Wilkinson, on Wilkinson's orders. Pike is not Jefferson's man.

Pike is what we would call an army brat. His father, Zebulon, no middle name, Pike, is alive and well in the summer of 1805 and recently retired, for the second time, from the United States Army.

Zebulon senior fought in the Revolutionary War, and then on the old Northwest Frontier when he rejoined the army in 1791. The father's most memorable battle was on the Wabash, in November 1791, when attacking Indians got into the baggage train of General William Butler's command and killed some two hundred civilians, almost all women, camp followers who performed all domestic and conjugal services for the enlisted men. Captain Pike took command of the shattered army and organized a retreat that was successful, except for the women.

In 1793, Captain Pike was given command of Fort Washington on the Ohio River and brought his family to live with him. The fort is General Wilkinson's headquarters, and the first experience of military life that young Zebulon has, at the age of twelve, is seeing General Wilkinson, a snappy if corpulent figure (something like Mr. Toad in *Wind in the Willows*) receiving the honors of command from an entire post, and not less from his own father, Captain Pike.

In 1795, the boy Pike accompanies his father and, more important, General Wilkinson, to the agreement of the Treaty of Greenville with the Indians. Amid the smoke of peace pipes and the odors of roasting beef, Pike watches Wilkinson take title, on behalf of the United States, to the Ohio country and most of Indiana. The Indians shift westward.

From that first summer at Fort Washington until the day he dies, Zebulon Montgomery Pike will want nothing in this world so much as the esteem of General Wilkinson. He simply adores the man. This explains almost everything that Pike will do in the years of 1805 to 1807. Pike may act without regard to his own safety, or his men's well-being, or his nation's interest. But he will please General James Wilkinson.

And the first thing he will do, a year after Lewis and Clark head up the Missouri, is move up the Mississippi River to find its headwaters, for that will be the northern boundary of the Louisiana Purchase.

In July 1805, having been chosen for this task by James Wilkinson, Pike begins to plan his expedition.

It is a curiosity, and one with no overt explanation, that Thomas Jefferson has no interest at all in determining the northern boundary, the line fronting British Canada that marks those limits of Louisiana. The logical reason is that relations with Britain are poor enough (her ban on trading with France and most of northern Europe and her impressment of American sailors are great irritants), and Jefferson doesn't need to add a squabble about boundaries to the mix. Wilkinson orders the discovery of the headwaters on his own authority, and for his own ends. Jefferson accedes, after the fact.

37

July 1805, To the Jefferson River

THE READER of the journals of Lewis and Clark is often frustrated by the missing interesting detail. On July 10, the men, now that the Iron Canoe is history, set about making several cottonwood dugout canoes. How many? We have thirty souls to transport, plus baggage. That couldn't mean many fewer than five boats, for six paddlers and polers is a lot of folks in one canoe. However many it takes, the men, certainly eager to get moving again, will make all the canoes in two days. That means everyone is working at once, several men to each log. Somehow they get it done without chopping off anyone's extremities. Lewis and Clark may find this prodigious work unexceptional, or, after the Iron Canoe perhaps Lewis is in no mood to comment on how swiftly and cleverly a canoe can be made by enlisted men from the raw materials at hand.

As they realize they are approaching the headwaters of the Missouri, a certain political responsibility begins to weigh on the captains. After leaving the Mandans, they name the two largest tributaries of the Missouri for their half-remembered girlfriends. Clark starts it with the Judith River, Lewis commandeers the next upstream tributary for Maria's River (later the Marias River). But after the long halt at the Great Falls, they remember to include their bosses. Just above the falls they name the Smith River for the secretary of the navy and the Dearborn River for the secretary of war. At the three forks of the Missouri, a flurry of debts are repaid: the Madison River for the ambassador who clinched the Louisiana Purchase, the Gallatin for the secretary of the treasury who's paying the bills for Louisiana, and the major tributary, obviously, the Jefferson River.

Sacagawea tells Charbonneau, who tells Cruzatte, who tells the captains and the rest of the men, that they are on the fringes of the country of her people, and this cheers "the spirits of the party who now begin to console themselves with the anticipation of shortly seeing the head of the Missouri yet unknown to the civilized world." Among the trials contributing to the lowered spirits of the party are a plague of mosquitoes and falling water levels that make paddling difficult, poling more necessary, and sometimes require wading and dragging the boats.

"I occasionally encourage them by assisting in the labor of navigating the canoes," Lewis writes, "and have learned to *push a tolerable good pole* in their phrase."

Fearful that their substantial armed party might frighten off the Shoshone, Clark has left Lewis with the men and is scouting ahead on foot with a few men, including York. You might think York, huge and very black, would frighten the Shoshone; he has already proven his ability to be seen as serious "magic." But Clark intuitively realizes it is no problem. After the parties meet, he and Lewis write that York seems no more remarkable to the Shoshone, who had never seen a European face before, than the captains and the other men. They only notice that York is not an Indian. He is just another them. He is an other.

Lewis never quite understands, or pretends to understand, the

Indian psychology. On the Jefferson, just above modern Three Forks, Montana, they camp "precisely on the spot that the Snake Indians were encamped at the time the Minnetaries of the Knife River first came in sight of them five years ago. Sacagawea our Indian woman was one of the female prisoners taken at that time; though I cannot discover that she shows any emotion of sorrow in recollecting this event, or of joy in being again restored to her native country." Lewis starts a new line in the journal: "If she has enough to eat and a few trinkets to wear I believe she would be perfectly content anywhere." There is something in her apparent serenity that annoys the mercurial Lewis.

Upstream, they name the three tributaries of the Jefferson for his virtues: the Philosophy (meaning science and the scientific method in these Enlightenment times), Wisdom, and Philanthropy Rivers. We know them now as the Beaverhead (from the mountain so shaped at its headwaters), the Big Hole, from the valley where it rises, and the Ruby, from the garnets in the mountain rocks to the southeast. There are a few artifacts of the original nomonology on modern maps: the major tributary of the Big Hole is the Wise River. The largest village in the Big Hole valley is Wisdom, Montana.

They are almost to the Continental Divide (and have been within a few miles of it several times) and they still have not found the Snake Indians, the Shoshones, Sacagawea's people.

38

꧁⁕꧂

July 30, 1805, Pike on the Mississippi

IN THE NEXT SEVERAL MONTHS, Lieutenant Pike will ascend the Mississippi. He has, as he will always have when working for Wilkinson, two sets of orders. One is private for the benefit of Wilkinson; one is public for the benefit of the public's opinion and the good of the United States of America. Here are his simple and public orders dated this day from General Wilkinson:

"You will proceed to ascend the main branch of the River, until you reach the source of it, or the season may forbid your further progress, without endangering your return before the waters are frozen up." To Pike's credit, he is considerably less fearful of ice and snow than of Wilkinson. To Pike's debit, he never seems to understand that ordinary men suffer when they are led into a wintry waste totally unprepared. He does not, as they say, get it.

Along the way, Pike will spend considerable effort attending to the needs of Wilkinson's purse and, given the general's corpulence, to his victuals.

Pike's command is composed of anonymous soldiers, whose names only appear in his journal when they commit some transgression or fall ill. They are not terribly reliable young men, but they will do, they suffice. And now, he is on his way up the Mississippi, at last.

39

Late July to Early September 1805, Burr in Motion

THE DAY that Lewis and Clark and the Corps of Discovery leave the Great Falls, Aaron Burr leaves New Orleans. He has spoken with everyone who might join him in this great escapade: capturing Mexico and the American west. He tells them he will be back in October 1806 with his army of volunteers.

After leaving New Orleans on the fourteenth of July, after promising the Ursuline nuns that he would lift the boot of Spain off the necks of their beloved Mexican peasants, Aaron Burr heads for Tennessee and Kentucky and on to Washington City, with a side trip to St. Louis. There is only one road from New Orleans (properly, from Natchez, Mississippi, upstream and on the east bank of the Mississippi, in undisputedly United States possession) that runs toward civilization. The Natchez Trace stays on the high ground, running parallel to the Mississippi and then the Ohio. It is almost a road, better than the mere trail that most roads are, and it has inns along the way. Once the northbound traveler reaches Nashville, he can take other roads that parallel the Ohio to Pittsburgh, or cut northwest to the suddenly important town of St. Louis, headquarters of the government of Louisiana Territory.

Burr stops and meets again with Andrew Jackson in Tennessee. His reception is cool this time. Jackson, who had given Burr a military escort to New Orleans in the spring, has had second thoughts. Jackson has heard rumors that Burr is not just interested in capturing Mexico, which suits Jackson just fine, but may want to separate the western states and the territory of Louisiana and combine it all with Mexico. Jackson is a devout nationalist and patriot, and it is hardly surprising that he has heard such talk, Burr has sprinkled those ideas across the west for months.

On August 2, while Burr is traveling alone on the Natchez Trace, the *Gazette of the United States,* printed in Philadelphia, reports on separatist movements in the west, and asks how long it will be before Burr takes the forts along the Ohio and Mississippi and the stores at New Orleans, all to "be used for the reduction of Mexico and the appropriation of her treasures, aided by British ships and forces." Burr has dropped so many hints along his trail that almost no one is unaware of his dream. Besides Jackson's suspicions of Burr, the formidable Tennessean is even beginning to wonder about General Wilkinson, much the cagier of the two conspirators.

It is as though everyone, with the possible exception of Thomas Jefferson, is in on the substance of the plan whether they approve or not. And Burr continues to let some very obvious hints drop.

When he arrives in St. Louis on September 12 to meet with Wilkinson, Burr seeks out a locally prominent politician, Judge Rufus Easton, and inquires of this civilian which of Wilkinson's officers could be trusted to lead an expedition to Santa Fe. Easton thought it would be a Lieutenant Bruff. This is a good choice. Bruff is the same man that Wilkinson asked, mere months before, to collect all available printed and anecdotal information on a route to Santa Fe. Wilkinson had told Bruff, as that young officer would later testify, that Wilkinson was contemplating a "grand scheme," one that will make a fortune for all who cooperate with it. Either Wilkinson, or perhaps young Bruff, must have spoken of some New Mexico scheme to Judge Easton, otherwise how would the judge know which local army officer was an expert on the route to Santa Fe? Burr continues to give the impression that he is not merely fomenting a conspiracy, he's virtually enlisting a public army to march on Mexico.

The introduction of the Santa Fe idea into the conspiracy doesn't attract attention. Western and eastern newspapers, like the *Gazette* in Philadelphia, stay focused on the Mississippi and New Orleans. What is surprising is how little stir it causes in Washington City or Monticello. Thomas Jefferson has a trait, not uncommon among geniuses, of simply not hearing or not seeing what he does not want to know. It simplifies his life to ignore rumors and speculations. It is a style of government, too. Avoid anxiety, avoid contention, avoid confrontations.

40

August 14, 1805,

Lieutenant Pike Meets Chief Quashquame

PIKE'S PRIVATE ORDERS from Wilkinson are simple enough. As he ascends the Mississippi, Pike is to keep an eye out for likely places to build trading posts. Wilkinson intends to create a monopoly in the Indian trading business to go along with his general's pay and his annual bribe from the Spanish government.

Pike is traveling through lightly settled country now. The lower Mississippi and Missouri valley has its small towns, mostly French-speaking villages. To the north, on both sides of the border, British-owned trading companies have their outposts in the northern woodlands surrounding the Great Lakes. The Mississippi valley is well known compared to the almost completely mysterious Missouri River country. Pike is not exploring so much as he is traveling from one known place to another. It is only the question of the exact point of origin of the Mississippi that remains to be solved. It simply had never been an issue, until Jefferson bought Louisiana and needed to know exactly what land was drained by the rivers.

On August 14, near where the Rock River enters the Mississippi (today's Montrose, Iowa), Pike enters a village of Sauk Indians, seeks out the chief, and asks the Indians to pick a site that they will give, or sell if necessary, to the army. The Indians demur. They explain, and Pike notes in his published journal: "That as for the situation of trading houses, they could not determine, being but a part of the nation."

The Indians suggest that Pike should visit the larger Sauk villages, or they will send messengers and Pike can wait for the Indians to come

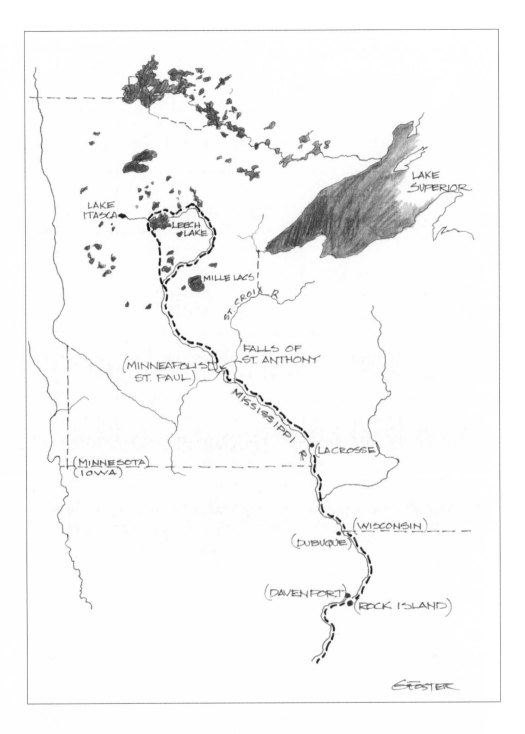

ZEBULON M. PIKE'S MISSISSIPPI RIVER EXPEDITION,
JULY 1805 TO APRIL 1806.

to him at Rock River. What they do not tell him is this: the chief of this small Sauk band is Quashquame, and he is a very unpopular man. The summer before, in June 1804, Quashquame was the senior chief when a delegation of five Sauk and Fox chiefs went to St. Louis and signed away their tribal claims to 15 million acres of land in Illinois, Wisconsin, and Missouri. They could stay until the white settlers arrived, but then they would have to move across the Mississippi. They were the first tribes to agree to Jefferson's first principle: the Louisiana Purchase will be a refuge for displaced Indians. The rest of the Sauk and the Fox Indians never accept that they must move, and the St. Louis treaty becomes the cause of the Blackhawk War of 1834.

Pike has no stomach for waiting around for a bunch of Indians to make up their minds. Without visiting the other Sauks or receiving a delegation, he sails on up the Mississippi toward the well-known lead mines of a Monsieur Dubuque, near the modern Iowa city of that name. Dubuque's mines are the most important source of lead in the west, an absolutely necessary commodity for a well-armed population. Dubuque's lead is traded up into Canada, out to the Great Plains, and down the Mississippi. Lieutenant Pike demands to inspect the mines. Mr. Dubuque, who is in the happy situation of owning a lucrative business that pays no taxes to any government, explains that they are several days' journey, far inland from the river. Lieutenant Pike sails on. As he does, he passes by the rubble of mine tailings excavated by M. Dubuque. The mines are right by the river. Lieutenant Pike is always in a hurry.

41

❧

August 11, 1805, Lewis Finds the Shoshones

As the Corps of Discovery ascends what they are calling the Jefferson River, Sacagawea points out the small mountain shaped like a beaver's head. She tells Charbonneau in Mandan (and he tells Cruzatte in French, and Cruzatte tells Lewis in English) that "we shall either find her people on this river or on the river immediately west of its source." That night he writes in his journal that his plan is to leave Clark with the main party "and proceed tomorrow to the source of the principle stream of this river and pass the mountains to the Columbia and down that river until I find the Indians."

Clark is not well. He is the only person in the party, as he would say in his laconic military style, "unfit for duty." Even Sacagawea, thought to be near death a week earlier, has recovered. The plague of boils which began in the winter camp near St. Louis and then followed them to the Mandans and on to the Rockies, skipping from man to man, has finally reached Clark. He has been doctoring boils for almost a year, and it is his turn. It is an untimely illness.

Because Clark is now essentially inseparable from little Pompey, he will keep Sacagawea (and Charbonneau) with him, while Lewis goes forward to find the Shoshone. At this critical moment, Lewis will dispense with his only Shoshone-speaking interpreting asset, the team of Sacagawea and Charbonneau. Although Lewis misses Charbonneau's sausages, he can barely stand the sight of the man. Clark, were he well, would be leading the small party to the Shoshones with Sacagawea and the child. And the explorers do not quite understand, as they will, how useful it can be to make their first acquaintance of a tribe with a woman and a toddler in tow. There are no camp followers on an Indian war party. The mother and child say "peaceful intentions" in a universal language. When Lewis sets out with a small group—Joseph and Reubin Field, the hardy brothers Clark recruited in Kentucky, and the useful, sign-language-literate Drouillard—Clark makes for him a rare journal entry, an entry of doubt and mild dismay: "I should have taken this trip [to find the Shoshone band] had I been able to march, [I am disabled] from the raging fury of a tumor on my ankle muscle." He misspells the important word as *tumer,* but it is not amusing to read.

Clark is left with the canoes, and Lewis goes on with his threesome of capable young men. Lewis, now hiking away from the river, is apparently unaware of how difficult it is for the men to push the heavy dugout canoes across the sand and gravel bars and beaver dams that increasingly bar their way, but push they must, for Lewis is determined to ascend to the parting of the waters by boat. He writes in his journal a description of the river which is both true and false, or, true and wildly optimistic:

"I do not believe that the world can furnish an example of a river running to the extent which the Missouri and Jefferson's river do through such a mountainous country and at the same time so navigable as they are." The men, horseless, hungry, heaving at the heavy dugouts, would not likely use the word *navigable,* were it in their vocabulary. "If the Columbia furnishes us such another example," Lewis continues, "a communication across the continent by water will be practicable and safe. But this I can scarcely hope from a knowledge of its having . . . a comparatively short course to the ocean, the same number of feet to descend which the Missouri and Mississippi have from this point to the Gulf of Mexico." He is righter than he knows.

On Sunday, August 11, 1805, at the virtual Continental Divide, Lewis sees an Indian. The man is mounted. It is the Shoshone at last, the tribe whose horses his party so desperately needs should they be unable to boat all the way down the Columbia, from its headwaters to the Pacific.

Following the instructions that he has asked from Sacagawea (and received from her, via Charbonneau and Cruzatte), Lewis shouts at the

Indian that he and his three men are "Tah-ba-bone." The Indian disappears instantly. It is difficult to reconstruct what is going through everyone's mind at that moment, but what Lewis is shouting is that he is "taibonii," meaning "from the trail of the sun," meaning from the east, which may mean "white man," or may mean anyone from the east and that would include the Rees and Blackfeet and Hidatsa who routinely assault the hapless, gunless Shoshone. Later, Lewis will think the word he shouted is the word for "enemy." He mistrusts Sacagawea's good intentions, and blames her for the difficulty. Lewis has no sympathy for the difficulty of translating from one language through two more to his ear. But that day, he blames Drouillard and the Fields brothers. They continue moving forward (they are walking abreast, like skirmishers or scouts) when he calls to them to wait. They cannot hear him. He assumes that the Indian fled from them.

"I now called the men to me and could not forbear upbraiding them a little for their want of attention and imprudence on this occasion."

Then, the Men from the East leave a small pile of trinkets from their rapidly diminishing store at the Indian's campsite. It is a gift, a peace offering, should the Indian return.

42

August 12, 1805, Communion at the Headwaters

ABSENT INDIANS, and joined by several other members of the corps, Lewis ascends the last tributary of the Jefferson/Beaverhead River, understandably named Trail Creek today. At the summit, Lewis writes, the corps finds "the most distant fountain of the waters of the mighty Missouri, in search of which we have spent so many toilsome days and restless nights.

"I had accomplished one of those great objects on which my mind has been unalterably fixed for many months . . . judge then the pleasure I felt in allaying my thirst."

After this first sacramental drink, Lewis crosses the divide to what is now Horseshoe Bend Creek, tributary to the Lemhi River, and the Lemhi is tributary to the middle fork of the Salmon, which today, even on simple road maps, carries the sobriquet River of No Return. Lewis, of course, does not know why it should someday earn that title.

"After refreshing ourselves [at the spring source of the Missouri]," Lewis relates, "we proceeded on to the top of the dividing ridge from which I discovered immense ranges of high mountains still to the west of us with their tops partially covered with snow." And then he drank from the waters of the Columbia.

While Lewis drinks both from thirst and ceremony, one of the party does the wonderful sort of thing that reminds us that they are all strong young men on an adventure: "McNeal had exulting stood with a foot on each side of this little rivulet and thanked his god that he had lived to bestride the mighty & theretofore deemed endless Missouri." And someone, no doubt spit across it. Or pissed across it. That would be something to brag about, someday.

43

August 12, 1805, Lewis Finds His Indians

MOST BRIEF ACCOUNTS of the meeting between the Corps of Discovery and the Shoshone Indians concentrate their attention on Sacagawea, who is reunited with her brother. As though it is all being scripted for Hollywood, her brother Cameawait turns out to be the true and veritable chief of this band of Indians. That happens, but it diverts attention from the real first encounter between Lewis and a few of his men with a scouting party—virtually a war party—of Shoshones.

First, Lewis spies three women, girls really, who are out foraging for anything edible—roots, berries, tubers. Then come some thirty Shoshone men, armed with bows and arrows, riding cautiously on their ponies, the very Indian horses that Lewis covets. It is all resolved when George Drouillard signs their peaceful intent.

One of the Shoshone men embraces Drouillard, then Lewis. It is a peculiar hug. Each man puts his left arm over the other's right shoulder, and then in this slightly offset face-to-face embrace, rub their cheeks back and forth against each other's. Peacefulness established, the other men of the corps and the rest of the Indian men join in the greeting:

"Both parties now advanced, we were all caressed and besmeared with their grease and paint [Lewis is presumably required to greet every Shoshone personally] until I was heartily tired of the national hug." They remove their moccasins, indicating to one another that they are not afraid and about to flee, and smoke. Lewis gives the chief an American flag and Drouillard signifies that it is "an emblem of peace among white men, now that it had been received by him it was to be respected as the bond of union between us."

The most remarkable visible traits of the Shoshone, even more than their bear grease and ocher war paint, are their eyes. They burn, in Lewis's words. In a few days he will realize that they burn not with emotion, but with the fever of starvation.

Clark and most of the men (and more important, Sacagawea) are somewhere downstream. His men continue doggedly to push the canoes up the ever-narrowing, ever-shallowing Beaverhead River. This leaves Lewis in a precarious situation. Not only is he undermanned, greatly outnumbered by the Shoshone, but Clark, with the canoes, has all the trade goods. Lewis has nothing to give but promises.

At his request, the Shoshone take Lewis over the divide to the

Lemhi River, the main tributary of the Salmon and thus the Columbia. The Shoshone chief informs him that it is "impossible for us to pass either by land or water down this river to the great lake where the white men live . . . this was unwelcome information. I still hoped that this account had been exaggerated with a view to detain us among them." Perhaps, although the extra mouths to feed are a problem. The Shoshone are trapped between the end of the summer run of Chinook salmon and the beginning of the very dangerous, but necessary, fall expedition to the plains east of the Rockies where they will try to take a few buffalo without attracting the notice of the Hidatsa, the Arikaras, or the Blackfeet.

The Shoshone are moderately generous, much more than Lewis realizes. He is given a piece of antelope meat "and a piece of a fresh salmon roasted . . . this was the first salmon I had seen and [it] convinced me that we were on the waters of the Pacific Ocean."

Lewis and his party camp for the night on the watershed of the Pacific Ocean. He is beyond Louisiana, in terra truly incognita. He worries about Clark, and more particularly about the promise made to the Shoshone that a large number of whites and parcels of rich trade goods would appear. His credibility is at stake, and he is almost alone, outnumbered ten to one.

44

Mid-August 1805, A Brief Glimpse of Aaron Burr

BURR, who keeps no diary and sends no important correspondence except in code, is moving from St. Louis, where he has just seen General Wilkinson, who is also Governor Wilkinson of Louisiana Territory.

On his way from St. Louis to Pittsburgh (and on to Washington and a meeting with Thomas Jefferson), Burr presents himself to William Henry Harrison, governor of the Territory of Indiana. Later, Harrison will recall that Burr is carrying a letter from Wilkinson to Harrison that suggests that Aaron Burr would make an excellent territorial delegate to Congress.

This is mildly bizarre. Wilkinson could just as easily make Burr the delegate from Louisiana as could Harrison appoint him from Indiana, but perhaps that would look just a little suspicious, since newspaper rumors are already linking Burr's alleged plot on Mexico with the commanding general of the United States Army.

Burr, once the vice president and a Princeton-educated member of the eastern elite, a delegate from a raw landscape of subsistence hog farmers scratching a slash-and-burn living out of what is truly Indian Country? It passes understanding. But we cannot complain; it is the only fact we will ever know about Aaron Burr in August 1805.

Harrison does nothing. He keeps silent for the time being.

Harrison is an underestimated man, and not just by Wilkinson and Burr. He is no fool, and he is a relentless expander of the American empire, responsible for the eventual extinguishing of tribal lands in Indiana Territory, leaving little but the name to remind us of what it was when Burr rode down some muddy track to find the governor's office.

45

August 16, 1805, Drouillard Feeds the Shoshone

LEWIS REMARKS that the entire band of Shoshone seems to own but a single firearm and has no powder or shot. On August 14, he conveys a simple message to Cameawait of the Shoshone, and his people. If the Shoshone remain true to their Father in Washington, they will have all the guns they desire.

Lewis, who has not given up the possibility that they can boat the Lemhi to the Salmon to the Columbia and the big ill-tasting lake, wants the entire band to leave the Lemhi, where there is at least the remote possibility of salmon, and return to the upper Beaverhead valley to meet Clark, the canoes, and the trade goods that will purchase their horses, and buy the Indians' labor to repack and move the party's stores over the divide and down to the Lemhi. This demand is met with a surly diffidence. At last he succeeds in persuading the Shoshone, although without quite understanding how he did it. One moment, they would not go with him, the next, as he describes in his journal entry:

"It appeared to me that we had all the men of the village and a number of women with us. This may serve in some measure to illustrate the capricious disposition of those people who never act but from the impulse of the moment.

"They were now very cheerful and gay, and two hours ago they looked as surly as so many imps of Saturn."

It is remarkable that they are the least bit cheerful, since they are basically starving. But, as Lewis and Clark often note of their own men, simply getting up and moving is a cheering activity for human beings.

Drouillard and the Field brothers, Lewis's constant companions, go hunting and somewhat to their dismay find themselves shadowed by mounted Shoshone. This interferes with surreptitious game-stalking.

Lewis has seen many things in his life and on this expedition, but he has been spared seeing mankind on the verge of starvation until Drouillard (of course) returns with the first deer, and, surrounded by a waiting throng of Shoshone horsemen, begins to gut and butcher the animal:

"They dismounted and ran in tumbling over each other like a parcel of famished dogs, each seizing and tearing away a part of the intestines which had been thrown out by Drouillard . . . each one had a piece of some description and all eating most ravenously, some were eating the kidneys, the spleen and liver and the blood running from the corners of their mouths. Others were in a similar situation with the paunch and guts, but the exuding substance in this case from their lips was of a different description."

This is part of the longest passage Lewis writes about Indians and their behavior for the entire trip. It is much abridged here:

"I really did not until now think that human nature ever presented itself in a shape so nearly allied to the brute creation," he writes that night by firelight. "I viewed these poor starved devils with pity and compassion," he tells himself, although he does not sound very convincing.

They are very hungry indeed, and of course the Indians are quite right to ingest all the organ meat and intestines that Drouillard discards. In them, and in the fat that coats them, lie the life-giving lipids and fats the Shoshone need. A second deer from one of the Field brothers produces the same scene. When Drouillard brings in the third, Lewis is able to watch with more attention to detail and less dismay about their manner of eating. He notices, rather more calmly, that when it comes to fresh venison, the Shoshone "eat the whole of them, even to the soft parts of the hooves."

On the eve of the deer hunt, Clark, still working his way upstream toward Lewis, notes in his journal that Charbonneau struck Sacagawea, "for which he was reprimanded." He does not explain further. So the battered Indian woman moves closer to a reunion with her people. They will meet on the top of the continent.

46

 (decorative ornament)

August 17, 1805, Sacagawea Finds Her Brother

WE CANNOT LEAVE the Corps of Discovery now; it is the defining moment of their unbelievably lucky, fortunate, serendipitous expedition. Lewis, for once, seems acutely aware that matters are out of his hands, his control is loosening, he has no option except patience to see how the cards are dealt. He writes at length on the evening of the sixteenth (and with such care that the reader assumes this is one of the many journal entries rewritten during the long winter to come by the Pacific shore) on the *possibilities* the future holds.

He is on the banks of the Beaverhead surrounded by Shoshone, with just three allies. Clark has not arrived with the boats, the extra ammunition, the trade goods, and the Indian woman. He speculates that the Indians are regarding this trip over the divide back to the Beaverhead as a ruse, a trap. He fears that they will disperse, taking their horses with them. This "would vastly retard and increase the labor of our voyage and I feared might so discourage the men as to defeat the expedition altogether. My mind was in reality quite as gloomy all this evening as the most affrighted Indian's, but I affected cheerfulness to keep the Indians so [that is, also cheerful] who were about me. My mind [was] dwelling on the state of the expedition which I had ever held in equal estimation with my own existence and the fate of which at this moment appeared to depend in a great measure upon the caprice of a few savages who are ever as fickle as the wind."

It is politically correct to remark on Lewis's low estimation of the Shoshone, from their table manners to their capriciousness. Shortly he will comment on their curious sexual mores. But the most important phrase in that night's writing, the one that will become the key to his next few years, is his ingenuous statement that the "state of the expedition . . . I had ever held in equal estimation with my own existence. . . ." We do well to remember that Lewis's life, in his mind, depends on the success of the journey to the Pacific. His very existence, he says, depends on finding a viable trade route to the riches of that distant, foreign shore.

He tries to keep the attention of the Shoshone. Several times he tells Cameawait that a woman of that tribe is coming with the other members of the corps. He offers more entertainment: there is a black man with "short curling hair," which excites "their curiosity very much and they seemed quite as anxious to see this monster as they were the merchandise which we had to barter for their horses."

Many years later, in Philadelphia, William Clark recalls the introduction of York, his man, to various Indian tribes. A Philadelphia scholar, William Biddle, is attempting to create a publishable manuscript out of the journals and daybooks of the expedition and he interviews Clark on matters that might intrigue the audience but are not clear from the journals. One particular interest is how York was perceived by the tribes.

Clark responds that "York made the Indians believe that he had been wild like a bear and then tamed. . . . Those who had seen whites and not blacks thought him something strange and from his very large size more vicious than whites. *Those who had seen neither made no difference between white and black.*"

The Shoshone are innocent of the appearance of white men and find the entire party quite remarkable. Lewis, when York and the main party arrives, does not realize that York's remarkable presence, the fascination he inspires in the Shoshone, is unrelated to his negritude: "Every article about us appeared to excite astonishment in their minds, the appearance of the men, their arms, the canoes, our manner of working them, the black man York and the sagacity of my dog were equally objects of admiration." York, who may have benefited among the Arikaras and the Mandans because of his uniqueness (they were all too familiar with European-Americans) is now, for the time, a peer of his fellows. He is no more "other" than his red-haired master. Oh, he is bigger and stronger than anyone, Indians included, and can dance on his hands, but he is just another Tah-boh-nee, another visitor from where the sun rises.

And Sacagawea? She recognizes her brother, Cameawait, and they greet, emotionally but decorously (incest taboos may well have required a certain restraint). Lewis is unable to fathom how relatives could greet each other without hugging. Later that day, Lewis notes: "The meeting of those people was really affecting, particularly between Sacagawea and an Indian woman who had been taken prisoner at the same time with her, and who had afterwards escaped from the Minnitaris and rejoined her nation."

With the Indian woman present at last, Lewis is able to make much more detailed speeches to the Shoshone. It is now a four-part translation: Lewis to Private Francois Labiche or Pierre Cruzatte in English, then his message goes to Charbonneau in French, Charbonneau to Sacagawea in Mandan, perhaps mixed with a little Shoshone, and Sacagawea to her brother, Cameawait, in Shoshone. Answers return up the same chain. Lewis at one point remarks that it is impossible to keep the attention of the Indians if too much is said, he does not seem to realize that the several minutes between question and answer, statement and reply, might contribute to a certain deficit in attention. This, in sum, is what he tells the Shoshone:

"We made them sensible of their dependence on the will of our government for every species of merchandise as well as for their defense and comfort, and apprised them of the strength of our government. The reason we wished to penetrate the country as far as the ocean to the west of them [was] to find out a more direct way to bring merchandise to them." More important, at that moment, there would be no trade until the corps of exploration went to the ocean and then returned to the east, so the Shoshone are well-advised to help them. It is true that the corps has shared food with the Shoshone, but they are all still on the edge of starvation, and these promises must seem terribly distant.

Cameawait, as Clark notes, is a person of "good sense and easy and reserved manners," the picture of calm self-confidence. This is what Cameawait says, first to his sister, as understood at last by Lewis, three translations later:

Cameawait is "sorry to find it would be some time yet before they could be furnished with firearms, but [says] they could live as they had done heretofore until we brought them as we had promised."

It will be a rather short time, in fact, before several Shoshone are furnished with firearms.

47

⚬⚬⚬

August 17–18, 1805, Merrymaking with the Shoshones

IN THE SPACE of a few days, Meriwether Lewis makes some of the most revealing entries in his journal. A number of things, a number of planets, so to speak, come into alignment: He reaches his own birthday, he has crossed the divide and learned (although he still does not quite believe) that an easy way to the Pacific is barred by topography, he has found the Shoshone but has not succeeded in acquiring the horses he desperately needs. Real conflict between his men and the Shoshone seems altogether possible, and he finally realizes that there is no Indian government with which to negotiate; he has no counterpart with his authority among the Shoshone.

The men of the Corps of Discovery are elated to arrive at the headwaters of the Missouri for two reasons, both dependent on the presence of the Shoshone Indians. The first joy is that Lewis's rigid insistence on exploring the Missouri by boat, even to the point of dragging the cottonwood canoes upstream until they are not floating, but scraping over the gravel, is satisfied. Since leaving the three forks (Madison, Gallatin, Jefferson) the men have spent more time pushing the canoes than paddling, more time lifting them over sandbars than poling them upstream. The second boon is the presence of a large number of women, and uninhibited ones, at that.

While the men are settling into camp, and beginning to regard their Shoshone hosts with some hope that certain pent-up desires might be gratified, Lewis is preoccupied with a more philosophical problem. It is his birthday, the eighteenth of August, and he reflects on that fact at, for him, considerable length. This passage from the journals is usually excused by historians with comments such as this: Young men of Lewis's era were expected to discuss their role in the world and make promises to improve their behavior for the benefit of mankind and therefore the reader should not pay much attention to this Enlightenment Analysis. Perhaps. There is here, underneath the platitudes, a slight tone of desperation. When you consider Lewis's eventual fate, the words are more poignant than trite:

> *This day I completed my thirty-first year, and conceived that I had in all human probability now existed about half the period which I am to remain in this sublunary world. I reflected that I had as yet done but little, very little indeed, to further the happiness of the human race, or to advance the information of the succeeding generation. I viewed with regret the many hours I have spent in indolence, and now sorely feel the want of that information which those hours would have given me had they been judiciously expended. But, since they are past and cannot be recalled, I dash from the gloomy thought, and resolve in future to redouble my exertions and at least endeavor to promote those two primary objects of human existence (happiness and knowledge) by giving the aid of that portion of talents which nature and fortune have bestowed on me; or in future: To live for mankind as I have heretofore lived for myself.*

It will never quite be enough for Lewis to ascend the Missouri and traverse the great divide to the western ocean. His triumph must also bring happiness and knowledge to his fellow man.

In one of the great understatements in his journals, Lewis writes on the eve of August 17: "The spirits of the men were now much elated at the prospect of getting horses."

The men, a marvelously uncomplaining lot, are unlikely to be as concerned as Lewis with the greater well-being of their race. They are also quite aware that the Arikaras, whom they left behind on April 8, routinely ride to the Shoshone country in a little over a week. If the point is to find the headwaters of the Missouri, it could have been done four months ago. What the men do not appreciate is how difficult it really is to cross the Great Plains of the Dakotas and Montana on horseback if you are not an Indian. They will all find out in the summer of 1806.

The other cause for joy, the availability of women, makes Lewis extremely nervous. The good will of the Shoshone leaders is paramount. They have horses and they know the country, two assets utterly lacking in the expedition's equipment. Without doubt, it is with some relief that Lewis, after careful observation, is able to make this entry in his journal on August 19, after two days of close contact between his men and his hosts:

"The chastity of their women is not held in high estimation, and the husband will for a trifle barter the companion of his bed for a night or longer if he conceives the reward adequate." Evidently this was not universal; from some experience, perhaps personal, Lewis adds that some women "appear to be held more sacred than in any nation we have seen.

"I have requested the men to give them no cause of jealousy by having connection with their women without their knowledge, which with them, strange as it may seem, is considered as disgraceful to the husband as clandestine connections of a similar kind are among civilized nations. To prevent this mutual exchange of good offices altogether I know it impossible to effect, particularly on the part of our young men, whom some months' abstinence has made them very polite to those tawny damsels. No evil has yet resulted and I hope will not from these connections."

One of the curiosities of the journals, Lewis's in particular, is how, under the greatest strain and in the most improbable and bizarre situations, the language never moves outside the limits of what one might write home to one's mother. His comments on what have must been a visible and audible orgy (more than twenty of the men would meet his definition of "young") are indistinguishable in tone from his own self-criticism on his natal anniversary. "Connections," indeed.

The possibility of conflict is exacerbated by the simple fact, which Lewis now realizes for the first time on the entire journey, that there is no central authority with whom he can deal. If the men do not behave properly with each and every willing spouse, "evil," in his words, may yet result. The problem arises from the long-standing practices of the American government to sort out the mysteries of Indian government by designating and ranking chiefs. The Corps of Discovery is carrying dozens of large silver medals for principal chiefs, and large American flags and dress-uniform coats for these same principals. Secondary and tertiary chiefs will get less. Now Lewis is faced for the first time with negotiating from a position of weakness (not only is he outnumbered, but the Indians hold the valuable commodity—horses). Fear of failure, like fear of being hanged, concentrates the mind, and Lewis realizes at last that his whole concept of what being a chief means has been wrong from the beginning of the voyage:

"Each individual is his own sovereign master, and acts from the dictates of his own mind; the authority of the Chief being nothing more than mere admonition, supported by the influence which the propriety of his own exemplary conduct may have acquired for him in the minds of the individuals who compose the band."

Now he has to negotiate for horses, and "in fact, every man is a chief." There is another problem with purchasing horses—inflation. The enlisted men of the expedition, distributing their own personal cache of trade goods—beads, needles, knives, the pocket stuff of the Western world—have given the impression that they are enormously wealthy. The Shoshone must be wondering: If a "connection," a temporary, fleeting "exchange of good offices" is worth a ransom, how much more valuable can a horse be to these footsore, spendthrift foreigners?

48

August 19–20, 1805, Mail from the Missouri

JEFFERSON, AT MONTICELLO to escape the heat (and attendant yellow fever and malaria) of Washington City, at last receives the first direct news from his Corps of Discovery. The mail is light, two parts of Clark's day journals, Clark's maps of the Missouri from St. Louis to the Mandan villages, and a letter from Lewis. It has been on its way from the Mandan villages since the ice went out in the spring.

The parcel post is more interesting. A package of skins, horns, and other biological samples arrives. Even better, a few cages of animals have made their way from the upper Missouri.

Lewis explains to Jefferson that the enclosure with his letter is "a part of Captain Clark's private journal, the other part you will find enclosed in a separate tin box." The obvious question: Where is Lewis's journal for the first leg of the expedition? Although he was not as regular a diarist as Clark, he has kept a journal when his health and his mood allowed it. Lewis must have realized that some explanation is needed, but he saves it, or only realizes it, later in the letter. Clark's journal, he writes, "is in its original state, and of course incorrect [Lewis is certainly referring to details such as spelling, not to veracity or accuracy], but it will serve to give you the daily details of our progress and transactions.

"Captain Clark does not wish this journal exposed in its present state, but has no objection that one or more copies of it be made by some confidential person under your direction, correcting its grammatical errors, &c." The subject of his own record of the first year is referred to only indirectly: "A copy of this journal will assist me in compiling my own for publication after my return."

And then Lewis promises to send along his journals from the headwaters of the Missouri. This is an odd idea. In April, when Lewis is writing to the president from the Mandan villages, he has the intention of sending a small party back from the Great Falls of the Missouri, which, as you know, he does not do. But from the headwaters? Surely that is the most improbable place to find a mailbox, the least likely place to detach a small unit of men and send them downstream to St. Louis.

The obvious answer is political, or geopolitical. Lewis is probably fearful that someone will intercept the letter from the Mandan villages. It could happen on the way downstream and is even more likely to happen somewhere within the federal post offices, or in the hands of some irresponsible, overcurious courier. It is just such illicitly opened mail that finally precipitated the duel between Burr and Madison—the first public reference to Madison's slandering Burr came from a private letter opened in upstate New York and subsequently printed in several newspapers.

Nowhere in the letter does Lewis mention that the expedition will continue to the Pacific. The reference to the headwaters of the Missouri is a ruse, should anyone open the mail. A Peeping Tom will see no farther west than the Continental Divide. The letters and animal skins and bones came down the Missouri to St. Louis in the care of an able young Corporal Warfington (who will be commissioned an officer in a few years). On the way, probably at Lewis's orders, he has acquired a couple of prairie dogs, a few magpies (a bird totally unfamiliar to Lewis), and a prairie chicken or two. These are sent by ship from New Orleans, and by the time the cages reach Washington, there are only two survivors.

Jefferson's butler (to pick a job title for this busy man), Etienne Lemaire, writes to the president at Monticello on August 20:

"The magpie and the kind of squirrel are very well; they are in the room where Monsieur receives his callers." Note that M. Lemaire, a Frenchman, knows the name of this rare bird sent at such great trouble from the Dakotas. And he knows that Jefferson knows it as well. Magpies are common from Europe through Eurasia, and on this side of the Pacific they thrive on both sides of the Rocky Mountains and down the east-running river valleys to the central high plains. Only eastern North America, of all the temperate woodlands of the Northern Hemisphere, is without its magpies. The "kind of squirrel" is a prairie dog, a genuine western rarity, and on its nearly immediate demise, will be skinned and given to the American Philosophical Society in Philadelphia. Jefferson, quite familiar with magpies from his years in France, never mentions the bird in any preserved correspondence or conversations.

49

Late August 1805, Pike Ascending

FOLLOWING GENERAL WILKINSON'S orders, Lieutenant Pike and a score of enlisted men proceed up the great river from St. Louis, bearing right, so to speak, at the junction of the Missouri and the Mississippi. It is not exactly an expedition into uncharted waters; the Mississippi has been a traveled river since the seventeenth century, and even its most remote headwaters are within the trading zone of the British-Canadian fur companies. Pike will seldom be out of earshot of an English speaker, even among the Indian tribes. As French is still a common language, reflecting the first two centuries of European exploration and settlement, Pike is carrying a French grammar, which he studies from time to time.

The effort to find the true headwaters of the Mississippi (and thus the putative northern border of Louisiana Territory) moves north on a pair of boats very like the much larger keelboat of the Lewis and Clark expedition. Pike's keelboats are propelled by sail in favorable weather, by oars in contrary winds. Each carries a large and visible cannon in the bow, and in no way resembles the modest craft of traders. They are as noticeable as battleships in a bayou.

Pike is entering a country of rapid change, as white settlements continue to press Indians to move farther west into the plains. Tribes once separated are now competing for scarcer resources from the same countryside. There are minor skirmishes between the tribes almost continually. The ascent of Pike's war craft is no inducement to a sense of security among the tribes.

"It is astonishing to me," Pike writes in his journal, "what a dread the Indians have of the Americans in this quarter." He hasn't spoken to an Indian since leaving the Sauks a month ago, so he is imputing motive without any firsthand knowledge. "I have frequently seen them go round islands to avoid meeting my boat. It appears evident to me that the traders have taken great pains to impress on the minds of the savages an idea of our being a very vindictive, ferocious and war-like people."

Pike believes he knows the motives of the traders, as well: "This impression was given no doubt with an evil intention." Confident of his own diplomatic skills and the righteousness of his cause, Pike adds: "When they find that our conduct towards them is guided by magnanimity and justice, instead of operating in an injurious manner, it will have the effect of making them reverence [us] at the same time as they fear us."

A few weeks into the voyage, at Prairie du Chien, a major trading post on the east bank of the Mississippi in what will become Wisconsin, Pike stops for rest and some recreation. The village is a mix of Americans, that is, traders from the United States and French Canadians. Besides whisky, and possibly women, although Pike never makes mention of sexual encounters, the major recreations at Prairie du Chien are limited to sporting events. Neither baseball nor soccer nor football have been invented, so the men are limited to foot races and jumping contests.

Pike cannot but notice the general friendliness and politeness of all the residents of Prairie du Chien. The town's name, by the way, literally means "dog prairie." But the animal in question is not a real dog, it is the "kind of squirrel" that Lewis and Clark have just had delivered to the president. As magpies are no surprise to any European, neither are prairie dogs to any French-Canadian voyageur.

The cordiality and the generosity of the Americans among the residents of Prairie Dog Town, Pike asserts, are "spontaneous effusions of good will and exultation in their countrymen, for it ever extended to the accommodation, convenience, pastimes, exercises, etc., of my men. . . . Whenever they proved superior to the French [in the foot races, the Americans] openly showed their pleasure.

"But the French Canadians were polite through their hypocrisy and, at the same time (to do them justice) natural good manners." And why were they so polite? Pike thinks he knows, for he has arrived in a fearsome boat and his men are uniformed riflemen: "Fear in them worked the same effect that natural good will did in the others."

And then Pike proceeds on up the Mississippi, satisfied with the awe-inspiring visit he has just made to the backwoods fur traders of Prairie du Chien.

50

⁂

August 25, 1805, Charbonneau's Mistake

THE ONLY THING Meriwether Lewis likes about Charbonneau is his cooking. And with a scarcity of game since the Great Falls of the Missouri, Lewis hasn't had a blessed thing to like. Clark is obliged to keep Charbonneau under control, and when Clark leaves to explore the upper reaches of the Middle Fork of the Salmon, Charbonneau has little to do except loll around with Sacagawea and little Pompey.

Charbonneau, Lewis knows, would rather go back to the Mandans than carry on. He is caught up in the forward motion of the Corps of Discovery, but not really a contributor. He is a bit of drag, really, useless in times of danger, another mouth to feed in times of need: that is Lewis's view.

At the Shoshone camp, Charbonneau does nothing to improve his standing. This is Lewis's account: On August 25, while Clark is still away assessing the possibility of running the Salmon River toward the Pacific, "Charbonneau mentioned to me with apparent unconcern that he expected to meet all the Indians from the camp on the Columbia tomorrow on their way to the Missouri. Alarmed at this information, I asked why he expected to meet them."

Charbonneau explains that the salmon run is played out, and the Shoshone will gather and join with other friendly Indians (the Flatheads, as it turns out), and then they will in some strength venture down to the Missouri and hunt buffalo, all the time, of course, keeping an eye out for the hostile Indians of the plains. If they do leave, Lewis has no horses to buy, no guides to a possible land route over the mountains to the Columbia River. The Corps of Discovery would be landlocked, on foot, and lost.

"I was out of patience with the folly of Charbonneau who had not sufficient sagacity to see the consequences which would inevitably flow from such a movement of the Indians, and although he had been in possession of this information since early in the morning when it had been communicated to him by his Indian woman, yet he never mentioned until the afternoon. I could not forswear speaking to him with some degree of asperity on this occasion."

Lewis immediately goes to Cameawait, smokes with him, no doubt suffers some of the "national embrace," and persuades him to delay until Clark has returned and the corps has traded for horses and, if necessary, engaged a guide. Charbonneau sulks. Charbonneau is uninterested in the larger purposes of the expedition. If the Indians want to go, what business is it of his? He has his talents, this tall, slow-moving human being. So far, Lewis only knows about his cooking ability, but Charbonneau has a few more strengths, none of which, to this point on the journey, have been required.

The patience of Cameawait is not to be underestimated. His people remain on the knife edge between hunger and starvation. The food they need is a hundred miles downstream on the plains by the Missouri. The red-haired captain does not believe him, and has gone off to explore the upper Salmon River even after he has been told that it is impossible. And the guns? There are guns promised, but there will be none at all, until the men from where the sun rises go to where the sun sets and then go back to where it rises and then, and only then, come back to see Cameawait bearing gifts. Is it a wonder that he doesn't bother to tell Lewis about his plans? What's he to Lewis, or Lewis to him, that he should wait for the captains to make up their minds?

51

❧

Late August 1805, Rumors of Burr

AS HE MOVES NORTH from New Orleans, staying a few days with General Andrew Jackson at The Hermitage, riding north again along the Natchez Trace, stopping in Nashville to test the waters of revolutionary sentiment, Burr's whole escapade becomes common knowledge.

British ambassador Merry, he of the overdressed encounter with Jefferson, writes to the home office that Burr's plans move along splendidly (true, to a point) and that there will soon be a convention of western states (presumably Kentucky, Tennessee, and Ohio) and the trans-Appalachian territories (Indiana, Mississippi, Louisiana, and Orleans) to vote for war with Mexico and for a declaration of independence from the eastern states (on this, he is wrong and wrong). The French ambassador notifies his office that New Orleans is to be the seat "of Mr. Burr's new intrigues; he is going there under the aegis of General Wilkinson (essentially true)." The Spanish ambassador, who is General Wilkinson's paymaster, is more skeptical, a perfectly understandable reaction. All this talk of invading Mexico, he reports to Madrid, is simply a way for Wilkinson and Burr to squeeze some cash out of an ingenuous England.

But these secret messages to the home countries had a tiny fraction of the information being published in the country's newspapers. The influential *Gazette of the United States,* in an editorial reprinted by papers on both sides of the Appalachian Mountains, asked, "How long will it be before we shall hear of Colonel Burr being at the head of a revolutionary party on the Western Waters? Is it a fact that Colonel Burr has formed a plan to engage the adventurous and enterprising young men from the Atlantic States to Louisiana? . . . How soon will the forts and magazines and all the military posts at New Orleans and on the Mississippi be in the hands of Colonel Burr's revolutionary party? . . . What difficulty can there be in completing a revolution in one summer along the Western States, when they will gain the Congress's lands, will throw off the public debt, will seize their own revenues, and enjoy the plunder of Spain [that is, Mexico]?"

It is an odd thing, this Burr conspiracy. It is conducted simultaneously in letters written in a difficult code between Wilkinson and Burr and in Burr's public speeches and dozens of his more private meetings that soon become public knowledge. Why cannot this well-groomed, charming little man keep from boasting about his plans?

52

August 28–30, 1805, Trading for Horses

THE SHOSHONE, from Lewis's detailed account of their material culture, appear to have almost no articles of modernity, no steel needles nor arrow points, no metal cooking pots, whether iron, brass, or copper. The only metallic weapon in the camp is Cameawait's musket, for which he has neither flint, powder, or ball. This suggests more than poverty (on the entire trip, it is only the Shoshone who are starving when the corps arrives), but lack of opportunity to trade. They are a tribe that only moves down out of the sheltering mountains to furtively kill, skin, and process a few buffalo before the Plains Indians, Crow or Blackfoot, Arikara or Sioux, can attack them. They do not visit the great trading centers of the plains.

He is not well-versed in trading, and perhaps because of that innocence, Lewis's negotiations for horses get off on a bad foot and limp home in worse condition. It is in part because the corps has already sent the Shoshone economy into a spasm of hyperinflation. Whatever the men are paying for sex becomes, one gathers, the minimum price of anything. When Lewis goes to hire men and women to pack goods back across the pass, he pays out more in beads and trifles than the Shoshone have ever seen in one place at one time. The women do most of the packing—"drudges," as Lewis notes—and their labors, whether in what Lewis calls "connections" or packing supplies, are surely overvalued by Shoshone standards. Sex and physical labor are the duties of women, after all. But now the captain wants horses, which are men's business.

When Lewis asks him to trade horses, Cameawait cheerfully agrees. This turns out in practice to be an agreement to let individual Shoshones trade their horses to the captains. Lewis is so pleased with the arrangement as he understands it that he orders the fiddlers to unpack their instruments, "and the party danced very merrily, much to the amusement and gratification of the natives, though I must confess that the state of my own mind at this moment did not well accord with the prevailing mirth as I somewhat feared that the caprice of the Indians might suddenly induce them to withhold their horses from us without which my hopes of prosecuting my voyage to advantage was lost." Within hours, the price of a horse escalates from a handful of metal (knives, mirrors, awls, fishhooks, needles) to at least two handfuls of better goods, plus tomahawks or blankets or clothing.

While the bartering continues, Clark explores the Salmon River with eleven men and concludes that the Middle Fork is unnavigable, with horrid rapids and sheer rock walls that would prevent portaging around the foaming broken waves, which today amuse and entertain recreational rafters and kayakers. Lewis is wrong, Clark learns, to dismiss the Indian view of the river as some kind of trick. It cannot be run in crude dugout canoes by the best of boatmen.

By the time Clark returns, the price of a horse has gone almost out of comprehension. The first horse Clark buys costs him "my pistol,

100 balls, powder and a knife." The second is dearer: "I gave my fusee [a rifled firearm] to one of the men and sold his musket for a horse which completed us to 29 total horses." With twenty-nine men, and goods to pack, not everyone would ride when the party proceeds. Not only are they expensive animals, but the Shoshone, planning a hunting trip to the plains, sell only poor specimens, young horses, and horses at least temporarily out of condition with sore backs. Clark, who has seen more of the western mountains beyond the divide than Lewis, is contemplating that the horses will not only carry some baggage, they may be the only available meat. He has the men pay "great attention" to the uninspiring band of horses. Clark, of all the men, is the first to realize what difficulties are yet to come.

53

September 10, 1805, The Lieutenant Is in a Hurry

ZEBULON PIKE'S two best qualifications for his assignments are simply understood: He adores General Wilkinson and he is, as they say in those times, "active." We might say hyperactive, but that would be reading our times back into an era we can barely understand. The curse of soldiering is always ennui and inactivity. Lieutenant Pike is quite the opposite. He is an eager, likely young man.

On the tenth, Pike's gunboat reaches the riverside home of the band of Mdewankton Sioux, a small part of the Santee division of the Siouan tribes that range from the Mississippi all the way west to the Black Hills. This is trader country, and the Mdewanktons are still rather badly soused from a day of bargaining and boozing with some French-Canadian voyageurs. Their chief is Wabasha, a man of apparent dignity and good sense. When Pike sends a messenger asking for a council, Wabasha sends back a request to put the meeting off until the next day: "Last night his people had begun to drink, and that on the next day he would receive us with his people, sober."

Pike pays no heed, lands his boats near the Mdewankton lodges, and is received as you might imagine an uninvited but unrefusable guest would be.

> On our arriving opposite to the lodges, the [Mdewankton] men were paraded out on the bank with their guns in their hands. They saluted us (with ball) [i.e., with real gun shots] with what might be termed three rounds, which I returned with three rounds from each boat with my blunderbusses.
>
> This salute, although nothing to soldiers accustomed to fire, would not be so agreeable to some people; as they had all been drinking, and some tried their dexterity, to see how near our boats they could make their balls strike."

That he is being teased or insulted is not a conclusion Pike allows himself to entertain.

The talks go well on the eleventh; neither Wabasha nor Pike are inebriated or intoxicated. The Sioux chief gives Pike an ornate pipe with his totem marked on it, for Pike "to show the upper bands [the Sioux he may encounter near the falls of the Mississippi], in token of our good understanding, and that they might see his mark, and imitate his conduct."

Pike dispenses small presents: two hanks of tobacco, four knives, a half-pound of vermilion pigment for face painting, a quart of salt. He adds an eight-gallon keg of whisky. Wabasha remarks, as Pike records, that the gifts "must come free as he did not ask for them. I replied that 'to those who did not ask for anything, I gave freely, to them who asked for much, I gave only a little or none.' "

While the brief talks are under way, a crowd of Sioux are trying to board the boats, but Pike is pleased that his soldiers "executed their duty with vigilance and vigor, driving women, children, and men back whenever they come near my boats."

When it is time to go, Pike is escorted back to his boats by what he calls "soldiers," that is, the armed young Sioux men. They have an odd request: "At my departure their soldiers said: 'As I had shaken hands with their chief, &c., they must with my soldiers.' In which request I willingly indulged them."

Pike and his men are off, alternately sailing and rowing the pair of keelboats beneath the bluffs that line the upper Mississippi. He carries a pipe that is certainly a great present, for whether Pike understands or not, believes or not, the pipe is, well, Big Medicine. And Wabasha has eight gallons of whisky, also a kind of medicine.

54

September 4–10, 1805,

Disappointment at Clark's River

THE CORPS OF DISCOVERY is, of necessity, unaware that it is undertaking to cross the mountains to the Pacific Ocean in the middle of a meteorological phenomenon now called the Little Ice Age. For entirely mysterious reasons, the Northern Hemisphere is astonishingly cold (which means no more than a few degrees below average, year after year) from the early eighteenth century to around the time of the American Civil War. Washington's troops suffer more at Valley Forge than a camper would today. From Montana to Switzerland, glaciers are temporarily advancing after ten thousand years of retreat. Except for a few shaded, northeast-facing gullies and bowls, the Rockies and

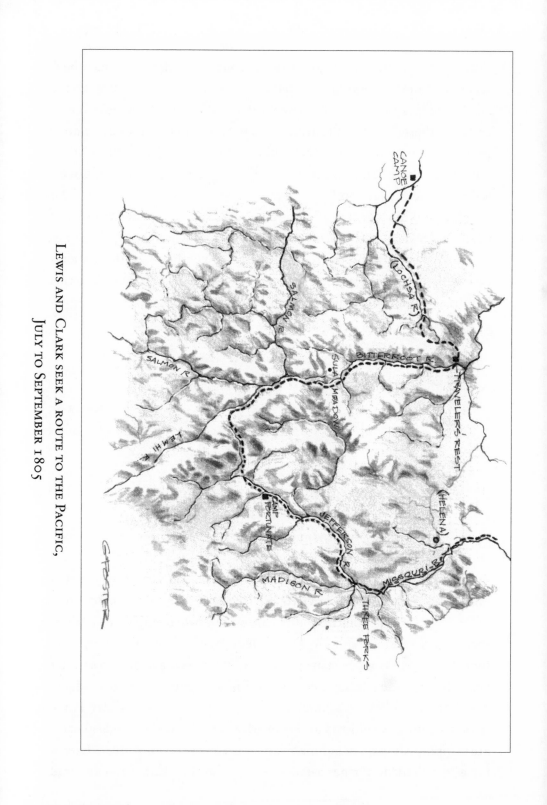

LEWIS AND CLARK SEEK A ROUTE TO THE PACIFIC,
JULY TO SEPTEMBER 1805

the Bitterroots today are often snow-free by mid-July, but when Lewis and Clark first see them, even the lowest mountains are snowcapped all about their summits.

It is impossible to tell how the corps moves from the headwaters of the Missouri across the Continental Divide to the headwaters of the Columbia—the east fork of the Bitterroot River near today's Sula, Montana. In haste, confusion, and anxiety about the motley crew of forty horses purchased so dearly from the Shoshone, neither Lewis nor Clark keeps a clear record of the transit of the divide. Meriwether Lewis may be in one of his periodic blue funks. It will be a few weeks before he writes a journal entry.

What we know is that they arrive at an open bowl, a high grass meadow, and find a band of Salish Indians, the ones erroneously called "Flatheads" by later explorers. To Clark, they are always "our beloved Salish." (Salish-speaking tribes along the Pacific Coast do practice head-shaping by tying a board to some infants' foreheads, giving them a straight-line profile from the tip of their noses to the crown of their skulls. The habits of some Salish speakers become a shorthand name for the entire language group.)

When the corps reaches the Bitterroot drainage, they find 33 elegant teepee lodges, 80 warriors (they guess about 400 persons total in the band) and, to their delight, 500 horses. Clark calls them "elegant horses." By signs, they discover that these are the same Indians that Cameawait and the Shoshone intend to meet on the upper Missouri this week. If the corps had arrived on the sixth of September, not the evening of the fourth, they would have found a deserted campground.

For reasons that actually baffle Clark, not a man given to much speculation, they are able to purchase horses cheaply, and even trade their lamest Shoshone horses for much better Salish-owned animals. By trading what Clark calls "a few articles of merchandise" and the seven poorest Shoshone horses, the corps acquires eighteen fit animals.

There are a few hints as to why negotiations at Sula go so well. Foremost, perhaps, the young men of the corps do not drive up the prices (or devalue their trade goods) by spending generously for sex.

The brief meeting at Sula does not provide time, or opportunity, for that kind of commerce. Secondly, Clark does not make Lewis's mistake and tell the Salish how rich the strangers from the east are nor does he promise to return with unimaginable gifts and generous trade goods. Third, unlike at the Lemhi pass, where the Shoshone women packed the corps' goods back to the main Shoshone camp, Lewis and Clark do not have to hire the Salish to do anything, another way that the value of trade goods could be discounted. Lastly, as the Salish prepare to go across the divide to the plains about the Missouri, they are also nearing the point of starvation: "We encamped with them," Clark writes, "and found them friendly . . . [they have] nothing but berries to eat, a part of which they gave us." So the Salish are in poor shape, economically, and they have no "exchange rate" for a knife or a twist of tobacco.

Or maybe they are generous, kind, and sympathetic. It takes all kinds, as true for an Indian world as any other.

Clark is made nervous by his sudden success as a horse trader. On the evening after the new horses are acquired, he sets a heavy guard over the herd. The main reason is he fears the Salish will decide the broken-down Shoshone horses and a handful of trade goods is a lousy deal and try to reverse the swap. Less probable, but he thinks possible, they might just steal back their own horses and leave in the night. But all is well. The Salish leave in the morning for the headwaters of the Missouri and their rendezvous with the Shoshone band. The corps descends the Bitterroot River to where it joins the Clark Fork of the Columbia in modern Missoula, Montana.

They still do not believe that there is no way to the navigable Columbia River, no way to the Pacific, except by crossing the Bitterroot Mountains that rise abruptly on the western side of the north-flowing Bitterroot River. The guide loaned to them by Cameawait marks Lolo Creek when they pass it a few miles upstream from Missoula, and tells them it leads to the Nez Perce trail that crosses the Bitterroots to that tribe's land on a tributary of the Columbia. They ignore the advice of their guide, an aged Shoshone named, by them, "Old Toby." At the Clark Fork of the Columbia, they meet a small group of Nez Perce who are trailing after a horse thief. By sign, they inquire about the river. It is like the Middle Fork of the Salmon, they are told; no one boats upon it. Even worse, Lewis learns that there are no salmon coming up from the Pacific here. Somewhere, downstream, there must be horrid rapids and falls of water that stop not only boats but prevent the great fish from ascending the waters. One of the Nez Perce (Lewis calls him a Salish, but that is most unlikely) agrees to take the corps to the beginning of the Lolo Trail, the horse route to the west.

The corps turns around. There is no way out but up and over the snow-clad, precipitous, forbidding Bitterroots. It is the tenth of September, and the search for an easy, sensible, tractable route to the Pacific is finally over. Except, as it will turn out, in Lewis's mind. Meriwether Lewis lets go of an idea very slowly.

55

꧁

September 16–17, 1805,

Lieutenant Pike Makes His Life Exciting

TODAY, FEW SECTIONS of the upper Mississippi resemble the riverscape of two hundred years ago. Now the river is a series of reservoirs and locks, a chain of artificial lakes from Minneapolis–Saint Paul to below LaCrosse, Wisconsin. These are built for the easy transit of barges.

When Zebulon Pike reaches the mouth of the Sauteaux River (today's Chippewa River, which flows into the Mississippi west of Eau Clair, Wisconsin) he reaches a natural lake in the great river. The Sauteaux/Chippewa "enters from the east and brings down more sand and gravel than the Mississippi can remove," thus creating a natural dam and raising a lake in the father of waters, already named by the Canadian voyagers as Lake Pepin. The lower end of the lake has long been a rendezvous where the Plains and River tribes meet, and where the northern woodland tribes come down to trade. In the more recent past, it is made more so by the seasonal French-Canadian traders who create an epicenter of commerce on the boundary between the northern woods and the eastern limits of the Great Plains.

Lieutenant Pike, after an early dinner (dinner in the old sense of the main meal, often taken nearer noon than evening), orders his boatmen to ascend Lake Pepin from the Grand Encampment. The men demur, "My interpreter telling me he had passed the lake twenty times, and never once in the daytime; rendering as a reason, that the wind frequently came and detained them by day in the lake."

Pike will not change his mind; it is part of his self-esteem, his reputation as "active," to press on. Rewriting his journals several years after the fact, he relates how he dismisses the advice of man who has been up the lake a score of times: "I believe the traders' true reasons (most generally) are their fears of the Sauteaux, as they have made several strokes of war at the mouth of this river, never distinguishing between the Sioux and their traders . . . accordingly, away we sailed."

Within a few hours, his sails gone, his keelboats dismasted, running before a suddenly rising evening gale, Pike careens back to a harbor of refuge near today's Stockholm, Wisconsin. He rises the morrow determined to carry on. He leaves after breakfast, headed again for Sandy Point (Point de Sable) on the Minnesota shore of the upper end of Lake Pepin. It is one of the charms of the journals of Zebulon Pike that he will remind the reader of his capacity for bravery and decisive leadership. The accounts sometimes describe what could be regarded as bravura.

On this second attempt to cross Lake Pepin, one of the daytime storms that he denies exist does come to life: "The sky became inflamed, & the perpendicular lightning seemed to roll in balls down the sides of the hills which bordered the shores of the lake. The storm in all its majesty, grandeur, and horror burst on our heads in the traverse which we were making to Point de Sable; and it required no moderate share of exertions and skill to weather the point and get to the windward side of it."

Pike rests at Sandy Point and goes sight-seeing. The reader may make of Pike's account what the reader chooses:

> *I was shown a point of rocks from which a Sioux woman cast herself and was dashed into a thousand pieces on the rocks below. [It is always said that persons who leap off rocks are dashed into a thousand pieces. In fact, they are not, as any emergency medical technician who has been to a jumper's landing will attest. Large mammals may splash quite a bit of serum and soft tissue, but they do not fragment.] She had been informed that her friends intended matching her to a man she despised, they have refused her the man of her choice. She ascended the hill singing her death song, and before they could overtake her and stop her purpose, she took the lover's leap and ended her troubles with her life—a wonderful exhibition of sentiment for a savage!*

56

September 10, 1805, Trouble Comes to Captain Clark

FROM THE DAY they leave the Shoshone and wander toward the Lolo Pass, Meriwether Lewis makes only two journal entries in two weeks. He is not well, and it makes perfect sense to believe he is depressed. This is not idle speculation. In years to come he will remain in what can best be described as a state of denial about the route he opened to the Pacific.

Climbing up to the head of Lolo Creek and then over the mountains to the headwaters of the Lochsa (and thus the headwaters of the Snake

River tributary to the Columbia), the corps effectively climbs above the normal range of the elk and deer that sustained them just a few days before in the Bitterroot River valley. We think of elk as mountain creatures that only come down to the plains when driven by winter snows. That is not natural. They were creatures of the valleys and plains. They are where they are now because we are where they should be.

A company of men used to eating an entire elk or several deer every twenty-four hours (on the order of ten pounds of meat a man a day) is quickly reduced in vigor when the protein disappears. One freezing evening, Lewis feeds most of the party with concentrated soup, the flesh of a scrawny coyote, and gives them each a tallow candle to chew and swallow.

Clark's brief journal entries describe the difficulties in unadorned prose. On September 14, he remarks that they kill and eat a colt at the end of a terrible march:

"The mountains which we passed today [are] much worse than yesterday, the last [mountains are] excessively bad and thickly strewed with fallen timber and pine, spruce, fir, hackmatack and tamarack, steep and stony. Our men and horse much fatigued." This entry ends with an unsteady pen stroke that trails off into a blank spot on the page.

They camp next to a snowbank. "We melted the snow to drink," Clark writes in his small, cramped, hand, "and cook our horse flesh to eat."

Clark is becoming disoriented. His journal entries misstate the day of the week or the date of the month, mistakes he will correct in the long Oregon winter ahead. Mental confusion is a classic symptom of hypothermia.

"Pines so covered with snow that in passing through them we are continually covered with snow. I have been wet and as cold in every part as I ever was in my life, indeed I was at one time fearful my feet would freeze in the thin moccasins which I wore." Clark begins to take on, briefly, the leadership of the corps, not overtly but by example. It is Clark who moves swiftly ahead of the corps, picking out a campsite and building a fire for the other men to huddle near.

In the deep snow, they lose sight of the Nez Perce trail on the ground. For two days, they struggle forward, finding the trail by the burnished scars on the trees where the Nez Perce horses have rubbed their packs against the rough bark of the ponderosa pines.

When it gets truly desperate, Clark takes six of the healthiest men, advises Lewis to move forward carefully, and then Clark and his men go on ahead looking for game to kill and hang for the trailing men in the corps. The best Clark can do (despite the help of the corps' best hunters) is leave another killed colt, partially eaten, by the trail side. It is enough to keep the men, and Sacagawea and little Pompey, from succumbing to hunger.

The desperate trek concentrates Clark's mind on small things. He not only fails to shoot the only deer he sees, but he snapped his flintlock seven times without even a flash in the pan, the "flint loose and wet." When they eat another horse, even the simple meal stands out in his mind: "Killed a second colt which we all supped heartily on and thought it fine meat."

Old Toby reassures them that they are almost out of the mountains. For some reason, they disbelieve him. Perhaps it does not seem possible that the excessively bad trail will ever end.

57

September 1805, Wilkinson Covers His Bets

GENERAL WILKINSON has an almost admirable enthusiasm for the American west. If he and Burr can't steal it entirely, Wilkinson will at least make money on it. After notifying the Spanish government about Lewis and Clark—encouraging the Spaniards to find and repel their expedition—and collecting his "pension" for that and similar pieces of information—Wilkinson comes up with a new scheme.

Resident in St. Louis, as both military and civil governor of Louisiana, Wilkinson observes the simple fact that the richest men in St. Louis are fur traders working on the upper Mississippi and lower Missouri Rivers. If Lewis and Clark open the upper Missouri to trade, and if the Americans can drive the English traders out of Minnesota and Wisconsin, Americans will be trading at the very font of furs. Someone is going to make money, and Wilkinson decides it might as well be him. He will leapfrog over the St. Louis traders and capture the headwaters.

What is difficult to realize, at this late date of established government and instant communication, is how free Wilkinson is to pursue his plans. He has already sent Pike up the Mississippi without any authorization from Washington City. And in the late summer of 1805, Wilkinson realizes he has the perfect excuse to put a stranglehold on trading with the upper Missouri tribes.

After Lewis and Clark depart the Mandans for the Rockies, a substantial number of Indians, most of them encountered the summer before by Lewis and Clark, comply for their own reasons with the government's request, assemble in St. Louis, and then travel east to see their Father in Washington face to face. In St. Louis, they become Wilkinson's charges, a motley crew of Arikara, Otoe, Missouri, Sioux, Sac, Fox, and Iowa chiefs. It is the Otoes and Arikaras who provide Wilkinson with the means to begin his attempt to capture the upper Missouri fur trade. The Arikara and Otoe chiefs fall ill, or feel ill, and demand to be returned to their villages. As Wilkinson writes months later the chiefs "clamored loudly & incessantly to be sent back, agreeably to the promise Captain Lewis made to them."

Wilkinson's men carry them back upstream, leaving the Otoes and some number of soldiers where the Platte enters the Missouri. The smaller group of soldiers and chiefs (there appear to be no records beyond a few bits of correspondence, so that exact dates and numbers of men involved have long since disappeared) carrying on a few hundred miles up the Missouri to the Arikara villages. While this happens, the soldiers at the Platte begin to construct a fort. This would give Wilkinson a stranglehold on fur trading up the Platte (which reaches into the Colorado Rockies) and since the fort is so near the Missouri, perhaps even a grip on the Missouri trade. It is of little matter that Wilkinson has no permission to build a fort on the Platte. Lieutenant Pike is ascending the Mississippi without permission from Washington, moving entirely on Wilkinson's orders, and Pike will be negotiating for trading posts and fort sites as well.

However convenient the chiefs' illnesses are for Wilkinson's desires to establish fortified trading posts, he is surely doing the right thing by agreeing to their demands to be sent home before they die. Indians have a habit of carrying out their self-prophesied deaths. Shortly after the remaining Indians set out for the Natchez Trace on the way to Pittsburgh, one of them gave a present to the escorting officer. Wilkinson tells the story in a letter: "In Kentucky, an Ioway chief gave away his tobacco pouch made of [turtle] shell, and then said, 'I have given away my tobacco shell, and this circumstance puts me in mind that I shall die in a few days.' " In four days, he did.

The fall of 1805 is a pleasant season for Wilkinson. His men are negotiating for, or actually building, forts along the upper Missouri and Mississippi. Although his attempt to help the Spanish capture Lewis and Clark has come to nothing, they are at least out of his territory. If they are still alive, they are over the divide. They are beyond the borders of Louisiana Territory, out of his jurisdiction.

Wilkinson's only discomfort is mental. Burr, moving up the Mississippi and Ohio, headed for Pittsburgh and the east, cannot stop talking about the next year's plans. Mention of him and his scheme trickles downriver to St. Louis. It is almost unanimously unfavorable. The trans-Appalachian west is more patriotic, less greedy, than Burr or Wilkinson imagine. As long as Burr is seen as a foe of Spanish Mexico, he is a hero. But genuine support for a separation of the west simply fails to materialize.

58

⁂

September 24–25, 1805, At the Falls of the Mississippi

INDIAN TERRITORIES are often defined by natural geographical barriers, and when Lieutenant Pike and his men arrive at the Falls of Saint Anthony and Saint Croix, they are at the northern and eastern boundary of the Sioux, and when they ascend the falls, they will be in Chippewa territory. These falls will be, when more Europeans come, the limit of navigation up the Mississippi. Freight and passengers arriving by boat will, in a few more decades, transfer to railroads. The paired falls will create, by their obstruction, the Twin Cities of Minneapolis and St. Paul.

Meeting with Sioux chiefs at the falls, Pike recounts his council with the Mdewankton Sioux. He has two purposes, one is to create peace between the Sioux and Chippewa (their habit of killing each other, and each other's fur-trading partners, makes economic development difficult) and the other is to begin to replace the British-American traders with United States traders.

It is never clear how much Pike understands of his orders from Wilkinson. He may think he is negotiating on behalf of Washington, he may understand he is bargaining for Wilkinson (and perhaps himself?). In any case, he sets out his demands for a trading post property and something to his surprise gets, or believes he gets, title to an estimated 100,000 acres. That is not as much as it might sound: a squarish chunk of land averaging twelve miles on a side would do it. Other than picking that very large number, Pike gives no other description of the parcel. He does estimate its value at $20,000, again for no apparent reason. He accounts for his expenses somewhat more accurately: "I gave them presents to the amount of about 200 dollars, and as soon as the council was over, I suffered the traders to present them with some liquor, which, with what I myself gave, was equal to 60 gallons."

The other request Pike makes is also granted: After he meets the Chippewa upstream from the falls, he wants to bring some chiefs downstream, past the Sioux, and on to St. Louis so that they too can see their Father in Washington. The Sioux (and these are the rather more tractable Mdewankton Sioux) cheerfully give him and any chiefs "a safe passport." As for peace with the Chippewa, the Sioux are really quite disinterested: Life itself consists of war with the Chippewa. Pike only remarks that the chiefs "spoke doubtfully relative to the peace."

The Mississippi is flowing at end-of-summer low water, and hauling the keelboats up the rapids and Falls of Saint Anthony and Saint Croix is taxing work. After a day at the haul ropes, Pike says, "at night the men gave a sufficient proof of their fatigue, by all throwing themselves down to sleep, preferring rest to supper."

Pike did not leave St. Louis for more than a month after he received his official orders from Wilkinson, and that was two months after he knew he was going to ascend the Mississippi to its source. Now, he is ascending the exposed rocks and barely flowing falls with enormous difficulty. Even rewriting himself for publication, he manages to sound peevish and avoids responsibility at the same time: "This voyage could have been performed with great convenience, if we had taken our departure in June. But the proper time would be to leave the Illinois [that is, the junction of that river with the Mississippi, in central Missouri] as soon as the ice would permit; then the river would be of a good height."

By the end of September they are past the falls, and headed upstream into the stronghold of the Chippewa and, more particularly, of the North West Trading Company of British America, longtime trespassers in French Louisiana and now in the sovereign territory of the Territory of Louisiana of the United States of America.

59

September 18 – October 8, 1805,

Among the Pierced Noses

A DAY AFTER Clark forages ahead, trying to stalk game in advance of the necessarily noisy passage of nearly thirty humans and forty horses along the Nez Perce trail, he takes time to explain it in his journal:

"The want of provisions together with the difficulty of passing those immense mountains dampened the spirits of the party which induced us to resort to some plan of reviving their spirits. I determined to take a party of the hunters, proceed on in advance to some level country where there was game, kill some meat and send it back &c."

It is the only entry in the journal where Clark admits to two things: that the men are discouraged, and that he makes a decision on his own. "I determined" is a unique phrase.

Before they can reach level country, they do encounter a fortuitous package of meat: a loose horse. This is the animal that Clark leaves most of by the trail for Lewis and the balance of the corps. It is a "liberated" animal, as Clark notes in his journal for September 19. When one recalls that Clark, his party, and Lewis, with his group, are all starving, there is a certain admirable understatement to Clark's entry; the men "beg leave to kill him which I granted, after they filled themselves, I had the balance hung up for Captain Lewis and proceeded on."

The mountains are as precipitous as ever, even though Clark and his men are almost to an open parkland on the banks of the upper Salmon River drainage. The last few miles are no easier for Clark than the first miles at Lolo Creek. And Clark is as laconic as ever: "I set out early and proceeded on through a country as rugged as usual."

Suddenly the land opens to the Camas Prairie, an open valley where a group of the Nez Perce are gathering the edible bulbs of the camas lily. The shock to the Nez Perce, not some minor modern psychological shock, but a sense that the world has turned upside down, cannot be imagined, nor exaggerated. No one ever comes over the mountains except their own brethren returning from a trip to the buffalo plains by the Great Falls of the Missouri. And these visitors, a half-dozen bearded creatures, may not even be human beings. One of them even has red hair. And eyes the color of water.

Clark chooses his words carefully when he describes the effect his arrival has on the large camp of Nez Perce. They come running to stare at his party in "great confusion."

The men buy some food with a few cheap trade goods, a kind of breadstuff made from cooked camas root and pieces of dried salmon. Within hours they are suffering from diarrhea and nausea. Whatever botulisms grow in the food are ones the Indians are immune to by reason of lifelong exposure. Clark, unfamiliar with the germ theory of disease, believes the trouble comes merely from "eating the fish & roots too freely." He sends two of the hunters back with salmon and camas to Lewis, with advice to eat carefully. Within days, everyone in the party is ill to some degree. "I am very sick today," Clark writes on September 21, "and puke, which relieves me."

The next day, every Nez Perce within reach of the Camas Prairie arrives to ogle. "The plains appeared covered with spectators viewing the white men and the articles which we had, our party weak and much reduced in flesh as well as strength."

Historians enamored both of Lewis and Clark and the Native Americans will point out that the Nez Perce could easily overrun the few men with Clark, and even the entire party when Lewis arrives. Clark and his men are outnumbered by several hundred to eight; they are for the most part lying on the ground in the grip of violent intestinal disorder. They have a comparative richness of trade goods to steal. Somehow it must be the innate kindness of the Nez Perce that keeps them from killing the white men. There is Nez Perce oral history that asserts that a woman who had been captured in a Blackfoot raid and rescued by whites told her kinsmen not to kill the whites. It is possible, but Blackfoot contact with whites or Nez Perce is infrequent in the late eighteenth century.

On the other hand, there are no bragging rights to be gained from killing a passel of incapacitated weaklings. And those weaklings have guns, which means no ceremonial fighting, no counting coups, nothing but death for a few Nez Perce until the white men are all killed. It is not a question of good character so much as that such a massacre of non-enemies would simply be out of character, outside the boundaries of the Nez Perce world. It is usually the case that first contacts are friendly (think of Cortez entering the Aztec kingdom, or Marco Polo in Central Asia). It takes some time to develop enemies, and there is no point, no honor, in fighting strangers.

Clark, pending the arrival of Lewis, begins to trade with the Indians. I "made three chiefs and gave them medals & tobacco & handkerchiefs & knives and a flag, and left a flag and handkerchiefs for the great chief when he returns from war." Compared to gifts to the Mandan, or even to the Shoshone and Flathead chiefs, this is paltry. But Clark is a long way from home and he is husbanding the corps's few resources for the tribes still unmet. When Lewis and the main party arrive, peace is assured, Clark thinks, in part because the arrival of Sacagawea and Pompey are a sort of insurance. There is no such thing in the Nez Perce world (as in most of the west) as a war party with women and children onboard.

From the twenty-fourth of September to the eighth of October, the reunited party works on dugout canoes along the riverbank, usually at half strength, as some succumb again to the camas and salmon pestilence. Clark is much of two minds about the Nez Perce and, being Clark, makes no attempt to reconcile the two realities he sees. When stores are accidentally soaked in a preliminary and unsuccessful test of the new canoes, Clark has "everything opened and two sentinels put over them to keep off the Indians, who inclined to thieve, having stole several small articles." But thievery seems to come naturally along with another trait: "Those people appeared disposed to give us every assistance in their power during our distress."

After the party launches their new canoes, accompanied by two Nez Perce chiefs who agree to introduce them to other Nez Perce bands living downriver, Clark reflects on this tribe's bundle of, to him, contradictions. He is as discreet as usual:

"The men expose those parts which are generally kept from view by other nations but the women are particular [more] than any other nation which I have passed in secreting their parts." And although the Nez Perce "appeared disposed to give us every assistance," Clark, after leaving them, comes to another, perhaps not contradictory, judgment: "They are very selfish and stingy of what they have to eat or wear, and they expect in return something for everything [they] give [us] as presents, [and for] . . . the services which they do, let it be however small, and [they] fail to make those returns on their part."

After a trip down the Columbia, a long wet winter with coastal Indians well accustomed to trading with white men, and a troublesome return up the Columbia to the Nez Perce country, Clark will have a mellower view, but not a romanticized one. He is not offended by anything, exposed "parts" or petty thieving or stinginess. Clark gets along. It is an underesteemed talent, getting along.

60

⁕

October 4 and 11, 1805, Lieutenant Pike at Play

in the Fields of the Lord

ASCENDING THE MISSISSIPPI into Chippewa country, just a dozen miles upstream from the falls (the Twin Cities today), Pike's party happens upon eight vandalized Sioux canoes. Stylized symbols carved on the handles of deliberately broken paddles indicate that both women and men were killed. Pike relates that his interpreter is "much alarmed, assuring me [that] at our first encounter with the Chippewas, it would be extremely probable they would fire on us, taking us for the Sioux's traders before we could come to an explanation." The interpreter recalls, for Pike's enlightenment, that just the previous spring three French-Canadian traders died at almost this exact spot.

It is sometimes easy to forget that this is all being related by Lieutenant Pike in an autobiography intended to impress the public with his courage and leadership. Thus, the following entry: "Not withstanding his information, I was on shore in pursuit of a flock of elk all the afternoon." Pike is not a terribly successful marksman. He always blames it on the light caliber of his rifles when yet another animal escapes, gut-shot, into the bush. No elk, but Pike returns to camp with a trophy. He captures a pocket gopher, an animal unfamiliar to him, and brings it back in the interest of science.

A week later, nearing the absolute head of navigation by any boat larger than an Indian canoe, Pike's eye is caught by a flash of bright color on the riverbank:

"I found a painted buckskin, and a piece of scarlet cloth, suspended by the limb of a tree. . . . I supposed [it to be] a sacrifice to Matcho

Manitou, to render their enterprise successful, but I took the liberty of invading the rights of his diabolic Majesty, and treated him as the priests have often done of old, i.e., converting the sacrifice to my own use."

And so, daring the immediate wrath of the Chippewa and the ineffable wrath of the Great Spirit, with a bit of Indian medicine tucked into his luggage, Lieutenant Pike continues on.

61

October 1805, Burr in the Wilderness

AARON BURR is somewhere between Indianapolis and Pittsburgh on his way to Washington City. That is all we know.

62

October 16–20, 1805, Descending the Columbia

THEY ARE A PECULIAR SIGHT, this Corps of Discovery paddling down the Snake and the Columbia, thirty-three human beings (counting the Indian woman, York, and Pompey) in crude dugout canoes, armed to the teeth with rifles and gleaming steel knives (most of the tribes along the Columbia are still in the Stone Age, without even metal arrow points). Only Sacagawea and two older Nez Perce chiefs who accompany the corps look like real human beings to the Indians; the rest are clearly aliens, and aliens, because they are unpredictable, are frightening.

For most of the descent, the old chiefs are able to placate the fearful bands along the river. The Yakimas and Wanapams speak a language so close to Nez Perce there is no language problem, and the corps moves peacefully, buying dogs, the only red meat available, from the bemused Native Americans, who have never seen anyone eat dog. Where they are well received, they are also given fresh salmon.

As they reach the Walla Wallas, the good offices of the accompanying Nez Perce chiefs have little effect. There are no more gifts of food. They are offered salmon to buy, but Clark declines: "The fish being very bad, those which was offered to us, we had every reason to believe [it] was taken up on the shore dead." Clark buys forty dogs for "articles of little value, such as beads, bells and thimbles, of which they appeared very fond."

At the Umatilla camps, the appearance of the corps paralyzes the Indians with fear. They will not come out of their wood lodges, and Clark, looking for more dog or salmon to buy, has to enter without ceremony. "When I went in, found some hanging down their heads, some crying and others in great agitation." Clark placates them with a few trinkets he has in his pockets, and when all the canoes arrive, the Umatillas regain their composure. It is, as Clark acknowledges many times, the appearance of Sacagawea and the toddler Pompey that reassures the tribes along their route. Clark remains struck by the despondency of the Umatillas and can find no better way to describe their utter resignation than to remark in his journal after leaving them behind: "I am confident I could have tomahawked every one of them."

The Nez Perce leave. They explain to Clark (and Lewis, perhaps) that they cannot speak to the Indians who live at The Dalles, the series of small falls and rapids where tribes gather to net and spear salmon. Their being with the party will only make things worse, the Nez Perce say, and they go home.

The Dalles is a threshold, a lintel, between the inland Indians and the Chinook language bands of the Pacific coast. It is also as far up the

Columbia as the British or American sailing captains have reached. It is the limit of European and American geographical knowledge, and when the corps passes The Dalles, their exploring days, their marches across land unknown to Europeans, are over.

63

October 16–17, 1805, The Mississippi Shrinks

BY THE FIRST WEEK in October, Pike and his party (nineteen enlisted men and a hired interpreter) are hauling the two large boats up the diminishing river and the weather is turning from rain showers to snow squalls and from chilly evenings to freezing nights. He should be turning around about now; he should have found the head of the Mississippi (and thus the minimum northern boundary of Louisiana Territory) and be on his way home. But Wilkinson gives the orders too late and Pike dallies and here they are pushing clumsy boats up rapids and over small waterfalls. It is worse than the last few miles were for Lewis and Clark on the Jefferson. They were pushing small dugout canoes and the weather was better.

It is not clear (it is seldom clear) if Pike has a plan, but he is apparently determined to rise as far up the river as possible with as much of his stores as he can keep with him (salt meat, flour, and whisky being the largest amount of goods). So it is that in the middle of a snowstorm, on October 16 the men are stumbling upstream, pushing the loaded boats over obstacles untold. We know almost nothing about the enlisted men in Pike's party. Much as in the journals of Lewis and Clark, only their last names, and sometimes their rank, are recorded in Pike's account.

Sergeant Henry Kennerman, Pike relates, "one of the stoutest men I ever knew, broke a blood vessel and vomited nearly two quarts of blood." This is a slight exaggeration; the average human being has but five quarts to begin with, and the loss of two would put even a hearty man flat on his back. "One of my corporals, [Samuel] Bradley, also evacuated nearly one pint of blood, when he attempted to void his urine," Pike adds.

It is difficult to peer so far backward and see what drives a Kennerman, a Bradley, to such exertion, to accept such abuse. Pike is sure that it is his authority and leadership.

"These circumstances," he relates, speaking of the ruptured arteries, along with "four of my men being rendered useless before, who were left on shore, convinced me that if I had no regard for my own health and constitution, I should have some for these poor fellows, who, to obey my orders, were killing themselves."

The large boats, armed with their swivel guns, are hauled ashore and the men set to different tasks. Some begin building log cabins to make a winter camp for the larger number (apparently some sixteen to eighteen men) who will stay behind while Pike presses on toward the headwaters of the Mississippi. A small group of hunters forage for game—deer and elk—and some begin making dugout canoes from the stately white pines that line the river. By these lighter and more agile craft, Pike will continue on to the head of the river. The men who winter at the cabins have a special responsibility—running a smokehouse. Lieutenant Pike has promised several dozen hams of smoked venison for General Wilkinson's mess.

64

November 1805, Burr in Washington

IN A PORTRAIT of Aaron Burr painted several years before his attempt to separate the west, a painting that now hangs in the New-York Historical Society, a viewer will see a remarkable profile. His nose ascends from its tip to his forehead almost entirely without deviation from a straight line. There is only the slightest deflection, an obtuse angle, where the nose joins with the cranium. The forehead, made even more obvious by Burr's receding hairline, seems to continue on the same angle as the nose before reaching a thin growth of hair near the apex of the skull. Burr resembles a Palouse Indian who had been tied facedown on a board as an infant.

Burr makes two lengthy visits that we know of when he arrives in Washington: with Anthony Merry, the British ambassador, and Thomas Jefferson, the American president. History is mostly gaps with a few stitches of fact holding it together. We know a good deal about what Burr said to Merry, we have but the barest notion what he said to Jefferson.

The conference with Merry begins on a bad note. London, the home office, has not even acknowledged receipt of Merry's first report on Burr and his request for funds to assist Burr in a war with Mexico and a separation of the western territories from the original United States. Burr is unfazed. We only have one version of the conversation— Merry's letter to London—but there is absolutely no reason to doubt it. Among other deficiencies, it seems that Anthony Merry has little imagination and no guile.

Burr suggests that he has, on his trip west, succeeded beyond his expectations. He is met everywhere with enthusiasm, and, Merry writes, Burr tells him that "everything was in fact completely prepared in every quarter for the execution of his plan."

What possible interest do the British have in Burr's scheme? Burr suggests to Merry that the western territories may ask to be returned to France, and that that implacable enemy of Britain will regain her colonies, take the Floridas by force, and perhaps Mexico. (France will take Mexico, in the short-lived rule of the Emperor Maximilian, whose execution will inspire Goya to a remarkable, if unfinished, painting.) Spain, in an uneasy forced alliance with France, is no friend of Britain, and Burr's plot, Merry tells London, will separate Spain from her wealth—the gold and silver of Mexico. It is all smoke and mirrors, this Burr hint about the western territories returning to French rule. France gave up all interest in the Americas before Napoleon sold Louisiana. France's attempts, in 1802 and 1803, at restoring her rule in Haiti (losing 30,000 troops in the process, most to yellow fever), ended her dreams of empire in the Western Hemisphere. The selling of Louisiana marked the end. London knows this. Burr may know it (being a brilliant if erratic mind). Merry has no clue.

London knows one more terribly important fact, a piece of news that has not yet reached the Americas when Merry meets with Burr. On October 21, Admiral Nelson's fleet destroyed the French fleet and drove the hapless Spanish fleet into harbor. Trafalgar, where Nelson enjoined every man to do his duty, has put an end to any possibility of a French or Spanish fleet sailing toward the Americas. Merry's long letter about Burr's plans will be treated like the last, as the home office treats all ridiculous messages—with silence.

Burr has dinner with Jefferson at the president's Washington home in late November. It is beyond imagining what they could have talked about for an entire dinner and a long, perhaps two-hour, conversation after dinner. Surely the election of 1800 is taboo, unless Jefferson has come to be amused by Burr's attempt to gain the presidency and there is precious little in the record to suggest the third president has anything resembling a sense of humor. If the prairie dog or the magpie are still alive, they might make a few minutes' dialog, although Burr's interest in natural history seems to be always limited to sexual explorations. Perhaps they talked of agriculture. It is a passion of Jefferson's, and Burr's son-in-law is a plantation owner. The death of Hamilton? One doubts it. Jefferson hated Hamilton and everything he stood for, but he despised dueling as much as one may hate an abstraction. And Burr is not known for speaking of the duel.

It is a ceremonial business, although without anything resembling the ceremonial rituals of the Corps of Discovery and the various tribes. One may be certain there is no "national embrace" as Burr departs to walk the dirt streets of Washington City toward his boardinghouse.

65

Mid-November 1805, Wilkinson Mends a Fence

WILKINSON, while Burr is on his way to Washington and Lieutenant Pike is on his way up the Mississippi, writes Jefferson. The letter arrives a few weeks after Burr dines with Jefferson. It is entirely mysterious what provokes the letter, but either Jefferson has questioned Wilkinson's judgment, or, more likely, Wilkinson has learned that some third party is snitching on him to the president.

The context is similar to Pike's exploration of the Mississippi. Wilkinson is trying to establish "military" trading posts on the Missouri to match the ones that Pike is negotiating on the Mississippi. St. Louis traders are already working both rivers, and intend, when Lewis and Clark return, to move much farther up the Missouri, into the distant Rockies. Wilkinson, by building military-run trading posts, including the one at the junction of the Platte and Missouri Rivers, would be competing against the civilian traders; they may be the ones he fears have compromised his reputation.

He writes Jefferson to explain that the establishment of a fort at the mouth of the Platte (a route to the central Rocky Mountains of Colorado) on the Missouri (the highway to the northern Rockies of Wyoming and Montana) really has nothing to do with trading. That is only incidental.

No, the problem is not of his making; he is setting up the fort at the Platte to take care of a problem with just a few Indian chiefs who are his guests in St. Louis. The troublesome ones are the chiefs of the Otoes and Arikaras ("Ottos and Riccari" in Wilkinson's spelling), who are in St. Louis at the request of Lewis and Clark, and who are supposed to be on their way to Washington to see Jefferson, their new Father.

The Otoes and Arikaras refuse to accompany the other chiefs to the east coast; they claim to be sick (or to becoming ill) and clamor "loudly and incessantly to be sent back [home] agreeably to the promise of Capt. Lewis." Wilkinson explains that his unauthorized fort on the Platte River is necessary to protect his men. They will take the Otoes to the Platte, which is central to their territory. Then a large body will escort the Arikara chiefs "eight or nine hundred miles higher up the Missouri." This is one of those moments where the close reader of Wilkinson's letter begins to wonder whether the general is terribly mistaken, horribly hyperbolic, or just plain lying. It is no more than 150 miles from the Platte to the heart of Arikara country. The soldiers at the Platte, he tells Jefferson, would build a fort and wait for the return of the party escorting the Arikaras.

Wilkinson tells Jefferson that another bunch of chiefs ("a conference of many Nations") is on its way to St. Louis and he has to get the Otoes and Arikaras out of town before the others arrive. That is why he has not asked anyone for permission to build the fort at the Platte. That is why he doesn't want the other chiefs to know about the escorts he is providing for the Otoes and Arikaras. If the other chiefs "found out they were not being returned" in the same style, "the jealousies which would ensue might prove fatal to Capt. Lewis, should he attempt to return by the Missouri." One may recall that this is the same General Wilkinson who notified the Spanish authorities of the departure of Lewis up the Mississippi and Missouri in the spring of 1804 and encouraged them to capture the Corps of Discovery and turn them back or kill them in the attempt, in order to protect the northern boundaries of New Spain.

Wilkinson's letter reveals his obvious nervousness about his reputation in Washington. He ends his letter with a protestation of his own honesty and his faithfulness to the orders of the civilian government: "I must declare that the establishment near the mouth of the Platte was intended for the safety and comfort of the party sent up with the Indian chiefs, pending the winter, to be confirmed or removed in the spring at the discretion of the Executive."

The fort on the Platte never becomes what Wilkinson desires—a choke point on the fur trade. The government trading posts never succeed, and independent fur traders pass them with impunity. The St. Louis traders will move far upstream from it in the following years, trading and trapping within the Indian-controlled land. That is very dangerous business, with many lives lost, but it succeeded, while the government traders waited for the Indians to come to them.

66

October 28–November 4, 1805,

Still at Play in the Fields

THERE IS A CERTAIN Boy Scout leader quality to Lieutenant Pike. This is deduced from his own words, virtually the only record we have of his brief life.

After giving up on hauling his large boats up the river, and while beginning to build a fortified camp, Pike sets about making dugout canoes to continue searching up the ever-narrowing Mississippi for its source. The first two canoes are a bit small, and when the men load them for the trip upstream, they sit low in the water. The next morning (why the canoes were loaded the day before is anyone's guess, but Pike is always edgy, nervous, uneasy when he cannot move at the first opportunity), one of the dugouts is found awash, sunk in the shallows by the bank.

Pike's solution to the problem is ingenious, or ingenuous. The water has soaked into his "cartridges," which are premeasured muzzle-loading powder charges for his rifle, each wrapped in thin paper so that they can be dropped down the barrel quickly and efficiently: "I had my cartridges spread out on blankets, and large fires made round them. At that time I was not able to ascertain the extent of misfortune, the importance of which *no man* can estimate, save only those, like us, who have been 1,500 miles from civilized society; and were in danger of losing the very means of defence and existence." Actually, he's more like 60 miles from some large North West Company British trading posts, and he's only about 700 miles (including the twists and turns of the river) from St. Louis.

Drying the cartridges with campfires didn't work, so on October 29, he tries a new trick: "I was at work on my cartridges all day and did not save five dozen out of nearly thirty [dozen], and in attempting to dry the powder, in pots, blew it up." He also nearly blows up three men he has set to cooking the black powder over a fire and the tent they're working in. With what was left after the explosion, he made a dozen new cartridges with the old wrapping paper.

While the new and larger canoes are being made and with the fortified camp finished, Pike finds himself with nothing to do. On Thursday, October 31, this unusual inactivity surprises him with a malaise:

"Found myself powerfully attacked with the fantastics of the brain called *ennui* at the mention of which I had always hitherto scoffed." It is not surprising that Pike knows the word. He is not formally educated, but aspires to knowledge, and is carrying a French grammar and vocabulary with him on this trip. "My books being packed up, I was like a person entranced, and then, could easily account why so many persons who have been confined to remote places acquired the habit of drinking to excess, and many other vicious practices, which have at first been adopted merely to pass time."

He shakes himself out of his blue mood, gathers a few soldiers, and sets out the next afternoon on a hunting trip, promising his enlisted companions a feast of fresh venison. Typically, he leaves the camp without bringing any provisions. The next day, he wounds two elk and three deer but does not take any of them into possession. This is partly due, he says, to the small caliber of his rifle, and "partly to our want of knowledge of the mode of following the track, after shooting them." Late in the second day of hunting he finally drops an elk with a decently placed shot "just behind the foreshoulder. He did not go 20 yards before he fell and died. This was the cause of much exultation, as it fulfilled my boast, and we having been two days and nights without victuals, it was of course acceptable."

67

December 1, 1805, Rumors Abound, Washington City

THOMAS JEFFERSON, like all leaders, gets his share of anonymous letters. Few survive; he is as likely to throw them away as anyone. But he keeps this one, received on the first day of the last month.

> *You admit him [Burr] at your table, and you held a long and private conference with him a few days ago after dinner at the*

*very moment he is meditating the overthrow of your Administra-
tion. . . . Yes, Sir, his aberrations through the Western States had
no other object. A foreign Agent, now at Washington knows since
February last his plans and has seconded them beyond what you
are aware of. . . . Watch his connections with Mr. M——y [that
would be Mr. Merry, the ambassador from London] and you will
find him a British pensioner and agent.*

The only trouble is that fomenting separation and rebellion in the
territories isn't illegal. It ought to be, and it will be in the future, but
at this precise moment in time it is not at all clear that revolution is a
crime. The Alien and Sedition Acts are long since repealed and Mr.
Jefferson has not yet disavowed his famous remarks about the tree of
liberty flourishing when its roots are watered with the blood of the
rulers, nor his comments about the right of the western territories
("our western sons") to go their separate way. But he saves the letter.

68

December 1805–May 1806,

Saber Rattling on the Sabine

BURR'S PLOT is approaching comic opera proportions. On one hand,
he is planning to separate the western territories from the original
states. On the other hand, he is promoting a punitive war against
Spanish Mexico (the "hated Don") to raise the almost revolutionary
army that will take New Orleans on its way to Mexico. And of course
his partner, Wilkinson, is on the Spanish payroll. If war with Spain, or

with Spanish Mexico, is what Burr, Wilkinson, and their co-conspirators require to raise a western army, Spain seems almost willing to oblige. If the reader is confused, that is Burr's fault, for it is he who has mingled anti-Spanish patriotism with secession from the United States and the creation of an empire that runs from the Ohio River to the Rockies and south to the Isthmus of Panama. As with most plots, not everyone involved knows everything. But, for now, all one must remember is that raising that army of western volunteers requires war with Mexico. And how much better if Mexico starts it?

The boundary between French Louisiana and Spanish Mexico (including what becomes the American states of Florida, parts of Louisiana, Texas, New Mexico, Arizona, and California) is not really clear at the time Jefferson purchases Louisiana. The western parts of northern Mexico are separated from any occupied parts of Louisiana by a vast unknown territory occupied, if at all, by Indians. And some of the Indians in Louisiana, especially the Pawnee on the fringes of Texas and New Mexico, are terrifying opponents.

The only point where the settled parts of Old Mexico approach the expanding settlements of Louisiana is near the Sabine River, which the Spanish assert is the eastern boundary of Mexico. The Sabine is easily found on a modern map; it is the squiggly border of Texas and Louisiana. The Spanish also claim the Red River as their northern boundary, and that makes up the squiggly line along the northern Texas–southern Oklahoma border. In short, the Spanish boundary claims are those of the Texas region.

The Americans, with little justification in history or geography, claim that Louisiana extends as far west as the Colorado, not the great Colorado across the Rockies, but a Colorado that drains through central Texas. When Jefferson is in a particularly grandiose mood, he claims that Louisiana extends all the way to the Rio Grande del Norte, the river that, in its lower half, makes up the uneven line of the current Texas-Mexico border.

The Spanish send troops to Nacogdoches, on the Sabine, and scout into Louisiana to Natchitoches, in disputed territory well east of the eventual border on the Sabine. And Jefferson orders Wilkinson to leave St. Louis, descend to New Orleans, and drive the Spanish back from not only Natchitoches, which is probably within the Louisiana Purchase, but push them back from Nacogdoches on the Sabine, which would mean going into Spanish Mexico.

Naturally enough, when an American president orders a general who is on the Spanish payroll (as Agent 13) to make war on his paymasters, things move slowly. From October 1805 to May 1806, Wilkinson vacillates. In the end, he negotiates a neutral zone between Natchitoches and Nacogdoches with Spain, and no one is killed, or even shot at. For negotiating this neutral zone (in direct opposition to his orders from the commander-in-chief), Wilkinson is neither dismissed nor reprimanded. He does ask the Spanish to pay him 150,000 pesos (a gold coin worth more than an American dollar) for refusing to fight, which they never do. The one thing the Spanish know about Wilkinson is that he has no fight in him, whether or not he is in their pay. They know him as a sometimes useful man whose major character traits are what one would expect from a traitor and a spy—deceptiveness and avarice.

On such a man, the president of the United States relies without doubt or fear. Wilkinson is a "Democratic Republican" and that is all that Jefferson needs, or perhaps it is all he wants, to know. Does the reader wonder how such a character has become the commanding general of the United States Army and the governor of Louisiana? In a long career, beginning in the Revolutionary War, Wilkinson has flattered and politicked the powerful and denigrated the abilities, even the loyalty of his fellow officers.

Among other adventures, he participated in a cabal to oust George Washington as commander of the Continental Army during the American Revolution. (This would be known to Burr and would recommend Wilkinson, for Burr and Washington loathed each other.) In a civilian pause between his military posts, Wilkinson ousted George Rogers Clark, our William Clark's older brother, as political leader of Tennessee when it was still a western extension of Virginia. On his return to the army, as second in command to Anthony Wayne, Wilkinson spent four years, 1792 to 1796, publicly quarreling with Wayne and privately questioning his sanity and intelligence. It is one of Wilkinson's achievements that General Wayne became known as "Mad" Anthony Wayne. On Wayne's death, in 1796, Wilkinson acceded to commander-in-chief.

President Adams (1796–1800) found him agreeable enough. President Jefferson merely continued to allow Wilkinson his way. The army, after all, was out on the frontier (Wilkinson's command moves from Detroit to St. Louis to New Orleans, frontier towns all).

One last explanation for Jefferson ignoring the warning signals about Wilkinson is that Jefferson had no use for a standing army, much preferring to rely on the state and territorial militias. Of all the armed forces in the United States, Wilkinson commanded the least admired and least relied upon. Any general, one gets the impression, would do.

69

December 1805, News of Trafalgar

DUE TO THE SLOWNESS of the mails, an account of the Battle of Trafalgar does not reach Washington until almost two months after the battle, a total victory by England. Admiral Nelson, before dying from his wounds, destroys the French fleet and drives the Spanish back to their home ports. Today, it means nothing to Americans, this epic sea fight. At most, we may know it as the time when Nelson signals his fleet: "England expects that every man will do his duty."

Even at the time, it does not reverberate in either meeting halls or distant vales. Few Americans have much stake in the outcome. But among those to whom it matters are Jefferson, Burr, and Wilkinson.

For the president, it is a mixed blessing. It marks the end of French influence in the Americas at least until she rebuilds her fleet. Spain, unlikely to dare sailing out of her ports, is reduced to an absentee land-lord, unable to project any force into the Americas. This is a plus, for it leaves disputed Spanish Florida at the sufferance of the Americans. But, ominously, Trafalgar infinitely enhances the power of Britain, who is already taxing American shipping with captures of goods headed for France and the impressment of American seamen whenever and wher-ever it can be condoned or concealed.

For Burr and Wilkinson, it threatens disaster. Their plot depends on the illusion of a great Spanish threat to the trans-Appalachian ter-ritories. Spain, they hint, may claim huge parts of the Louisiana Purchase, extending her Texas territory to the north.

Spain may bluster along the Sabine, but a Spain without a fleet capable of fighting its way to the Americas is an annoyance, not a threat. That the Dons of Mexico would make war on their own is ludi-crous. For more than three hundred years, Spain has made every deci-sion for all her colonies. (Even Wilkinson's pay is authorized in Madrid, not Mexico City.) The Dons are not going to do anything without permission from Spain.

Britain, from which the conspirators desire assistance in their grandiose plot to capture Mexico, has no need to get involved after Trafalgar. Spain is muzzled, and France is confined to the European continent. Britain's only viable enemy in the Americas is the United States itself, and that war has to wait until 1812, when a group of young trans-Appalachian congressmen are confident and angry enough to declare war on Britain. The worst news Burr can get is: "There will be no war with Spain," and that is exactly what he hears, however distantly, from the thunder of Trafalgar.

70

❧

December 1–7, 1805, By the Sea

AFTER LEAVING the Indian villages at the falls of the Columbia, the Corps of Discovery arrives at the huge tidal estuary where the Columbia meets the Pacific. William Clark writes (Lewis appears to be in one of his funks) the almost famous line: "Ocean in view. O, the Joy!" which is the last good thing anyone has to say about the mouth of the Columbia, about the salt water, the beaches, the estuaries, the tides, the surf, or the local Indians.

After a week on the northern side of the Columbia (modern Washington State), buffeted by winds and pelted by rainstorms, the corps takes a vote on what to do next. Not exactly a vote, but everyone's opinion was sought. The choices were: stay where they are; move across the river to higher, drier land with some four-legged food supplies; or, and this one makes no sense at all, go back up the river to The Dalles and wait there for spring to arrive. This is a moment touted as the first election in America where Native Americans (Sacagawea) and blacks (Clark's York) have a vote. Maybe, but it is also one of the first rigged elections, given the choices that the captains offer the party. Almost no one wants to stay on the beach without timber to build cabins or elk and deer to eat. No one wants to go back up to The Dalles, where they know they will be treated with the same contempt and discourtesy which those Indians showed them on the way down. The only choice is moving to the high ground south of the river, and that's the vote, with a single exception. One of the men has some hope that if they stay on the beach, they may catch a ride home on a trading vessel. As for Sacagawea's "vote," well, it is one of the few times that Lewis or Clark record her sentiments about anything. She votes with the same convictions that have made her a calming influence the entire trip. She is recorded as saying she thought it would be a good idea to move to a place where there was something to eat.

And so, with difficulty but without mishap, the corps moves south across the windswept Columbia in their canoes and sets up camp—Fort Clatsop—a few miles south of the river. They will spend four months there, subsisting almost entirely on bad elk, good dog, and a few fish they buy from the Clatsop and Chinook Indians. Several of the party will contract syphilis and/or the clap. The local Indians are too well acquainted with visiting sailors, and the only women available are semiprofessionals. It rains almost every day for the next four months. Life at Fort Clatsop is excruciatingly boring, but peaceful. The men do not fight. Charbonneau does not abuse Sacagawea. Lewis comes out of his blues and makes copious journal entries about flora and fauna, which Clark copies with regular bouts of misspelling. If this were a movie, the director would "cut to March."

71

Christmas 1805, Another Letter Ignored but Saved

WE KNOW that Thomas Jefferson has a blind eye to the faults of Democratic-Republicans like General Wilkinson. Underneath that public image of a man above partisan politics, that self-image of a rational man, lurks the venomous, the unforgiving, the vengeful Jefferson.

Far away, on the frontier of Kentucky, lives a young man with an unfortunate middle name and equally undesirable in-laws. He is Joseph Hamilton Daveiss, and he is the attorney general of Kentucky. He has two strikes against him: he is the son-in-law of supreme court justice John Marshall, whom Jefferson detests, and he is named in part after the late Alexander Hamilton, whose centralist, big-bank, big-government, oligarchic sentiments and actions were absolute anathema to Thomas Jefferson.

Still, Jefferson saves a letter sent to him by Daveiss. Somehow, probably by simply paying attention to barroom gossip and other indiscretions, Daveiss has a perfectly accurate understanding of the Burr conspiracy and General Wilkinson's place in it. In no uncertain terms, Daveiss tells his president that Wilkinson is not only conspiring with Burr to take New Orleans, Mexico, and as much of the trans-Appalachian United States as will join him, but Wilkinson is, and has been, a spy on the Spanish payroll. Daveiss urges the arrest of Burr on grounds of treason and the dismissal of Wilkinson.

Jefferson's response is not only to keep Wilkinson as commander-in-chief and governor of Louisiana, but make him both military and civilian governor of the Orleans Territory (the modern state of Louisiana). Daveiss writes more letters in the months to come, and Jefferson ignores him. On top of everything else, Daveiss is a member of the Federalist faction, or party, and not to be trusted by a Democratic-Republican president.

72

December 26, 1805–January 9, 1806,

Lieutenant Pike Carries On

THE COUNTRY AROUND the upper Mississippi (in modern Minnesota) is a mix of open prairie and woodlands where there is shelter from the boreal winds and moisture enough for trees. Across the open land, next to the now frozen Mississippi, Lieutenant Pike leads his men upward and onward. Where the shallow water of the river remains open, Pike's men drag the canoes across the snowbound prairie. Where the river is frozen, they slide the canoes on the ice.

As you might expect, they regularly break through the ice into the shallow waters, soaking their clothes, their shoes, and the contents of the canoes. On the fourth of January, Pike is encamped, attempting to dry his clothing. He never explains what kind of shelter his men take, but he has a double tent, a larger one over a smaller, the better to keep the snow and wind away. Pike's account of the night of January 4 and 5, 1806, has his usual ingenuous style:

> I was awakened by the cry of my sentinel, calling repeatedly to the men—at last he sung out 'God damn your souls, will you let the Lieutenant be burnt to death.' This immediately roused me, and at the first I seized my arms, but looking around I found my tents in a flame.
>
> The men flew to my assistance and we tore them down, but not until they were entirely ruined. This with the loss of leggings, moccasins, socks &c., which I had hung up to dry [over the fire inside his tent], was no trifling misfortune in that country, and on such a voyage.
>
> But I had reason to thank God that the powder (three small kegs) which was in the tent did not take fire when I should infallibly have lost all my baggage, if not my life.

Pike is one of those human beings utterly indifferent to the elements, supplied with a metabolism and a circulatory system beyond the imagining of the rest of us. This makes him a remarkable leader, in the sense that he is always capable of forging ahead in the worst of circumstances. For the next few days, he carries on without recording any personal discomfort, despite his lost leggings, moccasins, and socks. The cold is so miserable that he has to send someone ahead of the men, making fires every three miles. "Not withstanding which, the cold was so intense that some froze their noses—some their fingers and some their toes—even before they felt the cold sensibly."

Salvation comes from a source that Pike, who has postured, and may even believe, that he is entering a true wilderness occupied only by the wildest of Indians, is not expecting. They arrive at the shore of a large lake in the river's course, and "sometime after [we] discovered the lights of the houses; and on our arrival were not a little surprised to find a large stockade. The gate being open, we entered and proceeded to the quarters of Mr. Grant, where we were treated with the greatest hospitality."

Mr. Grant is a factor of the North West Company, the British trading company Pike has come to bring under the sway of, or to drive from the territory of, the United States Government and General Wilkinson's hoped-for fur-trading empire. For the time being, Pike behaves himself.

73

January 4, 1806, All My Children

JUST AFTER THE NEW YEAR, a horde of Indian chiefs, some recruited by Lewis and Clark, some by the St. Louis fur traders, and a few by General Wilkinson, descends on Washington City. They are on a public relations tour, intended to impress them with the wealth, the numbers of whites, and the enormity of the cities on the coastal plains. It helps, when reading Jefferson's speech to the Indians, to remember his way of regarding the Mississippi River as a channel, a barrier, between the settled states and Indian Country. And it helps to remember why,

when he writes of the "inalienable rights" of man, that he, and his contemporaries to a man, regard blacks and Indians as true human beings,
but trapped in a state of arrested development. They are like us, so to
speak, but fated never to grow up, as we do. Much is made of the
inconsistency of Jefferson's views of the rights of man and his suborn-
ing of slavery. There is no intellectual conflict, there is no psychological dissonance. Nonwhites are perpetual children. Jefferson may be
terribly wrong, but he is not confused.

So, that said, here is how he begins his address to forty-five Indians
from eleven tribes and subdivisions of tribes:

"My friends and children, Chiefs of the Osages, Missouris, Kanzas,
Ottos, Panis, Ayowas, and Sioux: [different spellings aside, the only
one that might cause confusion is Panis for Pawnee]

"We are descended from the old nations which live beyond the
great water," Jefferson explains, but we have lived here so long we are
sprung from the soil like you, "we are united in one family with our
red brethren." The most important message is simple: Jefferson is now
the Great Father. "The French, the English, the Spaniards, have now
agreed with us to retire from all the country between Canada and
Mexico, and never more to return to it."

In case the Indians have not gotten the message by traveling to the
great cities and through the well-settled farmlands of Pennsylvania and
Delaware and Virginia, Jefferson makes it clear: "We are become as
numerous as the leaves of the trees, and, tho' we do not boast, we do
not fear any nation. We are now your fathers."

Then, in a statement that would bring a shock of astonishment to
the St. Louis traders and General Wilkinson, Jefferson paints a picture
of a utopian and socialist trading system. Given that this is the same
man who encouraged getting Indian tribes into debt in order to have
an excuse to take over their tribal lands, the simplest explanation is
that Thomas Jefferson is lying through his teeth: "In establishing trade
with you we desire to make no profit. We shall ask from you only what
every thing costs us, and give you for your furs and pelts whatever we
can get for them again." Naturally, this will take some time, and until

this charitable program is under way, "the traders who have heretofore furnished you will continue to do so."

In case the Indian chiefs have not gotten the big picture, Jefferson closes with a plea for peace among the tribes and between Indians and whites. If peace is not gained, Jefferson makes the alternative perfectly clear:

"My children, we are strong, we are numerous as the stars in the heavens, and we are all *gun-men.*"

The forty-five chiefs took a few days to think all this through, and replied at some length, but with a single, simple request. If the white men are as numerous as stars and leaves, and as peaceable and just as Jefferson says, the chiefs would very much appreciate this: The Great Father should use some of his guns and some of his strong young men to keep white settlers from stealing Indian land.

And then the chiefs went home.

74

Early January 1806, News of Lewis and Clark

THOMAS JEFFERSON, at his Washington office, receives a letter from St. Louis with rather accurate information about his Corps of Discovery. The writer is Pierre Choteau, a member of an influential French family in St. Louis, a trader with the Indians, and a man heavily involved with Lewis and Clark. Choteau supplied them before their departure with trade goods and helped recruit the French boatmen who took the main party up to the Mandan villages in 1804.

The letter is a fairly accurate account of what has happened to Lewis and Clark, who promised to send back news from the headwaters of the Missouri, but who did not. The accuracy is all the more remarkable, considering the distance it has traveled, and the number of times the story has been retold before it reaches Jefferson. To the ordinary confusion of recounted information (as in the party game Telephone, with its inevitable and amusing mutations of the message) consider that the story has also been translated several times.

What we know of the letter comes from one written by President Jefferson to Meriwether's brother, Reuben Lewis, on January 12. If you would like to paint a mental picture of Jefferson at his desk, add in the newfangled letter-copying device he has acquired. The pen with which he writes is attached to one arm of a copying device, and a second pen moves across a separate piece of paper, making an automatic copy.

Jefferson tells Reuben Lewis that the news comes from the Indian agent who "informs me that some Osage chiefs had just arrived there who assured him that just as they were leaving their nation two Ottos [Otoes] arrived there with a *pretty direct* account that Capt. Lewis & his party had reached that part of the Missouri near the mountains where the Indian tract leads across (in 8 days march) to the Columbia, that he had there procured horses and had, with his whole party entered on the tract." (Jefferson uses *tract*, a common southern expression, comparable to "trace," or as we would say, "road," or "trail.")

This is a message worth parsing. The "8 days" to the Columbia recalls the Hidatsa's information given Lewis during the Mandan winter of 1804–1805. That was the number of days to ride from the Great Falls of the Missouri to the Pacific. "Eight" is a frequently encountered Plains Indian numerical adjective, probably meant to convey our idea of "several," rather than a specific number.

Just imagine how the news is transmitted. The only two tribes east of the Continental Divide who know firsthand about the horses and the decision to take the Nez Perce trail are the Shoshone and the Salish, who, after supplying the corps with horses, join forces and go down to the Missouri River plains to hunt buffalo together. Who would they tell? Was there a moment of conversation, a brief truce in an otherwise bitter feud with the Blackfeet? We know that the Hidatsa from the

Mandan villages rode west and attacked the Shoshones, but that was back in May or June, while the Corps of Discovery was toiling up the Missouri by boat. It could be the Crow that the Shoshone told; the Crow are a rather amicable group, and the Crow traded regularly with the Hidatsa of Knife River. The Blackfeet, if they learned from either the Salish/Shoshone or the Crow (likelier, the Crow manage to avoid most of the tribal conflict on the plains) could convey it indirectly through their Canadian trade partners who also traded south to the Missouri River. Somehow, the word got to the Otoes, who told the Osage, who told the Indian agent who wrote Jefferson.

75

January 21–29, 1806, Bloodsucker Lake

AFTER WEEKS of suffering from the cold before sheltering at Grant's trading post, Pike and his men encounter a new hazard when they set out to find the headwaters of the Mississippi. A strong January thaw makes it impossible to sled easily on the mush and also brings a flow of water down the surface of the ice-bound Mississippi. Pike is not exactly exploring for the source of the Mississippi; he simply is headed for what all the North West Company traders assume is the source, a lake known as Sangsue to the French-Canadians (in their patois it means "bloodsucker") and known as Leech Lake to the British-Canadians who are residents (and now for generations) in this northern extremity of the wooded country.

Pike's guide is a young Chippewa Indian whose name he does not know (or does not record). The Indian is amiable, competent, and Pike, as he writes, takes "him to live with me." That is, one assumes, to share the lieutenant's tent. They are headed for an unoccupied cabin, a "lodge" in Pike's phrase, a building intended to provide shelter to travelers between the North West Company trading posts at Leech Lake and the ones, like Grant's, lower down the Mississippi at Sandy Lake.

By this time, Pike is down to two companions; the dozen or so other men are lagging far behind with the provisions and the sleds. To lighten the sleds, Pike sends back all the "conveniences" on the sleds so that they might move expeditiously toward Leech Lake, "and in the hurry sent my salt back, also my ink."

Pike is if nothing else, "active." He and the Indian and a hapless soldier he calls "Foley" are fifteen to twenty miles ahead of the sled party, until January 23, when Pike says he "forgot my thermometer, having hung it on a tree. Sent Foley back for it." Pike sends him back the next day for another misplaced item, the Sioux pipe, given to him as a peace sign to the Chippewa. Foley now has marched almost twice as far as Pike, though not as rapidly; he does not return with the pipe until well after dark. And the next day, as Pike explains, "The Indian and I marched so fast that we left Foley on the route, about 8 miles from the lodge. . . . The Indian and myself arrived [at the intermediate sheltering "lodge"] before sundown. Passed the night very uncomfortably, having nothing to eat, not much wood, nor no blankets. The Indian slept sound. I admired his *insensibility*, being myself obliged to hover over a few coals all night."

Poor Foley, pipe in hand, arrived at 10 A.M., after a terrible trip, when, "sometime in the night, when not being able to overtake us, he made a fire and halted, but having no ax to obtain wood, was near freezing." Foley is actually John Boley, a minor character from the Lewis and Clark expedition, who wintered with them in 1803–1804, accompanied them as far as the Mandans, and then returned to St. Louis in the spring of 1805 with the big keelboat. Boley was not impressive enough to be enlisted for the entire Lewis and Clark expedition, but was above average among Pike's motley crew of misfits and malcontents.

The next day, the rest of the men show up, and there is no more trekking to do except the last leg to Leech Lake. Pike remarks, and the reader will understand, that "Foley [Boley] wished to decline going on with me." Another man is chosen, and at 2:30 in the afternoon, with the winter sun sliding across the southwestern horizon, Pike, the Indian, and a soldier named Theodore Miller arrive at Squaw Point on "Lake Le Sang Sue."

"I will not attempt to describe my feelings on the accomplishment of my voyage, this being the main source of the Mississippi." He and the Indian cross the ice to the North West Company trading post, arriving at nine at night: "Found all the gates locked, but on knocking was admitted and received (with my young man) with distinguished politeness and hospitality by Mr. Hugh McGillis. Had a good dish of coffee, biscuit, butter and cheese for supper." After several days of similar hospitality to Pike and the enlisted men who straggle in, Pike will make his wishes known to the North West Company in general, and the amiable McGillis in particular.

Leech Lake is not the source of the Mississippi, that is a much smaller lake farther north and west. Pike's error causes no geopolitical problems. Both lakes are well below the Forty-eighth parallel, which will become the U.S.-Canada border in northwestern Minnesota. The source lake is found and named fourteen years later by a Henry Schoolcraft. Almost as a joke, Schoolcraft gives it an aboriginal-sounding name: Lake Itasca.

The six letters of the lake's name are extracted from the center of the Latin for "true head" of the Mississippi: *Veritas caput.*

76

❧

January 10, 1806, Owning the Whale

SHORTLY AFTER NEW YEAR'S DAY, a whale washes ashore on the beach near the expedition's little salt factory on the Pacific shore southwest of Fort Clatsop. The men have almost all the necessities of frontier life—gunpowder, lead, medicines, and enough metal to manufacture small tools for trading with the Indians, but they are out of salt. The factory is two large iron pots, tended over campfires, and the evaporated salt crystals clinging to the sides of the pots are scraped and saved and carried back to the main camp.

The whale is another gift from the sea entirely. It promises blubber for oil. Oil and fat are precious commodities; the corps is losing weight and strength eating lean elk and venison. And it is entertainment. If there is one thing absolutely necessary to well-being in the coastal rain forest of Oregon, it is some kind, any kind, of diversion.

Lewis intends to lead the party, but Clark volunteers and takes eleven men and Sacagawea, who insisted on going along, and thereby taking Pompey, to see the whale. It is easy to understand why Clark replaces Lewis: Clark, given any choice, will never let Pompey out of his sight.

This is Lewis's account of Sacagawea's desire to see the whale: "The Indian woman was very importunate to be permitted to go, and was therefore indulged; she observed that she had traveled a long way with us to see the great water, and that now that [a] monstrous fish was also to be seen, she thought it very hard she could not be permitted to see either."

By the time the expeditioners get to the whale, the Clatsop Indians are stripping it to the bone. Since possession is entirely the law, Clark buys some blubber and renders some oil, and they return to camp with the first substantial fatty food anyone has seen since they left the Nez Perce in November. Lewis is so pleased with adding fat to his diet, he even makes a small joke about Jonah and the whale, remarking that he is swallowing the whale instead of the whale swallowing him, as it did with Jonah. Fat is so desirable that the next time, a month later, Lewis mentions food in any detail, he says his boiled elk dinner has "the appearance of a little fat on it." This, for Fort Clatsop, is living in high style.

The whale that swallows Jonah is the prophet's salvation. The whale fat ingested by the Corps of Discovery is likely the difference between scurvy or starvation and mere deprivation. They are, once again, all very lucky.

77

February 6–10, 1806, Pike as Diplomat

THE MEMBERS of Lieutenant Pike's company straggle into the North West Company fort on February 6, a day after Pike and his Indian lad. They are treated with the same consideration as Pike and his Indian tent mate. They need it. Each man suffers from frostbite, some on the hands, others on the feet, all of them about their ears, cheeks, and noses. When the last of the baggage arrives, they get their American flag out, and, Pike explains to McGillis, they plan to raise it over the British-owned trading post.

"Mr. McGillis asked if I had any objections to his hoisting their flag, by way of a compliment to ours, which had nearly [a misprint in Jackson's edition of Pike's journals, one assumes, for "newly"] arrived. I made none," Pike remarks, rather puckishly, "as I had not yet explained to him my ideas."

For the next three days, the men subsist on food supplied by the North West Company, and Pike is taken on tours of the lake and the interior in a low-to-the-snow sled drawn by horses, a "cariole," he calls it. Pike returns on the evening of the ninth, and on the morning of the tenth makes the sentiments expressed in his letter of February 6 (delivered on the seventh, the day after he allows McGillis to hoist the Union Jack) a little clearer to McGillis. The letter, addressed to the North West Trading Company care of their agent McGillis, is a stiff and formal set of demands to be met if the company plans to stay in business in the United States.

"Hoisted the American flag in the fort," Pike recounts in his journal. "The English Jack was flying at the top of the flag staff. Put the Indians and my riflemen to shooting at it; who, after some shots, broke the iron pin to which it was fastened, and brought it down to the ground."

After another meal is cooked and served by the resident Mrs. McGillis, a Chippewa woman, Pike retires to read by the light of the McGillis parlor fire. He is reading a book by the English author William Shenstone. Pike always has an educational book at hand. Shenstone is an author of enlightening and uplifting works. Pike spends the early evening reading Shenstone's "Essays on . . . Manners."

78

February 6 and 15, 1806, Mild-Mannered McGillis

PIKE'S LETTER to the North West Company trader at Leech Lake is more than a historical document. Pike would re-create this correspondence at a time when he is suffering considerable questioning of his motives and morals, including his possible role in the Burr conspiracy. (No copy of it is to be found in the North West Company's archives, although there is a reference to it.) Whether Pike gives an accurate recounting of the letter or not doesn't matter. What Pike writes, three years after the fact, is what he wants the reader to think of him and his personal character.

Pike's lengthy letter to Mr. McGillis, intended to be passed along to the North West Company headquarters and the colonial government of Canada, is a mixture of bluster, misunderstanding of geography, outright lies, and as with much of Pike's journal, unintentional character self-assassination. He accuses the company of invading "the center of our newly acquired territory of Louisiana," by which he may mean trading with the tribes at Fort Mandan, or else he has no idea what he's talking about. He is offended to note that the company has occupied every suitable place along the shores of Lake Superior, a place he has never been. He is shocked that they have come "down the Red River." This is the river that becomes the border of Minnesota and North Dakota, and since it runs north into Canada, it is not even within the limits of the Louisiana Territory (the headwaters of the Mississippi and its western tributaries).

"I have found, sir, your commerce and establishments extending beyond our most exaggerated ideas," and he accuses the company of acts "particularly injurious to the honor and dignity of our government." The most obnoxious act is showing the Union Jack over American soil. Even more serious are the stockaded trading posts, that is, the same two places of comfort Pike has been enjoying. The posts, he writes, "if properly known, would be looked on with an eye of dissatisfaction by our government for another reason, viz., there being so many furnished posts in case of rupture between the two powers, the English government would not fail to make use of those places of deposit of arms, to the great annoyance of our territory."

Then, he threatens McGillis personally: "Strict justice would demand, and I assure you that the law directs under similar circumstances, a total confiscation of your property, personal imprisonment and fines." And then comes the most curious sentence, until you remember that Pike is actually involved with his patron Wilkinson in setting up their own trading posts for their own profit, a sentence Pike inexplicably repeats in his edited journals: "But having discretionary instructions [that is, he is excused somehow from enforcing the law], and no reason to think the above conduct was dictated through ill will, . . . *I am willing to sacrifice my prospect of private advantage.*" Pike will allow Mr. McGillis to continue in business, so long as he refrains from raising the Union Jack, holding councils with the Indians, or distributing liquor to them.

The emphasis on Pike's "prospect of private advantage" is supplied. Pike is sacrificing his imagined right, and capability, of establishing trading posts for his and Wilkinson's profit, this far north and west of the Falls of St. Anthony, where he has already purchased land for a trading post.

Pike also relinquishes his government's right to confiscate all Mr. McGillis's trade goods, providing he promises to pay duty on them retroactively to the date of the Louisiana Purchase. He closes with thanks to McGillis for the hospitality shown him.

McGillis's reply, after he waits ten days to compose himself as well as the letter, promises to pay the necessary duties. He is even amused (for a Scot) by the suggestion that the North West Company's little trading posts could become British forts: We cannot imagine, he explains to Pike, "that such poor shifts will ever be employed by the British government in a country overshadowed with wood, so adequate to every purpose. Forts might, in a short period of time, be built far superior to any stockades we may have occasion to erect."

He regrets the flag incident (without reminding Pike that he had asked for, and received, Pike's permission to raise the Union Jack) and calmly remarks that: "The custom has long been established and we innocently and inoffensively, as we imagined, have conformed to it till the present day."

Neither Pike's letter nor McGillis's reply will raise much furor at the offices of the North West Company, and it is not clear whether McGillis forwarded the whole correspondence. There is a brief mention in company records to "Letters from Mr. Hugh McGillis, informing us that a party of American soldiers had arrived at his place in February last, commanded by Lieut. Pike . . . their errand was to oblige us to pay the usual duties at Mackinac for trading in American territories." And so they did, until the War of 1812 interrupted Canadian-American trade and had even more dire consequences for Zebulon Montgomery Pike.

79

February 1806, Burr in Winter

THE STRAIN of unusual inactivity during the fall and winter of 1805–1806 begins to take a toll on Burr. He loiters in the Washington City area, waiting for the summer months when he can begin his military campaign down the Ohio, to the Mississippi and on to New Orleans, and, if things go well, on to Mexico. The mere inactivity of the body after his long trek down the Mississippi to New Orleans and back through the woods of Kentucky and Ohio may be the cause of his altered mental state.

Sometime in the first months of the year, Burr begins to imagine a much greater coup than merely taking the west and invading Mexico and creating an empire that will run from Canada to the Strait of Darién. He visits the Spanish ambassador, the Marquis de Casa y Yrujo, in Washington City. Burr tells Yrujo that he believes he can raise enough opponents of the Democratic-Republicans to turn Congress out of the Capitol and Jefferson out of his office. What began as a dream to lead secession across the Appalachians has become the dream of a volunteer-military coup d'etat. Yrujo is interested.

Burr also tells the same plan to a curious figure, the adventurer William Eaton, who is in Washington to petition Congress. Eaton is an American popular hero, getting credit (probably deserved) for launching a campaign on North African soil a few years earlier. He attacks the Barbary pirates from land while American naval vessels bombard them from the Mediterranean Sea. (This is the "halls of Tripoli" in the U.S. Marine Corps Hymn.) Nothing Eaton does materially affects the resolution of that conflict, but his mere temerity is enough to make him a heroic figure in the popular press and thus the public mind.

Why Burr approaches Eaton is inexplicable. There is no reason for Burr to think Eaton will join him. That man's patriotism is evidently national, not regional, and Eaton has no reason to distrust or dislike Jefferson.

In fact, without revealing the details of Burr's fancied coup (is there some kind of honor among adventurers at work here?) Eaton does go to Jefferson and warns him that Burr is dangerous. Eaton argues that "Colonel Burr ought to be removed from the country," and suggests making him ambassador to Madrid, or to London. That would, and Eaton knows it, send Burr to the very people with whom he is plotting his adventures, from whom he is soliciting funds to carry them out. Eaton may have an ironical sense of humor or a taste for the absurd. He could just as easily suggest sending Burr to Paris or St. Petersburg.

Having gotten the thought, the fantasy, of a coup d'etat off his chest, out of his too-active mind, Burr never mentions it again.

80

❧

February 14, 1806, Lewis Examines Clark's Maps

IN THE TWO MONTHS after the corps settles into the new buildings at
Fort Clatsop, William Clark spends most of his daylight hours amend-
ing and correcting his field maps, rechecking distances traveled as
noted in his daybook, and adding details remembered but not drawn
at the time because of the daily pressures of the trek. The day Clark
finishes the maps, Lewis sums up their meaning in his journal: ". . . we
now discover that we have found the most practicable and navigable
passage across the continent of North America." Lewis will never
change his mind, and his mind will be gone before there is any evidence
to the contrary.

But it is remarkable, given the general modesty of both Meriwether
Lewis and William Clark, who manage to write thousands of boast-
free journal pages between them, that Lewis should be so sure that no
route existed less troublesome than crossing the Bitterroots, an awe-
somely young uplifted range, and therefore one with jagged and knife-
edged peaks and ridges, a country almost untouched by the gentling
hands of time.

Of course, Lewis understands that the final miles up the Missouri
and the trek from that river's headwaters to the Nez Perce Trail is useless for any traveler: "The navigation of the Missouri above the river
Dearborn is laborious and 420 miles distant" from the beginning of
the Nez Perce Trail. The Indians, both Salish and Nez Perce, Lewis
recalls, told him that from the Missouri by the mouth of the Dearborn
(a few miles upstream from the Great Falls) to the mouth of Lolo Creek
(Traveler's Rest Creek to Lewis and Clark) is a few days' ride over an
easy, low pass. The route up to the headwaters of the Missouri and

then back to Lolo Creek is "further by 500 miles" than the overland route from the Missouri to Lolo Creek. Not only further, "but much worse route if Indian information is to be relied on."

Lewis has always had trouble relying on Indian information, and he will have more chances to disbelieve them in the near future. Not only is he skeptical about the ease of the passage from the Missouri over to the Blackfoot River and the Clark Fork of the Columbia, he's still not convinced that boating from the confluence of the Bitterroot and the Clark Fork down to the main Columbia River is impossible. He even adds that the Salmon River from Lemhi Pass to the sea might be navigable, no matter what the Indians say. He has not seen the upper Salmon with his own eyes; Clark and a few of the corps are the only white men to look at the River of No Return.

Clark, as usual when Lewis is writing journal entries, merely copies them into his own book. He slightly modifies Lewis's hope that the Clark Fork and the upper Columbia might be boatable by adding this qualification to Lewis's enthusiasm: "Even admitting the Clark's river, contrary to information, to be as navigable as the Columbia below its entrance . . . the tract by land over the Rocky mountains usually traveled by the natives . . . is preferable."

It is an interesting and small distinction: Both Clark and Lewis argue for the Nez Perce Trail, but Lewis hopes the Indians are wrong about the navigability of the Clark Fork and the Salmon. William Clark doesn't much care if either might be rafted or canoed. He assumes that if the Nez Perce think their trail is the best, then it "is preferable."

What neither of them will countenance is the truth: They boxed themselves in by sticking to the Missouri to its headwaters and then by taking the only route known to the Indians they met along the way. South of their route, just off the upper Platte River, is the real way west, the South Pass of the Rocky Mountains, the route that will become the Oregon Trail. If they were denied the discovery of South Pass by following their orders from the president, that is not all bad. What neither of them yet understand is that sticking to the rivers has kept them alive. On the return trip, both Clark and Lewis will find out how difficult the prairie can be for a white man on horseback.

81

Late February 1806, Pike Commits Diplomacy upon the Chippewa

PIKE, apparently with the help of the local North West Company traders, arranges a council with several Chippewa bands. He declares, after their chiefs smoke with the Sioux pipe he is carrying, that peace has broken out between these hereditary enemies.

The great chiefs politely decline his invitation to travel to St. Louis, saying they should stay home and keep order. The minor chiefs that Pike invites demur; they say they are of "consequence insufficient" to be worth the trouble of ferrying them a few thousand miles through enemy territory. Pike tells them he is "sorry to find that the hearts of the [Chippewa] of this quarter were so weak" that the other tribes would laugh at them.

Pike is only inviting them to meet "the great war chief," not the Great Father, that is to say Wilkinson, not Jefferson. They barely understand his reasoning. He has come to make peace, bearing nothing more than the personal pipe of a great Sioux chief. One of the chiefs, Sucre, of the Red Lake Chippewa, tries to explain it to Pike: "There is my calumet, I send it to my father the great war chief. What does it signify that I should go to see him? Will not my pipe answer the same purpose?" Pike seems unable, or unwilling, to comprehend Sucre's reasoning. Pike brings messages and peace offerings from the Sioux by carrying their pipe to the Chippewa. Why indeed should it not work in the reverse direction?

Then, two young men volunteer to go to St. Louis. Pike (who has not met a Chippewa until this day) calls them the "most celebrated young warriors" in the tribe and adds that they were "adopted as my children, and had myself installed as their father." He swears they will "never regret the noble confidence placed in me, as I would have protected their lives with mine."

Now, having adopted two Indians, and enlisted them in his party, Pike gives the Chippewa some entertainment. "My soldiers [performed] a dance." The Indians were also entertained "with a small dram" of whisky. "They attempted to get more liquor," he preens, "but a firm and manly denial convinced them I was not to be played with."

Pike, who seldom drinks any liquor, gives the Chippewa a lengthy lecture on the evils of alcohol and promises that when the American traders arrive, they will not be selling that poisonous stuff. "But," he adds, "I have found the traders here with a great deal of rum in hand; I have, therefore, given them permission to sell what they have, that you may forget it by degrees."

As for criminal elements among the tribes, Pike tells the Chippewa to keep an alleged murderer out of his sight, else "I would be obliged to demand him of you and make my young men shoot him." Pike is outnumbered something on the order of 200 to 12 at this point, but he tells the Chippewa it is his manly self-restraint that keeps him from finding and executing the murderer: "My hands on this journey are yet clear of blood, may the Great Spirit keep them so."

So, having informed the Chippewa that war is abolished and prohibition is coming, Pike leaves the council in good spirit, sure that his words will work wonders, that not only has he found the source of the Mississippi, he has made the country safe for American commerce.

82

February 22, 1806, Burr Says Good-bye to Jefferson

HISTORIANS AND OTHER IDOLATERS like to believe that Thomas
Jefferson should be regarded as a man capable of rising above politics
and personalities, a sort of benign observer of the democratic process,
dismissive of its foibles, tolerant of its failings, serenely confident that
all will work out for the greater good. He is, to some, a presidential
Dr. Pangloss, and like Voltaire's character believes that everything is for
the best in this best of all possible worlds that is the United States of
America.

Certainly he keeps himself above public displays of partisanship,
and never more so than in his dealings with Colonel Burr. He invites
Burr to dinner. He has his carriage put at Burr's disposal for moving
about the rutted roads of the capital-in-progress that is Washington.
Even fully warned and very likely convinced of Burr's machinations, he
invites the little colonel to dinner on February 22.

We have no record of this private meeting except Jefferson's, and
that is composed nearly a month after the event, as though Jefferson
believes it is important to limn his interpretation and save it for pos-
terity.

Prior to their last meal together, Burr is prominently named in the
newspapers as the next ambassador to Britain, a rumor the colonel is
likely to have circulated himself. New Hampshire's Democratic-
Republican Senator William Plumer will tell a colleague that this is
absurd speculation, that "Mr. Jefferson has no confidence in him. He
knows him to be capable of the darkest measures—a designing dangerous man."

Yet they dine together. According to Jefferson, Burr says that although the president treats him politely, that is all. Burr takes credit for "bringing on the present order of things," which Jefferson takes to mean the second term of his presidency. Burr claims to always support the Jefferson administration. Then, by Jefferson's account, it turns nasty. Burr says "that he could do me much harm" and would wait for Jefferson to offer him some office, presumably to keep Burr from whatever harm it is he thinks he may wreak upon the administration.

It is difficult to imagine, these many years after, what Burr is driving at, where the weakness lies that he would exploit. The only political scandal-mongering against the president is an allegation that he somehow finagled the vote in 1801 that gave him the presidency and Burr the second office. Since that outcome was the clear intent of the voters, it is difficult to imagine what evil purpose Jefferson could possibly have. It is conceivable that Burr is really making a serious threat. Is it the forceful overthrow of the government, the plot he outlined to the Spanish ambassador, that he is hinting at?

In any case, Jefferson informs Burr that no office will be forthcoming. In Jefferson's account of the meeting, he says he simply told his guest that he has "lost the confidence of the public." Jefferson does not comment on his own feelings about Burr. He writes the account like a reporter, an observer only of what is said. It is a conversation in the third person.

In a curious finale, one quite inconceivable today, Burr makes a courtesy call at Jefferson's office the day he departs Washington to go west and attempt to divide the union. Jefferson, quite capable of mercilessly humiliating a Briton, poor and hapless ambassador Merry, treats the greatest of American scoundrels with all the external manifestations of respect. It is either Jefferson at his most notorious slowness to make up his mind, or else it is a way of honoring the colonel's previous service in the Revolutionary War. It also may be a reward for Burr's firm and capable behavior as vice president, once he loses his bizarre attempt to be elected as the chief executive. It is all so terribly decent as to pass understanding.

83

Early March 1806, Pike Exercises His Authority

AFTER BORROWING a sleigh and a dog team from the remarkably patient Mr. McGillis, Pike continues to explore the area around Leech Lake. It is not clear why he does this, perhaps only to visit other trading posts and make the same demands of them. Whatever he is up to, he does not account for it in his journal. It is altogether possible it is a habit of his, that he is simply moving, exploring, adventuring with no plan in mind.

Pike continues to set an example of hardiness that few explorers ever have, or ever will, attempt to emulate. There is no reason to disbelieve him. Moving between two North West Company stockades in the last week of February, he miscalculates the distance to be traveled and spends two unexpected nights sleeping on the snow. As he writes in his journal, he "took no provisions nor bedding."

In spite of this privation, he recalls that his "young warrior was still in good heart—singing and showing every wish to keep me so. My racket strings [that is, his snowshoe rawhide webbing] brought the blood through my socks and moccasins from which it may be imagined to what pain I marched." The small sled is meant merely for carrying goods, and so Pike is not greatly put out when he manages to simply lose one of the two dogs belonging to Mr. McGillis. A valuable animal, he notes in his journal, but evidently not valuable enough for Pike to offer any payment for the missing dog.

By the first week in March, Pike is finished with his survey of the trading posts and returns to his base camp, where the platoon of soldiers who accompanied him that far are waiting for him and also waiting for the ice to go out so that they may head downriver for St. Louis.

Pike's authority, and there is no question he can demand obedience, even something like loyalty from his men, is not something that continued in his absence.

Sergeant Henry Kennerman is in charge of the base camp, and when Pike returns he discovers that Kennerman has eaten all the smoked venison hams intended for General Wilkinson and other gentlemen friends of Pike. Kennerman "also made way with two barrels of flour, nearly all the whisky (publicly sold it to the men), one barrel of pork and a keg of private whisky of my own, also broke open my trunk and sold some things out of it, traded with the Indian, gave them liquor."

The only punishment Kennerman receives is that he was reduced in rank, for he is Corporal Kennerman on Pike's next expedition. For any one of those offenses, you will recall, a member of Lewis and Clark's corps would expect at least a hundred lashes, well laid on a bare back.

Pike has opinions about his men, many of whom follow him first up the Mississippi and then to Colorado the next fall. He calls them "rogues," and still takes them the next year. They, in all fairness to Pike, seem willing to follow him. It is an interesting conundrum. One believes, in the long run, that life in the United States Army in 1805 and 1806 is very boring. Pike, at least, is not boring.

84

The Ides of March, 1806, At Fort Clatsop

POLITICALLY SENSITIVE, if not correct, readers of the fine print in the journals of Clark and Lewis never fail to point out that neither captain is capable of saying a good word about the Chinook Indians who reside about the mouth of the Columbia. Proof of their insensitivity to the Chinook culture is particularly evident in the "friend or foe" password for entering the palisaded camp. The answer to "Who goes there?" is "No Chinook."

The local tribes are well aware that the Corps of Discovery will depart when spring arrives. The bustle of preparation is both obvious and materially rewarding. In mid-March, Lewis trades his last respectable piece of clothing, a dress blue uniform, for one of the Clatsop's elegant, large, light, cedar-plank canoes. The thought of paddling clumsy dugouts upstream against the swift waters of the Columbia is on the edge of inconceivable.

Both Chinooks and Clatsops, regular daytime visitors to the fort, see all the men, and Sacagawea, busily preparing for the trip. On March 12, Clark notes that the men have completed 358 pairs of moccasins for the trek home. They are rawhide elk-leather footwear that the men know, by experience, will each last a week or less of hard use. Although the party has clever carpenters and ironworkers, it apparently has no one capable of tanning leather, except, of course, the Indian woman, who makes elegant soft deerskin clothes for herself and the boy Pompey, and for Charbonneau himself. Her dresses and his shirts are sometimes mentioned as trade goods highly sought after by indigenous Indians.

On a Saturday afternoon, March 16, Lewis observes the anxiety of the Chinooks to cash in before the corps departs: "We were visited this afternoon by Delashewilt, a Chinook Chief, his wife and six women of his nation which the old bawd, his wife, had brought for market. This was the same party that had communicated the venereal to so many of our party in November last [almost the very day they arrived in Chinook country], and of which they have finally recovered. I therefore gave the men a particular charge with respect to them [the six women] which they promised me to observe."

The old bawd, her husband, and the women set up camp just outside the palisade, Lewis notes on Monday, and they "seem determined to lay close siege to us but I believe notwithstanding every effort of their winning graces, the men have preserved their constancy to the vow of celibacy which they made on this occasion to Capt. Clark and myself."

After trading Lewis's dress uniform for a canoe, the corps is out of capital to exchange for anything precious: "We want another canoe," Lewis writes, "and as the Clatsops will not sell us one at a price which we can afford to give, we will take one from them in lieu of the six elk which they stole from us in the winter." Clark's journal entry has a little more detail: ". . . as the Clatsops will not sell us one, a proposition has been made by certain of our interpreters and several of the party to take one in lieu of 6 elk. . . ."

And they did. They would much rather steal a canoe from the despised Chinooks, but those are kept on the north side of the Columbia, while the local Clatsops leave their canoes unguarded on their own lands, on the south bank near Fort Clatsop. Drouillard, master hunter, is one of the ringleaders of the theft and sequestering of the canoe. He is surely one of the "interpreters" who suggest stealing what cannot be bought. After all, they are his elk; he is the man who spends the winter slogging through the marshes, shooting the elk that winter in the lowlands, dragging their carcasses to dry land for the benefit of the corps. He is also half or more Indian, and stealing a canoe, like stealing a horse, is part of the game, part of life. It is the only serious "theft" perpetrated by the Corps of Discovery. It is politically incorrect by modern standards. Critics (and there are many) should try walking from Fort Clatsop to the Nez Perce country, carrying all their possessions, before rubbing the corps' noses in this particular dirt.

85

❧

April 9–11, 1806, Blood Money,
New York and St. Louis

HENRY DEARBORN, the secretary of war, has some troubling news for General Wilkinson. On top of arranging with Lieutenant Pike to acquire some personal trading posts on the Mississippi, informing the Spanish of everything they want to know (except, of course, his and Burr's plan to take Mexico) and arranging a cease-fire along the Nacogdoches River (for the benefit of Spain and also to keep himself a long distance from shots fired in anger), Wilkinson now has to commit a difficult act of diplomacy. This is the beginning of Dearborn's letter from Washington, sent April 9:

"The Missouri and Mississippi Indian Chiefs will leave this place tomorrow for Pittsburgh, from whence they will descend the river & proceed on to St. Louis. Several have died; but what is more especially to be regretted is the death of the very respectable & amiable Ricara Chief, which happened on the 7th instant."

The Arikaras are a critical tribe to remain friendly with; they are the first choke point on the Missouri and not easily placated. It is the Arikaras, the previous summer, who dismiss Lewis and Clark's offer of whisky with the understandable complaint that no true friend would offer them that "which makes us fools."

Dearborn, an old border fighter and thoroughly acquainted with the average army soldier, orders Wilkinson to send a message of condolence to the Arikaras "in a light boat, with a sober, discreet Sergeant & four faithful sober soldiers." From Washington, Wilkinson will receive and send upriver "the Big Medal, clothes, trinkets, &c., &c. of the Old Chief, to his favorite son, together with something like a commission to him of a Chief. And it is thought advisable to send presents to his wives and children, to the amount of from two to three hundred dollars, which you will please to have selected from the Factory Goods." Almost as an afterthought, Dearborn orders a present of "100 lbs of powder, corresponding amount of lead, to be distributed generally." That's not really enough to start a small war, but it does amount to some three thousand charges for a muzzle-loading rifle.

President Jefferson, in a separate letter, adds his own thoughts and sends them to Wilkinson to be communicated to the Arikaras: Speaking of the late chief, Jefferson writes:

> *Wishing to see as much as he could of his new brethren, he consented to go towards the sea as far as Baltimore and Philadelphia. He found nothing but kindness and good will wherever he passed. On his return to this place he was taken sick; everything we could to help him was done; but it pleased the Great Spirit to take him from among us. We buried him among our own deceased friends and relatives, we shed many tears over his grave. . . . But death must happen to all men; and his time was come.*

Since the Arikara chief will not be making any speeches to his tribesmen, Jefferson thoughtfully encloses a copy of the speech he made to all the assembled chiefs just two months before the Arikara died. The chief is buried among the Great Father's friends and relatives Jefferson writes, and they are, as he noted in the speech copied and sent to the Arikaras, "as numerous as the stars, and . . . are all *gun-men*."

It will be the summer of 1807 before Dearborn and Wilkinson and Jefferson have the opportunity to assess the effect of their diplomatic words, medals, trade goods, and one hundred pounds of powder and an amount of lead necessary to make bullets to match the powder.

86

❦

April 2, 1806, Clark Is Impatient

WHEN DESCENDING the Columbia the previous fall, the Corps of Discovery had passed by the mouth of Oregon's major river, the Willamette, without seeing it. Islands formed by silt from the Willamette's annual floods are tree-covered and obscure the powerful river which drains the rich western valleys of the Cascade Mountains.

While the corps is outfitted with a sufficiency of moccasins, they remain extremely short on food, and Clark forages up the Willamette. Along the banks, Clark's party comes upon a village of substantial wooden houses. He goes ashore, hoping to barter for food. Clark, who is almost always amiable and patient in his dealings with Indians, finds the Indians on the Willamette a difficult people: "I entered one of the rooms and offered several articles to the natives in exchange for Wapato," he writes that evening. "They were sulky and they positively refused to sell any." Wapato is a kind of biscuit made from the dried roots of a marsh plant, arrowhead, also called duck potato.

That is understandable; the Indians up and down the Columbia, like Indians everywhere, are always shortest on food in the spring, before the plants develop, the migratory birds arrive, the grazers grow fat on the new growth and the fish run upstream to spawn. In fact, Lewis and Clark know that the Indians along the Columbia are suffering this annual famine, and know they will have difficulty buying food for the trip upriver to the Nez Perce and the mountain road home. Offering to buy food, especially with the minimal amount of trade goods the corps has left, is not exactly a position of power.

From time to time, the corps has entertained Indians with "medicine" shows. Lewis's powderless air-powered rifle is always a hit.

Magnifying lenses used as burning glasses may amuse some spectators. Clark's York may be magic, depending on the sophistication of the tribe he visits. This is one of the few instances that they use magic malevolently, and the only time that Clark is mean-spirited.

"I had a small piece of port-fire match in my pocket, off of which I cut a piece an inch in length and put it into the fire," Clark explains. He also revolves his compass about a magnetic catch in the lid of his little portable ink-stand, so that the needle revolves about its center. "The port-fire [cannon fuse, left over from the upstream voyage in the armed keelboat] caught and burned vehemently, which changed the color of the fire." All this "astonished and alarmed these natives and they laid several parcels of wappato at my feet & begged me to take out the bad fire, to this I consented, and at this moment the match being exhausted was of course extinguished."

The Indians were reduced to cowering, except for an old man who chanted loudly, as Clark writes, "apparently imploring his god. I lit my pipe," he recounts, "and gave them smoke and gave the women the full amount [for] the roots which they had put at my feet."

The men hate wapato—they had to eat far too much of it at Fort Clatsop—but it is going to be a long march to the Nez Perce.

87

Mid-April 1806, A Lackadaisical Filibuster

IN THE SPRING, Aaron Burr resumes his correspondence with a peculiar character he has known, although only by letter, since the summer of 1805. This is Harman Blennerhassett, who much to the surprise of anyone reading his name is an Irish immigrant. He lives with his wife and a few servants in almost total seclusion on an island in the middle of the Ohio River, about halfway between Pittsburgh and the Mississippi River.

One of the reasons that Blennerhassett lives so far from ordinary contact is that he is involved in a semi-incestuous marriage (and one certainly illegal in Ireland) with his first cousin. Like many a man on any frontier, Blennerhassett is on the lam.

Burr's 1805 trip down the Ohio, testing the waters for the rich tangy scent of rebellion, is the basis for his pen-pal association with Blennerhassett. That summer, when he encountered Mrs. B on Blennerhassett's Island, she was alone. Mr. B was off trying to scare up some more money to pay for their extravagant lifestyle, including house servants and gardeners to maintain the English-garden landscaping of this odd island sitting in the middle of, if not a howling wilderness, then certainly and literally in the center of a bumptious and boisterous western waterway. Burr is his usual woman-charming success with Mrs. B., although it does not extend to fornication, a frequent result of a visit from Burr when a husband is absent. That he is so circumspect in 1805 suggests how much Burr wants the support of Blennerhassett himself and the use of the island as a staging point for his filibustering expedition down the river to New Orleans and, by God, to Mexico! (The only extant portrait of Mrs. Blennerhasset shows a face distinguished by a very weak chin, thin lips, and dull eyes. This may have helped Burr maintain decorum.)

But in the spring of 1806, Burr's enthusiasm, or his optimism, is waning. The main problem is the lack of war with Spain. A war with Spain's Mexican provinces would enlist all the energies of westerners and the United States Army, and provide the perfect cover for a citizen's army to march on New Orleans and Mexico.

Curiously, as the reader knows, the one man capable of starting a war with Spain is General Wilkinson, who rather than fight has allowed the provincial troops from Mexico almost free rein along the Louisiana-Mexico border.

So, this is all Burr can promise Blennerhassett in April: The "business ... in some degree depends on contingencies not within my control, and will not be commenced before December, if ever." The reasons are financial, Ambassador Merry cannot provide funds from Britain, and Ambassador Yrujo continues to regard the whole enterprise as nothing more than a way to extort money from the Spanish government.

Burr needs a war, and Wilkinson appears unwilling to give him one. Wilkinson may have two quite separate reasons: It is too soon, Burr is not ready, or Wilkinson, in the pay of Spain for decades, has some loyalty to that country. And there is a third possibility. Wilkinson might actually find himself in close proximity to war if he starts one on the Texas border. War has so many unforeseen consequences, such as being shot. By the winter of 1806, when Burr moves downstream, Wilkinson will have another chance to create a war with Mexico, if that is what he wants. And even better, it would begin a great distance away. The only military officer in harm's way in this situation will be the newly promoted Captain Pike.

88

April 11–13, 1806, Honor Among Thieves

THE CHINOOKIAN BANDS along the Columbia River are on, even before he sees them again, Captain Lewis's shit list. They were no help on the downstream journey, and the memory of a winter among their language-brothers on the coast always puts Lewis in a foul mood and his enlisted men in a near-murderous frame of mind. The Chinooks were not so much more difficult than some other tribes had been— petty thievery and extortionate prices for traded goods (or thought to be extortionate, which is the same thing, psychologically): all this had been encountered. The difference at Fort Clatsop was that the corps couldn't get up in the morning and set off to meet more amicable Indians.

The tribe at the Oregon Cascades, which Lewis calls the "War-clel-ars" and are now called the Watlala Chinookians, are extremely jealous of their title to the river at that point. The myriad rapids push migrating salmon toward the quieter waters along the bank where they can be harvested more easily. And it just may be the case that, as other tribes steal horses almost for the hell of it or modern tribes like ours adore almost any game played with a ball, the Watlala Chinookians enlivened their boring existence between the hurly-burly of a salmon run with recreational thieving.

From Fort Clatsop to the Cascades, petty thefts and petty revenge keep the Corps of Discovery on the edge of vicious retaliation. They arrive at the turbulent low falls and begin hauling the boats by tow ropes, the men slipping and falling and cursing, but knowing every step was a step home this time. The captains do not even pay a courtesy call on the Watlalas and are soon assailed for their impertinence.

The other thing about the Corps of Discovery, besides attitude, is that they are all poorly dressed, looking much more like vagabonds than when they descended the river in 1805. The last items of European-style clothing have long since rotted away in the Oregon winter and none of them appear any better than disreputable. In any case, they get no respect.

"Many of the natives crowded about the bank of the river where the men were engaged in taking up the canoes," Lewis writes that evening. "One of them had the insolence to cast stones down the bank at two of the men who happened to be a little detached from the party at the time." Shortly after the stone throwing, John Shields, one of the large, active, and imposing young men, gets in an argument over a dog he is trying to purchase, one of the smallish, short-haired dogs tolerated, if not encouraged, among the Indians throughout much of North America. It ends up with pushing and shoving until Shields draws his extremely large knife (an "Arkansas toothpick," as they are known along the Mississippi River) and offers to slit all their throats. The final insult, and a curious one, is that in the middle of all this dog purchasing, a couple of Watlalas decide to steal Seaman, Lewis's gigantic Newfoundland retriever. Three armed men from the corps pursue and rescue Seaman, who is apparently following the Indians of his own free will, unaware of the consequences. Lewis says Seaman was "decoyed . . . nearly half a mile."

The men of the corps desperately want to get away from the Cascades, although not looking forward to portaging The Dalles. They would be happily shed of the whole Columbia River, for that matter. There is something unpleasant about their reception on this return trip, and the men know it.

Lewis promises to purchase horses as soon as they reach a tribe with animals to sell, and they will walk and ride directly, overland, to the Nez Perce. There, they hope to find the horses they left behind when they took to canoes on the upper Columbia, horses the Nez Perce have promised to keep safely for them. But they will not leave the Columbia without a few more meals of dog, which Lewis, in this extremity, has finally learned to eat:

"The dog now constitutes a considerable part of our subsistence and with the most of the party has become a favorite food; certain I am that it is a healthy strong diet, and from habit it has become by no means disagreeable to me. I prefer it to lean venison or elk, and it is very far superior to the horse in any state."

He knows that if venison and elk are scarce at the Nez Perce villages, they will all eat horse again on the trail over the Bitterroots. But sufficient to the day is the evil thereof.

89

April 15–18, 1806, Horse Traders at The Dalles

THE SPRING SALMON and steelhead runs are late when the Corps of Discovery reaches The Dalles, the broken boulder and ledge–strewn rapids of the Columbia. There are Indians galore, and the one thing on everyone's mind is food. The corps wants two things at The Dalles, provisions and horses for the overland journey to the Nez Perce. They get very little of either.

While Lewis and most of the party begin the arduous work of portaging The Dalles and packing for the trip, Clark and a few trusted men cross the Columbia to trade for horses with the Indians on the north bank, tribes with forgotten names, bands with unpronounceable names—Chilluckquittequaw, Skillkoot, Eneeshur.

Clark takes Charbonneau, who is not on the list of worthy expedition gentlemen, but who Clark seldom lets out of his sight. It is likely (neither Lewis nor Clark mentions it one way or the other) that Sacagawea and little Pompey crossed over with Clark. The presence of Sacagawea with her child always has a soothing effect on Indian bands.

William Clark has many talents, and he will live a long, prosperous, useful life, but there are two things he cannot do to save his life— spell and bargain. Incapable of haggling, and well aware how inadequate he is in such negotiations, Clark makes two calculations. He sets a goal for horses to be acquired, and assesses the amount, very small by now, of trade goods he can offer. Then he does something that while perfectly logical must have puzzled the Indians. They are all traders, and negotiations are not only necessary, they are enjoyable, and may even be necessary, a sort of financial foreplay.

Clark divides the available trade goods into piles. He does not record the contents, but it is surely no more than a handful of beads, something manufactured out of scrap iron like an awl or a small knife, perhaps some colored cloth, certainly some body-paint pigment. He does not record the number of bundles of trade goods, but it is apparently less than a dozen, and then he waits for the Indians to accept his, so to speak, final offer. They do not. He sends Drouillard and Silas Goodrich off to the Skillkoots, to see if they are amenable to a swap. Charbonneau and George Frazer go off to the Chilluckquittequaws to see if they have horses. And no one swaps with Clark.

Charbonneau, who is able to annoy Lewis merely by existing, manages to pique Clark when he returns with a "very fine mare" from the Chilluckquittequaws.

Clark, almost palpably envious in his journal entry, asks Charbonneau what he traded for the horse and with some bitterness notes that it merely cost Charbonneau an ermine pelt, "elks teeth, a belt and some other articles of no great value." What the Indians want most is what the corps has least: large iron cooking pots. Two days after Charbonneau scores with his handful of trinkets and a belt (possibly nicely decorated by the always-sewing Sacagawea), Lewis surrenders a large kettle for an entirely indifferent horse.

Clark, for all his ability to make fun of Indians (as in remarking a month earlier that he entered a house of Indians so fearful that he could have tomahawked them all), does get along with them much more easily than the short-tempered and, more disabling, the overly fastidious Lewis. It is Lewis who twice in this week threatens all-out slaughter if the locals do not stop attempting to pilfer small items. Clark does not even repeat the threats in his copying of Lewis's journal entries.

With his quite genuine common touch, Clark finally succeeds in acquiring two horses, but only after he stops trading to doctor the "wife of the principal chief." Never mind that he thinks her ailments are hypochondriacal at best (she is "somewhat afflicted with pains in her back") and finds her an ungrateful patient—he calls her "a sulky bitch." He does treat her with warm flannel dressings on her back, plus a little rubbed-on camphor, that pungent, warming salve he prescribes for any and all mysterious aches and pains. The chief trades him two horses; Clark says only, "I made him an offer which he accepted." It is likely that the offer is more than the pathetic little bundles Clark offered before, but the value is enhanced by his "medicine."

Clark may not be the very picture of rectitude (modern politically correct historians never fail to point up his occasional lapses), but he is perfectly transparent. Writing of attempts to trade with the Klickitats at The Dalles the day after doctoring the sulky bitch, he notes that the locals are poor, dirty, and indolent, but also, in a word that Lewis never uses, he notes that they are "kind." And then Clark, pencil in hand, writes one more true sentence in his journal. He remarks that he is using "every artifice decent and even false statements to induce those poor devils to sell me horses."

Charbonneau, to the astonishment and almost palpable envy of Lewis, will acquire yet another horse for himself, giving him enough mounts for himself, his wife, and one left over for carrying their few possessions. Clark, so much closer to that family, is the journal-keeper who knows how Charbonneau works this magic and he adds the facts to his copy of Lewis's entry: Charbonneau gets his fine horse for three objects that Sacagawea made during the winter at Fort Clatsop, one of his elk-skin shirts and two of her dresses. She is a woman of great value.

They leave the Columbia without enough horses to ride. The few they have are carrying their diminishing supply of trade goods and necessities (for all the animals killed and ammunition traded, they are still freighted down with several lead boxes of gunpowder and their few remaining mess kettles and extra rifles). They are able to trade for more and much better horses when they reach the Walulas, a tribe they got to know briefly the previous fall. Clark and Lewis and the men provide two nights of entertainment for the Walulas, and speeches are given about the rosy future of American-Indian relations, the benefits of peace, the prosperity of trade. Yellepit, the Walula chief, invites every Indian within reach to visit, to observe his close relationship with the Corps of Discovery. He wants them to understand that he, Yellepit, will be a big man when Lewis and Clark fulfill their many promises.

Flattery will get you everywhere. The corps leaves the Walulas with two dozen excellent young horses. That is enough to carry the stores and give an occasional ride to one of the footsore soldiers. They will be back with the Nez Perce in a week.

90

Early June 1806, Aching to Go Home

WHILE THE CORPS OF DISCOVERY spends a few happy weeks with the Nez Perce, waiting for the snows to melt in the Bitterroots, nothing happens. The Nez Perce tell them to wait, but Lewis insists on trying to take the Nez Perce Trail, which is as clogged with snow as they warned him. Everyone goes back to the Nez Perce village and hangs out. Some readers of the journals find complicated messages in this period. There are references to games played, footraces, meals, fiddle music, a little discreet sex. This is the moment when some writers discover the first game of baseball played west of the Mississippi. It is not. Lewis refers to a game of "bases," in the context of running competitions. It is a back-and-forth relay race, not a ball game.

At last the high snows melt, the party heads over the mountains, and on July 1, the corps finds itself back at "Traveler's Rest," a group of hot springs next to Lolo Creek, just a few miles from the conjunction of the Bitterroot River and the Clark Fork of the Columbia. A few horses fall down, a few boxes are smashed on the slippery trail, but nothing really happens.

91

June 15, 1806, Pike Delays, Fortunately for Him

IT IS DIFFERENT in St. Louis, where the corps hopes to be within two months. A great deal is happening down at the mouth of the Missouri, and after all these years, it is as mysterious, curious as ever.

Lieutenant Pike has safely descended the Mississippi to St. Louis, bringing back his purported location of the headwaters of the Mississippi and information on the future locations for trading posts along the river. For his efforts, Wilkinson promotes Pike to captain and orders him to undertake another expedition to the borders of Louisiana.

Wilkinson's orders to Zebulon Montgomery Pike are difficult to understand. There are public orders, private orders, and third-party versions. The one thing that will become clear is that for most of the next year, Lieutenant Pike will not have a clear notion of his role, and will resolve that ambiguity—as is his habit—by attempting heroic deeds and presenting a public persona of enormous moral rectitude.

On the tenth of June, now well-rested from his exertions on the Mississippi, Pike receives his orders from Wilkinson. He is to depart St. Louis on the fifteenth of June. He has several tasks to perform on this; his second exploration, which, like the first, will be of a distant border territory already occupied by Europeans. The major difference is that this time Pike will approach, if not enter, Spanish New Mexico; while he was on the Mississippi he carefully avoided the Canadian border.

Wilkinson's public order to Pike, the one kept in official files, gives him several tasks. Pike will return some Osage prisoners to their village on the river of the same name in modern Kansas, and then move out onto the Great Plains by horseback and make contact with the Pawnee, one of the horse tribes that occupies, and rules, the vast prairie

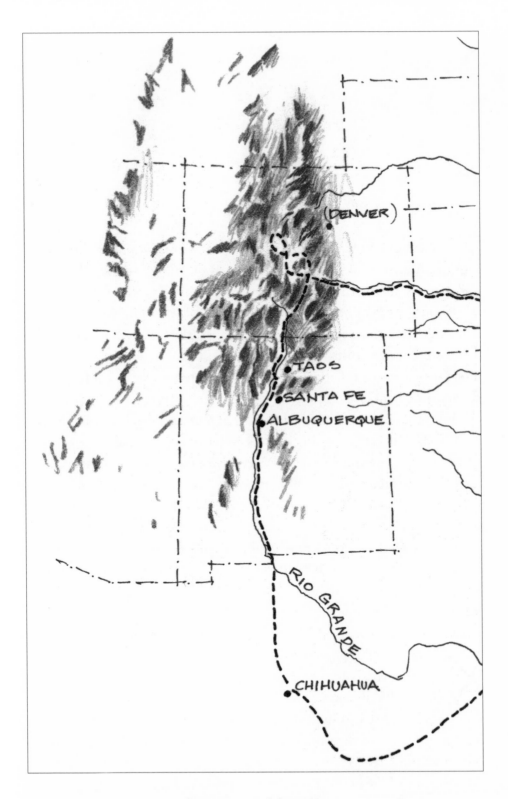

Pike enters Mexico,

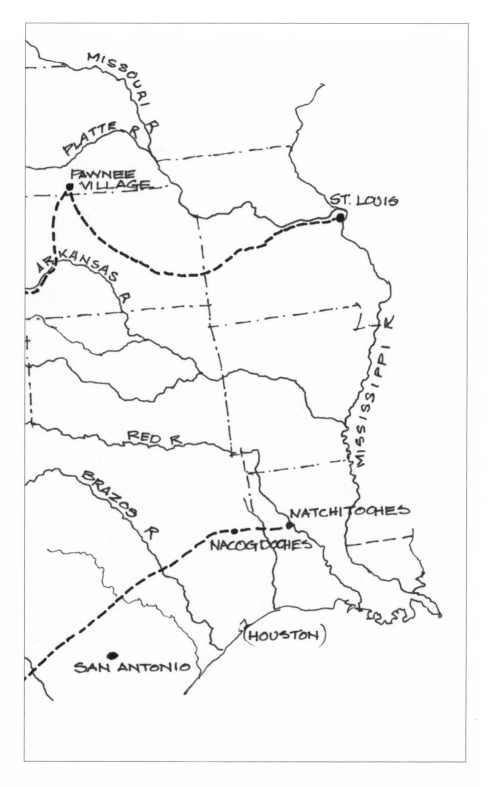

July 1806 to May 1807

between the Mississippi and the Rocky Mountains. Moving south and west (the Pawnee country is on the Kansas-Nebraska border, in modern political geography) he should encounter the Comanche, who roam in the western plains from what is now Texas north to Colorado. His orders are to draw the Comanche into the sphere of influence of the United States (and General Wilkinson). They will get medals and flags and such trade beads as will make them willing allies of the Americans in general and of Wilkinson in particular. For the public record, Wilkinson cautions Pike to avoid a clash with the Spanish:

"As your interview with Comanche will probably lead you to the head branches of the Arkansas and Red Rivers, you may find yourself approximated to the settlements of New Mexico, and it will be necessary [that] you should move with great circumspection, to keep clear of any hunting or reconnoitering parties from the province."

Pike must, according to his official orders, "prevent alarm or offense" and most particularly because "the affairs of Spain & the United States appear to be on the point of amicable adjustment." Wilkinson has created that amicable solution, he knows whereof he speaks. It is important to remember that Pike is absolutely ordered to do two things:

Stay out of New Mexico.

Stay away from Mexicans.

On June 15, the day that Lieutenant Pike is supposed to be leaving for the west, a young officer, Lieutenant Don Facundo Melgares, leaves Santa Fe with a small company of mounted regular troops, dragoons, and an accompanying troop of New Mexican horsemen. The provincial government of Mexico has been informed of Wilkinson's orders to Pike and means to intercept him. Melgares and his men will cross over the mountain pass south and east of Santa Fe, ride past the pueblo at Pecos and enter the high plains, the domain of Kiowa, Comanche, and Pawnee. They are looking for Lieutenant Pike. Their orders are to arrest him. As far as they are concerned, once he moves west of a line drawn northward from the Colorado River in Texas (not the great river across the continental divide), he is in Spanish country. They are not so numerous because they fear Pike, but because they want so over-whelming a presence that the Plains Indians will remain amicable.

The hundreds of horsemen sweep east and north; they stop at Pawnee and Comanche encampments, they ride hundreds of miles up to the Platte River. Along the Arkansas River, which they believe Pike is ascending, they leave a track on the arid, burnt, summer short-grass prairie as wide as a football field and as obvious as a brush stroke on a bare canvas. And they head home, empty-handed, about the time that Pike actually gets under way.

Pike has been delayed. One could imagine he knew about the New Mexican posse out to get him and waited for them to clear the terri-tory before he lit out for the headwaters of the Arkansas River. But one does not have to do that. Pike was over a month late leaving on his Mississippi trip the previous summer. For an active, truly daring sol-dier, Pike is notoriously slow to get on the trail. He makes up for it by haste once he is under way. Delayed as he is, he leaves St. Louis poorly prepared for the journey ahead. July 15 is less than two months from snow season in the Rockies, and Lieutenant Pike is dead set on not only reaching the Rockies, but crossing them.

92

July 2, 1806, Traveler's Rest

AFTER DESCENDING from the high country, following the Nez Perce Trail to Lolo Creek, the corps stops at the hot springs, the place they named Traveler's Rest on the outbound journey. The mineral springs soothe aching muscles and pinched nerves.

While most of the men rest, a few move down into the Bitterroot

River valley and hunt. Lewis begins a lengthy journal entry, then breaks up the day by going out with a shotgun looking for specimens. He shoots a large, blackish woodpecker. By a series of coincidences, it is the only biological specimen collected on the entire journey that we can be sure survives intact, with provenance, and can be seen today.

The bird is skinned, carried home without incident, shipped to Jefferson, and donated, with so many other things, to the American Philosophical Society. The Society, having no place to display natural history items, gives the woodpecker skin to one of its members, Charles Willson Peale, best known as a portrait painter.

Peale is running a small museum, open to the public for a charge, and he will put the bird, now known as Lewis's woodpecker, *Melanerpes lewis,* on display. (*Melanerpes* is Greek for "black creeper," the generic name for several North American woodpeckers; *lewis,* of course for the captain.) Alexander Wilson, author of the first bird encyclopedia for North America, draws the woodpecker as it was mounted in Peale's museum and prints its portrait five years after it arrives in Philadelphia. When Peale's museum closes, some of the contents end up at Harvard University. To this day, Lewis's very own Lewis's woodpecker lies in a drawer on the fifth floor of the Peabody Museum of Comparative Zoology on Oxford Street in Cambridge, Massachusetts. It is easy to find the original woodpecker in a drawer containing more than two dozen stuffed *Melanerpes lewis.* All the others are lying on their backs in classic museum storage poses: beak pointed straight forward, parallel to the bottom of the drawer, feet stretched back in the opposite direction, also parallel to the drawer. Lewis's personal woodpecker lies with its beak pointed up, at right angles to the body, and the two feet also sticking up, fixed forever as though they clasped an invisible tree trunk. It is the same bird, looking exactly like the one in Wilson's *American Ornithology.*

Downstairs in the Peabody Museum are some badly moth-eaten and seam-sprung stuffed North American mammals. They look old enough to be from Lewis and Clark's expedition, and are mounted clumsily enough to have been in Peale's museum. But you cannot be sure. The woodpecker is different. You have the painting in *American Ornithology* for evidence. The anthropology museum at the Peabody has other souvenirs and relics of the expedition, Indian clothing and tools, a bow and arrows, gifts to Lewis and Clark. They, too, traveled from the Academy to Peale to Harvard. So much distance traveled. So little left.

93

July 1, 1806, A Division of Force

THERE COMES A TIME in almost all military campaigns when commanders let down their guard, underestimate their enemy, exaggerate their own strength. It is necessary to remember that the Corps of Discovery is a military unit on a mission into at best neutral, and occasionally unfriendly, territory.

This time comes for Meriwether Lewis as he and his men soak in the pools at Traveler's Rest. This is not criticism of Lewis—he will always be remembered as one of the most successful and resourceful leaders in the history of exploration. But to understand what happens in the next month, it is necessary to recapitulate what has gone before.

The corps is almost finished with a journey of more than five thousand miles, counting all the twists and turns, and no one bears a scar left by either wild beasts or human inhabitants. They all remember moments of danger, but even those are perhaps a half-dozen events scattered over two years. They have overcome every obstacle, they believe that they are masters of their expansive universe. And they are wrong.

For two years, no one has been added or subtracted from the corps.

Every man is necessary, Lewis remarks on more than one occasion. He says that nothing but their strength in numbers has prevented disaster more than once. And at Traveler's Rest he decides that unity is no longer necessary. That is the first mistake. The second one is easier to understand. Lewis decides that a small party of men will ride across the open plain from the headwaters of the Yellowstone to the Mandan villages and then on to the Sioux villages on the Assiniboine River and "prevail on the Sioux chiefs to join us on the Missouri and accompany them with us to the seat of the general government." What Lewis does not realize is that while the corps are masters of the western waters, they are innocents, "pilgrims" in western slang, when they venture out onto the high plains.

Counting the small party that will go overland to the Mandans, Lewis breaks the corps into four groups:

The first: Lewis will take "six volunteers to ascend Maria's River with a view to explore the country and ascertain whether any branch of that river lies as far north as latitude 50, and again return and join the party who are to descend the Missouri, at the entrance of Maria's River." (Lewis spells the river's name with the accurate apostrophe, now lost. It is Marias River today.) The purpose is simple, Lewis is hoping to push the watershed of the Missouri well north into British Canada. This will be at the minimum an excellent bargaining point when it comes time to fix the U.S.-Canada boundary (which will be set at the Forty-eighth parallel of latitude).

The second: After the balance of the corps retrace their route to the headwaters of the Jefferson, in Shoshone country, Clark, the Charbonneau family, and five soldiers will continue on to the Yellowstone, make dugout canoes, and float down to the Missouri and rejoin Lewis.

The third: Nine men and Sergeant Ordway will retrieve their old canoes and stored goods at the headwaters of the Jefferson and run down that river to the Missouri and on to the Great Falls. They will excavate the buried pirogues and the cache of trade goods and scientific specimens left there the previous August, portage the falls, and descend to the entrance of Marias River and combine forces with Lewis and his men.

The fourth: Sergeant William Pryor (probably the best frontiersman of the noncommissioned officers) and two men will go overland from the head of the Yellowstone to the Mandan and the Sioux villages, as we have described.

There are minor changes in the numbers assigned to each group before the plans are carried out, but the principle remains. Two groups will leave the shelter of the rivers and traverse the high prairie for hundreds of miles.

Having made his plans, and written them in his journal, Lewis spends the rest of the day entering a lengthy description of the prairie dog, an animal he has not seen since the previous August. It is not an entirely odd sequence of subject matter, although, sitting by a bubbling warm spring in a pine and fir forest, Lewis's mind is already fixed on the short-grass prairie of Blackfoot Indian country.

94

Early July 1806, Wilkinson's Boast

THIS BUSINESS OF BURR, Pike, and Wilkinson is difficult to untangle. The first is a dreamer who writes mostly in an indecipherable code during his campaign to take the west; Pike is not the most reliable reporter; and Wilkinson is, as his rise in the army demonstrates, not unwilling to commend himself for his purported actions. Still, we must take them at what little words they leave us, for what they are doing is so bizarre that we could not imagine such goings-on.

Much later, after all is calm again on the border, Wilkinson's behavior throughout this year prompts a judicial inquiry. One witness is an obscure (but at least not notorious) judge, Timothy Kibbey of St. Charles in the upper Louisiana district (Missouri, today).

It is a concise deposition, worth reading carefully:

> *A few days previous to the departure of Lt. Pike . . . I asked the General if Mr. Pike was sent by the Government of the United States, he replied, no, that it was his own plan and if Mr. Pike succeeded he, the General, would be placed out of reach of his enemies and that in the course of eighteen months he would be in a situation (if the plan succeeded) to call his damned foes to an accounting for their deeds. I asked the General if he did not apprehend danger from the Spaniards, knowing their jealous disposition, on Mr. Pike's account with a party of American soldiers at Santa Fe. He answered that Mr. Pike and his party would have documents to show which would make them as safe as in Philadelphia.*

Wilkinson also indicates to Judge Kibbey that not only is the expedition secret, but Pike "as yet" is ignorant of its real purpose. Note that Kibbey understands from the first moment that Pike is not headed to find the headwaters of the Arkansas River, a western boundary of Louisiana; he is headed for Santa Fe, the capital of Spanish New Mexico.

This is difficult stuff. Even as Wilkinson speaks with Kibbey about Pike's guaranteed safety, Lieutenant Melgares, the Santa Fe military commander, is scouring the Colorado prairie trying to capture Pike. Melgares is a month early. Is this because Wilkinson lied about the date of Pike's departure? Just because Pike doesn't leave as publicly ordered, that doesn't mean Wilkinson doesn't privately tell him to delay. On the other hand, if Pike thinks he is safe from Melgares, much of what he is going to do on the plains of Colorado makes no sense at all.

If it is not an official presidential expedition (and at least that much is true) then the only "papers" could be ones supplied by Wilkinson.

That is the last we hear of papers. By his account, Pike is carrying nothing resembling a passport, a secret commission, nor as much as a letter from Wilkinson. But Pike may be lying.

In short, Wilkinson is lying about some things. And Pike will lie. But not about everything: The expedition certainly is Wilkinson's child, and if his plan succeeds, he will truly be out of the reach of his enemies. He will be the field marshal of all Mexico, serving the Emperor Burr.

The one thing that seems likeliest to be true is this: Pike hasn't got the foggiest notion of what's going on.

95

July 3–4, 1806, Trail to the Sun

LEWIS AND CLARK part company at the confluence of Lolo Creek and the Bitterroot River. Clark will, without incident, retrace their steps: up the Bitterroot, over a path the Nez Perce know well (Chief Joseph will use it some sixty years later on his epic flight from Idaho through Yellowstone Park to his surrender near the Canadian border), to the Big Hole River (Clark's "Wisdom River") and then to the Shoshone country on the Jefferson, retrieve what's left of the canoes and the cache of goods and descend to the three forks of the Missouri. There, part of the group descends the Missouri to the Great Falls, while Clark and the balance enter unknown country, stumble through a vast beaver swamp, and at last take a route that Sacagawea knows over the hills to the Yellowstone River valley. All is well when Clark's party reaches the Yellowstone. The canoe trip to the Great Falls is uneventful for the other men.

Meanwhile, a short day's march brings Lewis and his group to the entrance of the Bitterroot at Clark's River, the Clark Fork of the

Columbia in modern Missoula, Montana. His two Nez Perce guides wish to go no farther. They give Lewis quite precise directions: where to ford the Clark Fork (a dozen or so miles upstream), which side of the Blackfoot River to ascend (the northern), and when they have crossed the Continental Divide, how to descend to the Missouri (along the Dearborn River to a point midway between modern Helena and the Great Falls).

And then, the Nez Perce want to go home. Lewis, not particularly fond of Indians or comfortable in their midst, makes an exception for the Nez Perce. Lewis knows them as life-savers after the party descended from the Bitterroot Mountains in 1805. The few weeks of amicable socializing while waiting for the snows to melt in this spring of 1806 are just further signs of the gracefulness of this relationship.

Before departing for the Blackfoot River valley, Lewis directs "the hunters to turn out early in the morning and endeavor to kill some more meat for these people whom I was unwilling to leave without giving them a good supply of provision after their having been so obliging as to conduct us through those tremendous mountains."

It is impossible to know how much these two Nez Perce understand of Lewis's plans. But he obviously intends to do exactly what their tribe does—cross the divide and enter the buffalo plains, and do it on horseback. They would not know exactly how Lewis and Clark arrived at the Nez Perce in 1805, but they know precisely how Lewis intends to return to the plains. When the Nez Perce go buffalo hunting they move en masse, with all the warriors and all the allies they can muster. Lewis and just nine other men will ride onto the short-grass prairie while the bulk of the party heads for the headwaters of the Missouri. The Nez Perce guides do not approve of this idea. Ten men, no matter how brave or how well armed, should not go wandering into Blackfoot country.

On the Fourth of July, somewhat to Lewis's astonishment, the parting is on the verge of tearful: "These affectionate people, our guides, betrayed every emotion of unfeigned regret at separating from us; they said that they were confident that the Pahkees [a word meaning any and all of the Plains Indians] *would cut us off.*"

Lewis comes very close, within hours, of never seeing the Missouri again. As they go to ford the Clark Fork, both the men and horses swimming across the current, Lewis takes charge of the two men in his party who cannot swim. After everyone else is across, they board a rude raft and paddle for the far shore. They are "soon hurried down with the current a mile and a half before we made the shore. On our approach to the shore the raft sunk and I was drawn off the raft by a bush and swam ashore." Being swept off a water craft by an overhanging tree is the commonest of all ways to drown in a swift river. The two men stick with the raft, and arrive wet and frightened a little below where Lewis swims ashore.

The valley of the Blackfoot River gets its Plains Indian name from its use as a highway in both directions. The Nez Perce and the Flatheads and the Shoshone use it to make their brief forays into Blackfoot territory in pursuit of buffalo. And the Blackfeet use it when, for lack of something to do, they come over the divide and pillage the settlements of the inoffensive and vulnerable Flatheads. But except when foraging and raiding parties move through it, the Blackfoot valley and the Dearborn as well are empty of Indians. Lewis and his nine companions move warily, but they see not a hint of an Indian between the Clark Fork and the Missouri. It is open, parklike country between dense stands of timber, easy riding, good visibility. They are on the Missouri in two days.

96

July 22 (?), 1806, Pike as Correspondent

PIKE, A WEEK into his journey toward the Rocky Mountains and the headwaters of the Arkansas River, stops to write a letter to General

Wilkinson. Or claims he does. The letter is so dated, although there is an odor about it as if it were written before he departs. But Pike is always catching up with things, and he may be on the prairie when he writes. On the other hand, the mails are slow between the Osage villages and St. Louis. Some date before July 15 is as likely as July 22. It would also be a rare letter from Pike that makes no mention of his most recent triumph over some travail.

> With respect to the Ie,tans [Comanche] the General may rest assured I shall use every precaution previous to trusting them—but as to the mode of conduct to be pursued towards the Spaniards I feel more at a loss; as my instructions lead me into the country of Ie,tans—part of which is no doubt claimed by Spain . . . in consequence of which should I encounter a party near the village; in the vicinity of Santa Fe—I have thought it would be good policy to give them to understand that we were bound to join our troops near Natchitoches but had been uncertain about the headwaters of the rivers over which we passed.

It might be good policy, but it would be hard to swallow. To get from St. Louis to Natchitoches one would ride south by west some 600 miles. To go via Santa Fe Lieutenant Pike will be saying he thinks it's reasonable to take a 1,600-mile round trip—as the crow flies—in the wrong direction. And in the wildest imaginings, Santa Fe, a Spanish capital established long before there was a United States, is not and never was within the boundaries of Louisiana.

Then Pike, in a train of thought and an estimation of his own importance really without parallel in American letters, tells Wilkinson what he will do if the Spanish commandant wants him to go to the provincial capital and explain himself:

"We would pay him a visit of politeness—either by deputation or the whole party, but if he refused [their voluntary visit of politeness, Pike would] signify our direct route to the posts below . . . if not I flatter myself, this [show of determination to go to Natchitoches] will secure us an unmolested retreat to Natchitoches."

When Pike comes to publish this letter in his journals, he omits one phrase. After saying that if they are allowed to approach Santa Fe and then go directly off to Natchitoches, the original letter to Wilkinson contains this phrase: "This if acceded to, would gratify our most sanguine expectations." In short, they would have spied out a route from Louisiana to Santa Fe and gotten away unscathed, if not undetected. This intent, to find a "Santa Fe Trail" has given rise to the myth that Lieutenant Pike blazed that trading route. Hardly. On his circuitous path to Santa Fe he will be scores, sometimes hundreds, of miles north of the Santa Fe Trail.

Then Pike speculates on what will happen if the Spanish take them prisoner: "I trust to the magnanimity of our country for our liberation—and a due reward [that is, a "just desserts" or punishment] to their opposers for the insult and indignity offered their national honor." Pike is a worse stylist by far (if a better speller) than William Clark. He means "to *our* opposers for the insult and indignity offered *our* national honor." Pike tends to elevated language at the risk of clarity.

Then Pike asserts it will not be a less than honorable imprisonment: "However, unless they give us ample assurances of just and honorable treatment—according to the custom of nations, I would resist, *even* if the inequality [of forces] was as great as at . . . the Straits of Thermopoli."

That is the place where several dozen Spartans held back the invading legions of the Emperor of Persia. Pike is the invader here, but the braggadocio transcends the solipsism.

A very generous historian, Donald Jackson, has written that this letter is just an explanation—before the fact—that if Pike is captured, he will simply *pretend* to be lost. We will see. This tolerant historian also believes that when Pike does approach Santa Fe, he actually *is* lost. Perhaps. The main thing to remember is that Pike is not supposed to be spying for General Wilkinson and mapping an invasion route to capture Santa Fe as part of Aaron Burr's Mexican empire. He is not supposed to be doing that at all. And when Pike edits out the part saying that if he can get close enough to Santa Fe to map the route and then escape unharmed that this "would gratify our most sanguine expectations," it can hardly be argued that Pike doesn't at least know that he's spying for Wilkinson. And he most certainly would alter his own letter in order to protect Wilkinson. If there is any man whom Pike loves more than himself, it is Wilkinson.

97

July 11–18, 1806,

A Week on the Marias and Missouri Rivers

WHEN LEWIS and his share of the Corps of Discovery come to the Missouri after ascending the Blackfoot to the Continental Divide and descending to the Missouri, they find the buffalo already assembled. The young horses they ride, most acquired from the Nez Perce, are frightened by the great animals. Buffalo in any season may affright an innocent horse; even a shaken buffalo robe in the distant east may disturb a colt who has no knowledge of the animal. And this is an even more agitated herd than usual, as Lewis notes on the evening of July 11:

> *It is now the season at which the buffalo begin to copulate and the bulls keep a tremendous roaring. We could hear them for many miles and there are such numbers of them there is one continuous roar. Our horses had not been acquainted with the buffalo, they appeared much alarmed at their appearance and bellowing.*

Several horses disappear that night, and Lewis suspects they have been stolen, either by the Blackfeet or their allied (and subordinate) tribe, the Gros Ventres. George Drouillard, who gets all the hard jobs, is sent to find the horses and the horse thieves, if there are any. He finds an abandoned Blackfoot camp, and no horses.

While invisible Indians are somewhere nearby, the corps is more immediately threatened by the usual complement of grizzly bears that accompany the buffalo herds. The grizzlies of 1806 are of a different character than the reclusive mountain dwellers of today; they live on the open plains and regard anything that moves as a meal. The men have one of their last encounters with a grizzly at the Great Falls of the Missouri on July 16. Private Hugh McNeal, on horseback, is startled by a charging grizzly, thrown from his horse, and reduced to the simplest self-defense. He swings his rifle with both hands and strikes the "bear over the head and cut him with the trigger guard of the gun and broke off the breech [that is, broke the gun in half at the point above and slightly behind the trigger guard where the powder charge sits]. The bear, stunned with the stroke, fell to the ground and began to scratch his head with his feet." McNeal flees the bemused bear, climbs the closest tree, and is stuck there until evening when the gun-struck grizzly gives up and goes away. To this saga, Lewis appends a note which is as true today in the plains of Montana as it is in 1806: "Awful mosquitoes."

On July 17, while the rest of the men retrieve their stored goods and prepare for the downstream trip, Lewis and his three selected men, Drouillard (of course) and the two Field brothers, set out for the Marias River. Lewis cannot help but be in a terrible mood. When the cache is opened, he finds that all his hundreds of botanical specimens and animal skins collected on the way west are spoiled by dampness, all useless, all ruined. If a summer's scientific work is lost, the present is no happier. He understands that the Marias River is Blackfoot territory: "The Blackfoot Indians rove through this quarter of the country and as they are a vicious, lawless and rather an abandoned set of wretches, I wish to avoid an interview with them if possible." The reader may remember that word, *interview.* It is the same word Burr uses for his duel with Madison. An appointment in that phrase is not about commerce, it is about killing.

"I have no doubt," Lewis continues, "but they would steal our horses if they have it in their power and finding us weak should they happen to be numerous will most probably attempt to rob us of our arms and baggage." And having said that, he splits the tiny unit into three parts, sending Reubin Field to scout for Blackfeet in one direction, and detailing Drouillard to follow a wounded buffalo and see if it carries an arrow that will identify the Indians who shot it, while he and Joseph Field scout ahead toward the Marias. Any two or three Blackfeet will "happen to be numerous" compared to the corps.

It is dangerous country. The open and treeless prairie gives the illusion that you can see clear to the horizon. But it is not so level and simple a landscape as it appears. It rolls, it breaks, it has its secrets.

98

July 22 – 23, 1806, Clark Writes a Speech

THE CORPS SOLDIERS who will explore the Yellowstone River reach the vicinity of modern Big Timber, Montana, on July 22. They come over the shortest route from the three forks of the Missouri, the Bozeman Pass, as it is called today, named for a cattleman who will find it yet again seventy years later. By so doing, the corps avoids the Big Belt Mountains to the north: "The Indian woman who has been of great service to me as a pilot through this country recommends a gap in the mountains more south which I shall cross," Clark enters in his journal. The other thing they avoid is the permeable barrier between Crow

Indian country along the Yellowstone and the prairie country north of the river, occupied from time to time by any of the Plains Indians who chose to hunt there. These are the Indians, Blackfeet and Gros Ventre, that Lewis expects to find quarrelsome and difficult. The Crow, as a nation, are not assumed to be so preoccupied with war, rapine, and pillage. When the western Indians, Shoshone or Nez Perce or Flathead, ventured onto the plains, they too stayed closer to the Crow Country.

It is from here on the upper Yellowstone, within traditional Crow territory, that Sergeant Pryor and two enlisted men are detailed to ride directly across the high plains to the Sioux encampments near the Missouri, find the local trader (and translator) and through him invite the Sioux to send chiefs along to the Mandan trading villages, there to join with the returning party and visit the Great Father. They are lucky to have the horses to do it, as twenty-four of their thirty-odd horses disappear in the night, cut out of the remount herd by Indians, almost certainly Crows. This is not a great difficulty. Clark and the remainder will be descending the Yellowstone by dugout canoes hollowed out from the great cottonwoods that flank the river.

And it is here, on the upstream border of Crow country, that Clark makes ready to meet the tribe. He writes a speech. It is his first and last— Lewis is always the orator when they travel together. Clark expects that Charbonneau will be able to translate; he believes (wrongly) that the Hidatsa language of Charbonneau's mother is closely allied to the Crow tongue. In any language, it is a remarkable piece of work.

"Children," he inevitably begins, "the Great Chief who is benevolent, just, wise & bountiful has sent me and one other of his chiefs (who is at this time in the country of the Blackfoot Indians) to all his red children on the Missouri and its waters quite to the great lake of the West where the land ends and the sun sets on the face of the great water, to know their wants and inform him of them [upon] our return." In hindsight, the problem here (and Lewis will make the same mistake in a day or two) is that the last thing the Crows would want to hear is that their needs and desires were on a par with those of such implacable and truly dangerous enemies as the Blackfeet.

Clark has a sense of humor; it is a rare commodity among the corps. Leaving a blank for the number of days (since he does not know when he will have a chance to speak to the Crow chiefs), he remarks in a most diplomatic manner that "I heard from some of your people [blank] nights past from my horses who complained to me of your people having taken 24 of their comrades."

Having made that point, Clark makes great offers of unlimited trade goods in the future and inquires of the Crow where in particular they would like to have this trading post built. "Children," he continues, "the people in my country are like the grass in your plains, numerous. They are also rich and bountiful and love their red brethren who inhabit the waters of the Missouri."

On the other hand, neither Clark nor his interpreters are going to make much of an impression as ambassadors of a rich nation. And so he is humbled, and acknowledges his weakness:

> I have been from my country two winters. I am poor, naked, and have nothing to keep off the rain. When I set out from my country I had plenty, but I have given it all to my red children whom I have seen on my way to the great lake of the west and now [I] have nothing.

Having been so desperately honest, he concludes with a severe exaggeration: "The red children of your great father who live near him and have opened their ears to his counsels are rich and happy, have plenty of horses, cows & hogs, fowls, bread, and so forth and so on ["&c., &c." in the original]."

All the Crows have to do is take up the plow and build the pigpen, he is saying, and all will be well. And he invites the Crows to send two (no more) principal chiefs to accompany him to the Great Father, and they will come back "next summer loaded with presents and some goods for the nation. You will then see with your own eyes and hear with your own ears what the white people can do for you."

With the great good fortune that precedes and follows the Corps of

Discovery, Clark and his party slip down the Yellowstone River without even seeing a Crow. The speech is never delivered, and the amity of the Crow Nation is not tested. All the party sees is game, so much that after a few days' entries, Clark swears he will stop mentioning the enormous herds of elk and buffalo. He does not want to bore the reader. He is true to his word, except for one last time. Just before reaching the planned rendezvous site where they will look for Lewis on the Missouri, Clark and his party have to stop paddling. Their way downstream, and then quickly, upstream as well, is blocked by a buffalo herd that fills the wide Yellowstone from bank to bank and as far upriver and down as the eye can see. It is the last great herd they will meet, and it parts for them, and sweeps around them, and leaves them awestruck.

99

July 27–29, 1806, Lewis Interviews the Piegans

THE EXPEDITION up the Marias River, where Lewis hopes to find an extension of the Missouri tributaries that rises up well into British Canada, is dogged with problems. The river, which promisingly came down from the north, shifts to course from the west and then the southwest. At the apogee of that curve, Lewis waits a few days, trying to get an astronomical fix on the river's northernmost bend. It is too cloudy. And then, on July 26, as the group of four heads back to the mouth of the Marias, they encounter eight Piegans, the small tribe with a distinct language that survives on the plains by maintaining a subordinate alliance with the more numerous Blackfeet.

The Piegans are the Gros Ventre—the Big Bellies—of the northern plains, named after a misunderstanding by the French-Canadian trappers who misread the Plains Indian sign language for the tribe. It is a motion in front of the stomach as though the hand were caressing a full, protruding, belly. So it is, but it is the swollen belly of starvation. The sign for Piegan is simply the universal sign for hunger, and on the plains, hunger is famine.

Lewis, who hopes to avoid any meeting with the Blackfoot confederation, and realizing he is outnumbered, orders Drouillard to make signs of peace and an invitation to smoke. As he and his men are nervous about turning their backs on the Piegans as dusk falls, Lewis chooses to camp and spend the night with them. Lewis cannot resist, since his hand is forced, making a speech. He lies, of necessity, telling this small band of adolescent Indians "that I had come in search of them in order to prevail on them to be at peace with their neighbors, particularly those on the West side of the mountains and to engage them to come and trade with me when the establishment is made." The Piegans agree that they would trade, if there is a trading post. Lewis says they all readily gave their assent. As for peace with the Indians across the mountains to the west, that would be peace with the Nez Perce.

They "declared it to be their wish to be at peace with the Tushepahs [Lewis's name for the Nez Perce, whom he also called the Chopunnishi] whom they said had killed a number of their relations lately and pointed to several of those present who had cut their hair as an evidence of the truth of what they had asserted."

All that would sit well enough, but Lewis continues on and explains that his expedition would not only bring a trading post to the Blackfeet (one directly competing with the North West Company posts in British Canada) but the same benefits would come to the Indians across the mountains: the Shoshone, Nez Perce, and Flathead. Even the Crows will get trade goods. Lewis thinks he is demonstrating the benevolence of the Great Father to all his red children by telling the Blackfeet that their enemies are about to be armed by the Great Father.

He is telling them, apparently in all innocence, that their great tribal advantage over the other tribes is over. As he speaks, the Blackfeet can trade for guns and are well armed; the Indians to their west cannot and own only a few captured weapons. He also promises, if that is the right word, that the Blackfeet should come to Crow country to trade.

It is an interesting scene. On one side of the campfire are four well-armed white men, poorly dressed in unadorned and untanned and untailored elk and deerskin garments, riding indifferent horses. The Piegans, with perhaps no more than a single rifle among them (Lewis's account is ambiguous) have better horses and, heedless of mosquitoes and cactus stickers, are lightly dressed, their skin glowing in the firelight.

Lewis explains that he must leave in the morning, his many men (he exaggerates) are waiting for him at the mouth of the Marias. He invites the braves to come along, and suggests there may be ten horses and some tobacco if they ride with him. In fact, all he has to offer in trade is some tobacco, and as soon as he embarks on the downstream trip, he will turn the horses loose. It is not much of an offer, and he notes, "To this proposition they made no reply."

Lewis sets watches, taking the first one himself, sure that without vigilance the Piegans will try to steal their horses. Still, he is able to sleep soundly. A "profound sleep," he recalls. It is very dark. That is all he remembers of the night.

100

Ca. July 26, 1806, Sergeant Pryor Builds a Boat

AFTER CLARK'S main party begins to descend the Yellowstone, Sergeant Pryor and two men make their last camp before setting out on horseback to find the Sioux and their white trader. They will ask the trader to translate an invitation to join the returning Corps of Discovery to go to St. Louis and then to see the Great Father in

Washington. They are not expected to negotiate with the Sioux, but they do carry a letter from Lewis, written over a month earlier, encouraging the Teton Sioux to accept the Americans and become part of the trading system up the Missouri from St. Louis, and most important, refrain from interfering with boatmen on the Missouri.

It is a straightforward task. And the men wake up in the morning to a surprise. Soundlessly, effortlessly, the Crow have stolen all their horses. Now there are three men, afoot, in the middle of the wilderness.

Sergeant Pryor is an estimable man, and he remembers something from the winter of 1804, from the Mandan villages. He recalls the Mandans and the Hidatsa crisscrossing the Missouri, before it froze solid. They used the simplest of boats, each constructed from a single buffalo hide stretched into a half-sphere with willow branches. The boats are almost impossible to steer, but they are equally impossible to sink, and the Mandans and Hidatsas cross the rapid river with impunity, bobbing haplessly until the little boat bangs up against the far shore.

If there is one thing that abounds on the Yellowstone, it is buffalo. It takes but a day to kill, skin, shape, and sail away in three tubs made of buffalo hide. They move so swiftly, bobbing like leaves, that they will catch up with the stodgy dugouts before the Yellowstone enters the Missouri. The three isolated men have no idea how lucky they are. Their good fortune has but one source: The river is in Indian country, but it is in horse-Indian country. In boats, the men might as well be in another, parallel world.

❦

101

July 27, 1806, Lewis Concludes His
Interview with the Piegans

JOSEPH FIELD, handpicked, along with his brother Reubin and the estimable George Drouillard as Lewis's companions on this dangerous mission, has the last watch of the night. The Field brothers, part of the "young men from Kentucky" recruited by William Clark, is the corps's champion athlete at running bases and a good shot. But he is not invincible. Sitting up on watch, he falls asleep just as the first light creeps over the valley of the Two Medicine River. Two of the Piegans, taking advantage of the dimmest of dawn illumination, creep up to the sleeping soldiers and grab all four of the rifles—both guns belonging to the brothers Field, Drouillard's, and Lewis's. As Lewis re-creates the scene in his journal entry for July 27, which he surely writes at least two days after that date, the startled-awake Joseph Field turns to see a Piegan with two rifles, his and his brother's, and he shouts and wakes Reubin Field, and they chase after the too enterprising Piegan, and the Field brothers are both notoriously good runners. Their Piegan quarry, known in oral tradition as Sidehill Calf, is burdened with some fifteen pounds of awkward rifles, and he hasn't got a prayer: "They pursued the Indian . . . whom they overtook at the distance of 50 or 60 paces from the camp, seized their guns and wrested them from him, and R. Fields, as he seized his gun, stabbed the Indian to the heart with his knife."

That part of the story is reconstructed from talking to the Field brothers. Lewis first learns what is happening when he hears Drouillard shouting at a Piegan who is stealing his rifle: "His jumping up and crying, 'Damn you, let go my gun' awakened me." Lewis sees Drouillard wrestling with the Indian, and then, still shaking off sleep, realizes that another Piegan is running away with his rifle:

> I then drew a pistol from my holster and turning myself about saw the Indian making off with my gun. I ran at him with my pistol and bid him lay down my gun which he was in the act of doing when the Fieldses returned and drew up their guns to shoot him which I forbid as he did not appear to be about to make any resistance or commit any offensive act. The Piegan dropped the gun and walked slowly off.

Drouillard, who recovered his rifle and ammunition then asks Lewis for permission to kill his thief, "which I also forbid as the Indian did not appear to wish to kill us."

Now, the Piegans, seeing the four rearmed men, three of whom clearly would like to shoot themselves an Indian, run off toward the mingled herd of horses. The Indians drive as many horses as possible, and Drouillard and the Fieldses chase the main body of Indians (and the main body of horses) up the Two Medicine River. This is how Lewis explains what happens next:

> I pursued the man who had taken my gun, who, with another, was driving off a part of the horses which were to the left of the camp. I pursued them so closely that they could not take twelve of their own horses, but continued to drive one of mine with some others. At the distance of three hundred paces they entered one of those steep niches in the bluff with the horses before them. Being nearly out of breath I could pursue no longer. I called to them as I had done several times before that I would shoot them if they did not give me my horse and raised my gun, one of them jumped behind a rock and spoke to the other who turned around and stopped at the distance of 30 steps from me and I shot him through the belly. He fell to his knees and on his right elbow from

which position he raised himself up and fired at me, and turning himself about, crawled in behind a rock. He overshot me. Being bareheaded, I felt the wind of his bullet very distinctly.

Not too make too much of a disjointed account, but:

As Lewis chases the Piegans, they have one horse of his, and he has kept them from taking twelve of their own.

As Lewis races after them, he shouts orders at them in a language they have no possibility of understanding.

As the Piegan stops and turns around, Lewis shoots him through the belly, surely a mortal wound. Then, the Indian fires at Lewis.

The four members of the corps kill two and drive away six Indians who leave almost all their worldly goods in the camp. Lewis and his men keep their best four horses and take the best four of the Indians' herd and prepare to ride toward the juncture of the Marias and the Missouri. "While the men were preparing the horses," Lewis continues, "I put four shields and two bows and quivers of arrows which had been left in the fire, with sundry other articles. They left all their baggage at our mercy. They had but two guns with them and one of them they left. The gun we took with us. I also retook the flag, but left the medal about the neck of the dead man that they might be informed who we were."

Lewis is sometimes accused of actively placing a medal around the dead Indian's neck in "a final act of defiance," or similar words. Not true. This is the Indian Joseph Field has slain, the one still wearing the medal which Lewis gave to him the night before the altercation. The other Indian is the one Lewis leaves for dead, gut-shot in a coulee a few hundred yards from the camp.

Changing horses, stopping only briefly to rest, the four men ride nearly 100 miles between the morning of July 27 and the middle of the night, 2 A.M., on July 28. At first light, they continue on, reaching the mouth of the Marias just as the main party is descending by canoe and also aboard the red pirogue that they had stashed at the Great Falls the previous summer. Everyone is safe. The Field brothers and Drouillard can forget Lewis's final order: "It was my determination that if we were attacked in the plains on our way to the point [of reunion at the Missouri] that the bridles of the horses should be tied together and we would stand and defend them or sell our lives as dear as we could."

They abandon the small red pirogue—it is rotted beyond repair—and retrieve the white pirogue that lies buried at the mouth of the Marias. They move swiftly downstream aboard five canoes and the pirogue, filling their stomachs daily with deer and elk meat. On July 31 alone, Lewis notes that the men kill 15 elk, 14 deer, 2 bighorn sheep, and a beaver (Lewis is rather fond of sautéed beaver tail). That is at least two tons of meat, without picking the bones, more than 210 pounds per man. A few days later they kill 29 deer. They are eating just the best parts of the animals now. There is no other explanation. The next day it is 6 elk and 4 deer. "In short," Lewis seems obliged to explain, "game is so abundant and gentle that we kill it when we please."

102

Undated, 1806, Lewis Confronts Himself

IN THE CASE of Zebulon Montgomery Pike, we have his rewritten journals and most of the original manuscript on which to rely. Everything Pike published, whether it is about exploring the Mississippi or seeking a route to Santa Fe, is his considered self-serving reflection. With Meriwether Lewis, we have his journal entries, which were never intended to be published in their unvarnished entirety. In rare occasions, we have his rewritten account. The interview with the Piegans is one of the few events that have two accounts.

Lewis alters his journal account of the interview with the Piegans when it comes time to write a lengthy letter, one intended to find its way into newspaper accounts, of the exploration. They are small changes, but worth noting. History, as usual, is written by the victors.

Given the unhappy outcome of the Marias trip, Lewis quite reasonably explains in some detail why he undertook an expedition that was so likely to end so badly. The trip up the Marias had little to do with establishing a claim to the northernmost possible boundary between the United States and Canada. It is assumed, and has been since the peace treaty ended the Revolutionary War, that a line of latitude would make up the boundary across the high plains. In the east, the line of latitude setting Vermont and New Hampshire off from Canada is the Forty-fifth parallel. In the west, it is likely to be a line that begins at Lake of the Woods. On a modern map, Lake of the Woods lies on the east-west border between the provinces of Manitoba and Ontario, and toward its south end, reaches to the northern border state of Minnesota. At that point on the map, the eventual line across the prairie will be drawn at the Forty-eighth parallel, beginning at the southernmost edge of Lake of the Woods. But it is not settled yet, and when Lewis is in the west, that line is up for grabs.

So, adding material not in his journal at all, Lewis's letter explains that this dangerous mission into Blackfoot country is "to explore the River Maria completely with a view to establish, provided it so existed, that some of its branches extended so far north as latitude 49′ 37″ north, [putting it] on the same parallel of latitude with the north west extremity of the Lake of the Woods. Good grounds [existed] to hope that it extended to latitude 49′ 37″ north." This makes his survey "of the highest national importance as it respects our Treaty of 1783 with Great Britain." That treaty settled the boundaries between the original states and British Canada, and left unsettled the possible future boundary west of the Great Lakes. It was, in fact, unclear which part of the west was of the United States and which would remain Spanish (or French, should that country reassert its claim to Louisiana). A line running west from the Lake of the Woods was assumed, but from which part of that lake was undecided.

It is a measure of the man that for all the errors and misconceptions that led to the bloody confrontation on the morning of July 27, Lewis makes only small changes about a few moments of that fatal dawn. The rewriting does something to improve his reputation, and it may even be the truth, although it is inconsistent with his journal.

Just before everyone retires on the night of July 26, Lewis writes in his journal that he has invited the eight young Indians to accompany him to the mouth of the Marias. To this offer, his journal says, "they made no reply." The letter, contrarily, omits his request that they stay with him and go downriver to the Missouri. It omits his promise of horses and tobacco when they reach the river and his other companions. The letter says only: "These people appeared extremely friendly on our first interview & insisted on remaining with us all that night to which I consented." According to the journal, they were not all that friendly and, it should be repeated, staying together that night was Lewis's idea.

That is not bad, just one self-serving moment in recounting three years of exploration. It is just enough of a foible to make Lewis mortal.

103

August 6, 1806,

Wilkinson Natters On About Something

THE CORRESPONDENCE in August between General Wilkinson and Lieutenant Pike is as difficult to decipher as were the letters and orders in June. There are any number of reasons that no modern author wants to write a biography of Zebulon Montgomery Pike, and one of them is that the few scraps of document we have today are ambiguous.

Readers (who are very different creatures than historians) may well enjoy puzzling out what is going on here in the summer of 1806. Surely, the reader's guess will be as good as anyone's. In that spirit, here is the essential part of a letter:

August 6, 1806, Wilkinson to Pike

> In regard to your approximation to the Spanish settlements, should your route lead you near them, or should you fall in with any of their parties, your conduct must be marked by such circumspection & discretion as may prevent alarm or conflict, as you will be held responsible for the consequences.

Now, that sounds just like the letter written in June, the public, official, for-the-record letter ordering Pike to stay away from the Spanish settlements. We know Pike has secret orders to approach them. We have a letter from Pike in July explaining to Wilkinson exactly what lies he will tell to excuse his presence on the outskirts of the capital of the Spanish province of New Mexico. He will claim he got lost while marching from St. Louis to Natchitoches, in New Orleans Territory.

If that is true, we might assume that in August, Wilkinson is just creating another public statement of the purity of his motives by making it perfectly clear that Pike is to stay away from Spanish settlements and Spaniards in person. We might be, could be, would be, wrong. Here is the second important part of the letter of August 6:

> By return of bearer you may open your correspondence with the Secretary of War, but I would caution you against anticipating a step before you, for fear of deception or disappointment.

That is a difficult sentence. What it means is best understood by comparing what Pike is ordered to write to the secretary of war and what he is to write to Wilkinson:

To me you may & must write fully & freely, not only giving a minute detail of everything past worthy of note [that is, everything important that has happened to the date of his correspondence] but also of your prospects & the conduct of the Indians. . . .

In other words, and see if you agree, Wilkinson is ordering Pike not to tell the secretary of war that he is headed for Santa Fe (that is the "step *before you*" which Wilkinson underlines in his letter). Pike should hide this information to prevent "deception or disappointment" if the central government knows his plans. But, Wilkinson adds, "to me you may & must write fully & freely, not only giving a minute detail of everything past worthy [of] note, but also of your prospects. . . ."

Now, it is all very well to know that Wilkinson, a habitual liar, is not to be trusted in this letter. He has, you remember, notified the Spanish of Pike's expedition, and as this letter is being delivered, some five hundred mounted Spaniards from New Mexico are concluding their search for Pike.

But here is the odd part: If the letter is just Wilkinson covering his trail, why does he order Pike not to be forthcoming with the secretary of war? That is insubordination, to put the best face on it. It borders on treason. Surely Wilkinson does not want Secretary Dearborn to read that sentence. So, does that make it the true part of the letter and the part about avoiding the Spanish the false part? Or has Wilkinson changed his mind? Is he trying to stop Pike from completing his expedition to Santa Fe? In the months to come, will Pike be disobeying Wilkinson?

It begins to be a puzzle like the old conundrum: Can you believe the Athenian who says, "All Athenians are liars"? Among other faults Pike has as a subject for a biography is that you can barely begin to understand what he is supposed to be doing in the summer and fall of 1806 and the early winter of 1806–1807. The best thing to do is just keep an eye on him for the next few months.

Oh, there's one more possibility. Wilkinson may not have actually sent the letter. The only way to figure that out is to maintain a close watch on Pike. What he does may tell us if he got the letter, and whether he understood what to ignore and what to believe in the letter. Or maybe not.

104

August 11, 1806,

Pierre Cruzatte Makes a Serious Mistake

A FEW MEMBERS of the corps are almost full-time hunters. The party is eating its usual ten pounds of meat per person per day and wasting a good deal more of it. There is no human possibility that they ate everything they killed on August 6: six elk and a deer—over a thousand pounds of boneless meat from the easiest parts of the animal to butcher.

If hunting is a chore for Drouillard, the Field brothers, and a few other picked men, it is a form of recreation for Meriwether Lewis. He is an excellent shot and enjoys both the chase and the execution.

On Monday, August 11, Lewis gives up on taking a meridian reading; they are still on the water at noon and he misses the 12:00 opportunity by twenty minutes or so. Just then they approach an island in the middle of the Missouri. It is densely covered with willows, and as the boats approach Lewis sees a herd of elk browsing on the thick growth.

Lewis decides that he might as well kill some elk for supper and takes one of the men along with him. He picks a companion with no particular aptitude for elk hunting. This is Private Pierre Cruzatte, a man of several talents, hired and then enlisted into the party for his skills as a boatman. He plays the fiddle and has entertained Indians from Nebraska to the Pacific Ocean and back. In a pinch, he can translate with some tribes in their tongue, and as we know he usually translates from French to English for Charbonneau. Cruzatte apparently has some skill with sign language as well. He is honest and industrious.

Unfortunately, he is also blind in one eye and nearsighted in the other. Why, out of at least two dozen candidates for companionship, Lewis picks this man is inexplicable.

They are not ten minutes into the hunt, deep in the willow thicket, when Lewis is shot in what he always refers to as "my left thigh." The wound is "about an inch below my hip joint," he writes later, which would make it a wound in the left cheek of his butt. Fortunately, the shot misses bone and artery, and he is able, until it stiffens, to run. And he will run.

"I instantly supposed that Cruzatte had shot me in mistake for an elk as I was dressed in brown leather and he cannot see very well; under this impression I called out to him, 'Damn you, you have shot me,' and looked toward the place from whence the ball had come." There is no answer, and Lewis concludes that if the shooter is not Pierre, it is the Indians, and he races back to the boat and raises the alarm that they are being attacked by Indians. Lewis, his wound stiffening, stays at the boats while the corps fans out in the willows to find the hostiles.

"In this state of anxiety and suspense I remained about 20 minutes when the party returned with Cruzatte and reported that there were no Indians nor the appearance of any; Cruzatte seemed alarmed and declared if he had shot me it was not his intention." Lewis does go on about it for a few days, even to the point of examining the caliber of the ball, which is recovered from his pants leg. The ball stops when it exits the wound, creases the other cheek, and hits the leather clothing. It is determined to be a large slug, .54 caliber, matching Cruzatte's rifle.

"I do not believe that the fellow did it intentionally but, after finding that he had shot me, was anxious to conceal his knowledge of having done so." So Lewis writes later that week, all the time lying on his stomach in the white pirogue.

The day after the hunting accident, Lewis and Clark are reunited, just below the entrance of the Yellowstone. Clark immediately gets to work on the wound, debriding the dying flesh, packing it with a cone of bandage lint to allow drainage and to let the wound heal from the inside toward the entrance and exit holes. That evening, after copying Lewis's account into his own journal, Clark adds only this remark: "This Cruzatte is near-sighted and has the use of but one eye, he is an attentive, industrious man and one whom we both have placed the greatest confidence in during the whole route." On the other hand, in a few months Lewis will take a roster of the members of the corps and make notes about their contribution and make a few recommendations that certain men receive extra pay. Of Pierre Cruzatte, Lewis never has another word to say.

105

August 11, 1806, Burr Is Sighted in Pennsylvania

AARON BURR, last seen by us having his final dinner with Jefferson, has been lying low, gathering financial backing from associates in New York for his filibustering plans. He leaves New York (the murder charges from the duel with Hamilton have been quietly dropped) and goes on to Philadelphia and then to Pittsburgh, from whence he plans to descend the Ohio to Mississippi, the Mississippi to New Orleans, and march on Mexico City. One of the odd facts (one of the few facts, for that matter) that we have about this trip is that he passes through

Chambersburg, Pennsylvania, on August 11 and arrives in Pittsburgh on the twenty-first.

The newspapers of the day cannot be trusted in matters of politics or personalities. Each paper is a sectarian organ, a party platform, or merely the splenetic and invective-filled rag of a publisher's personal whim. But they are probably very reliable on dates. Burr passing through Chambersburg on the eleventh of August and arriving in Pittsburgh on the twenty-first is the kind of fact that the most irresponsible of newspapers will not fabricate. Why do we pause to dwell on his journey's details? Because, in spite of his reputation and the widely rumored plan to raise an army and march on Mexico (and perhaps lead a secession of the west), it is his rate of travel that seems noteworthy, not his destination. It is a matter of intense reader interest that it takes Burr (or any other traveler) exactly ten days to ride from Chambersburg to Pittsburgh. In 1806, that is news you can use.

You and I have real trouble imagining what it is like for Lewis and Clark and their party to go by boat and horseback on a 6,000-mile round trip. The average citizen in 1806 not only understands what it is like, but can give a pretty reasonable estimate (providing they can multiply three- and four-digit numbers) of how many days of travel it will take for Lewis and Clark to get out there and back. The west may be more dangerous than the east, but not much.

Once in Pittsburgh, Burr socializes, enlists young men in his vague adventure. He tunes his agenda to suit the ear of the listener—a liberation of Mexico, an invasion of Texas, a separation of the southern and western territories from the United States. A few well-to-do adventurers join up, including one who supplies his own elegant riverboat. Burr is collecting an army of sunshine traitors.

And he is talking. Burr cannot shut up. Visiting the country estate of a Colonel George Morgan, a somewhat eccentric but perfectly sane Revolutionary War officer, Burr is intent on enlisting Morgan's two sons. At dinner with their father, Burr tells Colonel Morgan that the eastern states are now wicked and weak. He repeats his favorite boast: With two or three hundred men he could take Washington and drive the government into the Potomac River. With twice as many men, he could capture New York City.

Morgan, a member of the American Philosophical Society and a supporter of Jefferson and the Democratic-Republicans, is appalled. As soon as Burr has left, Morgan writes the president and also notifies several distinguished officials of Pittsburgh and the state of Pennsylvania that Burr is a traitor. No one believes him. Or, no one wants to believe him. Or, they are quite willing to sit on the sidelines and see how the game progresses.

Some even thought Morgan a bit over the edge. Months later, one of Morgan's confidants recalled that the colonel "was a good deal indisposed, & his disorder considerably affected his brain—he talked much of Burr—& seemed deeply impressed with an opinion that he had it in contemplation to effect a separation of the States." Of all the people Morgan warns, not one does a thing. They wait for events to unfold, and only recall what serves their interest. Some biographers of Burr seize on these men and their inertia and insist that Burr has no intention of raising a revolution in the west; it is just a game, and only old and addled people like Morgan believe it is true. It is too preposterous to be true. Burr is a great prankster. All well and good, but who is the audience for the joke? And if it is a joke, who are those young men building boats and buying arms and food for an expedition down the Ohio?

The one thing we know for sure: Burr passes through Chambersburg, Pennsylvania, on August 11, 1806.

106

꧁꧂

August 14–16, 1806, Reunion at the
Mandan and Hidatsa Villages

THE CORPS arrives at the villages of their winter companions in much less grandeur than in the fall of 1804. The white pirogue is battered, the red pirogue replaced by a few dugout canoes. They, who left with enormous riches stowed in the pirogues, return essentially penniless. Lewis is bedridden, flat on his stomach. Clark is in charge.

Almost the first Indians they see are old friends, the "Mah har Chief" as Clark styles the chief of the Awaxwahi Hidatsas who live in the Mahawah village on the banks of the Missouri just upstream from the Mandans. It is easy to forgive Clark for not remembering the chief's name, or not attempting to write it; the chief is Taluckcopinreha.

Clark writes, "The Chief of the Mah har has told me if I would send [someone] with him, he would let me have some corn." A sergeant and two men walk up to Mahawah and return "loaded with corn. The chief and his wife also came down. I gave his wife a few needles, &c." Clark has nothing left but a few needles. The *et cetera* is not even worth elaborating.

On the next night, Lewis still abed, Clark, with Charbonneau translating and Drouillard backing him with sign language, tries to enlist Hidatsa and Mandan chiefs to make the trip downriver on the way to see the Great Father in Washington. Nothing will persuade them. First the Hidatsa decline. The Mandans explain that they fear the Sioux also, and if they go, they too will die on the way. At last, they offer Clark a young man. A young man of bad character. Clark recognizes him as the youth who begins the day by stealing a knife from one of the enlisted men.

I then reproached those people for wishing to send such a man to see and hear the words of so great a man as their Great Father; they hung their heads and said nothing for some time when the chief spoke and said they were afraid to send anyone for fear of their being killed by the Sioux.

To most purposes, this refusal puts an end to the very last duty of the expedition. It is their last task, and the Mandans and Hidatsas will not cooperate. There is nothing left but to go home.

On the sixteenth, a party of fur traders from Illinois arrives at the Mandan villages. They are headed up the Missouri to trap and trade, and Private Joseph Colter, one of the rambunctious "young men from Kentucky," asks Clark if he can be released. Colter has no desire for civilization. Clark discharges him most amicably: "We were disposed to be of service to any one of our party who had performed their duty as well as Colter had done. . . . We gave Joseph Colter some small articles which we did not want and some powder & lead. The party also gave him several articles which will be useful to him on his expedition."

As they are leaving, Charbonneau happens to tell Clark something he has learned. It is probably just as well he waits until they finish with their councils. The year before, while the party was moving up the Jefferson River toward their meeting with the Shoshone, some Hidatsas from the upper village, Menetare, followed them closely. After the party leaves the Shoshone and heads for Ross's Hole to meet with the Flatheads, the Hidatsas fall on the Shoshone. Two of Sacagawea's kinfolk were killed. It was an ordinary summer expedition, just like the one that had captured Sacagawea some six years earlier. Now, Clark is truly discouraged. The Hidatsas' promise to stop killing the Shoshone turns out to be just one more convenient lie. They push off for St. Louis. There will be no more Indian diplomacy this year.

107

⚜

August 30, 1806, The Last of the Teton Sioux

WILLIAM CLARK is in a foul mood for the entire last two weeks of August. It starts with the Hidatsas and most of the Mandans refusing to send chiefs to the Great Father. It gets worse when the Mandans try passing off one of their juvenile delinquents as an ambassador. The expedition's old friend Sheheke, a Mandan chief, does accompany them, but one chief for six villages and two cultures? It is not enough. Clark's spirits get even lower when Charbonneau tells him that the Hidatsa did not, and do not, have any intention of making peace with the Shoshone or any other tribe they can harass.

Clark must be regretting one of his last attempts to seal good relations with the Mandan-Hidatsa villages. Anticipating no need for it, he has just a few days earlier given away the cannon from the white pirogue. Even that generosity won't convince the chiefs of the upper Hidatsa village to come to Washington. Clark attempts a negotiated peace among the tribes that trade at the Mandans, and no one is interested. The one thing all the Indians have in common is simple: They are afraid of the Teton Sioux; it is all the Sioux's fault.

So, black thoughts aboard, the corps rows and paddles downstream from the Mandans, collecting a few animal skins to replace the ones lost to mildew at the Great Falls. In particular, they look for trophy-size mule deer and antelope.

On a Saturday morning, the thirtieth of August, they see Indians on the west bank of the river. Cautiously, the corps stops on an island in the river. Some young men swim out from the shore and approach the boats. Clark, for really the first time on the entire journey, loses his temper completely when he sees that they are Teton Sioux. The arrogance of the Sioux is exceeded only by their ferocity; the mere sight of them arouses Clark. It is very difficult to shout at someone through an interpreter, but that is all Clark can do. An old trader who lives at the Mandans, the same René Jusseaume who remarked on the young sol-diers' eagerness to attract the buffalo during the Mandan winter, is along for the ride and he translates for Clark.

The Indian boys who swim to the boats are ordered off. Clark says he "directed them to return with their band to their camp, that if any of them come near our camp, we should kill them certainly."

In the midst of all this, a Pawnee-speaking Indian appears on the bank, and as a few of the men aboard the boats can speak a little Pawnee, the argument escalates with two translators, one for Clark to the Sioux via Jusseaume, and another Indian, perhaps a Pawnee or per-haps a Teton Sioux with language skills, to pass along the insults from the Pawnee-speaking members of the corps. Clark writes that he began with this speech:

> *Whenever the white people wished to visit the nations above they would come sufficiently strong to whip any villainous party who dare to oppose them and words to the same purpose. I also told them that I was informed that part of their bands were going to war against the Mandans &c. and that they would be well whipped, as the Mandans and Minnitaris (the Hidatsa) had a plenty of guns, powder and ball, and we had given them a can-non to defend themselves. . . . I directed them to inform their chiefs what we had said and to keep away from the river or we should kill every one of them, &c., &c.*

As always, so much is lost in the record. Here are a few boatloads of white men dressed in ragged elk hide, screaming threats at elegantly mounted and war-painted warriors. Ragamuffins railing at the rich, that is what it amounts to. Besides killing every one of them, what else could Clark promise, what is the *et cetera, et cetera*? The corps embarks, and the Teton Sioux appear in even greater numbers on the bank above the river. It turns into a generalized shouting match between Indians who cannot speak English and Clark, who must rely on Jusseaume, who is an indifferent speaker of Sioux. Presumably, Drouillard can swear in sign language.

Clark does not attempt to record the insults hurled back and forth across the muddy water. It is amusing to imagine the poor trader, caught in the middle translating an insult to Clark, waiting for a reply, and then shouting back a return insult. Toward the end, as can be imagined, the argument, with the men joining in, shifts from words to that universal language of contempt, the finger, the whole arm, pumped in a silent "fornicate you." Some of the corps may have exposed their buttocks to the Indians, and the Indians may have done the same. It is hard to tell from the record, but that is hinted. It is a curious thought, the Corps of Discovery mooning the Teton Sioux, the Tetons making some kind of graphic obscenities in reply.

The men paddle and row for home. The expedition is truly over when the Teton Sioux disappear from sight.

108

Ca. August 20, 1806, The Spanish Meet the Pawnees

IT IS DIFFICULT to understand what it is about Pike's expedition that so upsets the government of New Spain and, most particularly, of New Mexico. The legal boundary between Spain and Louisiana is a bit vague, but for two centuries it has not mattered very much. The real barrier between New Orleans or St. Louis and Santa Fe is not a customs service, it is several tens of thousands of mobile and hostile Indians. Native Americans own the plains, and New Mexicans,

Spanish and Pueblo alike, huddle on the western side of the mountains, far from the buffalo herds and the buffalo people that follow them. Only the Pecos pueblo, soon to be abandoned, is east of the Sangre de Cristo Mountains, where it serves as an uneasy trading center, mediating between the Pueblo and the horse Indians.

What passes for settlement in French Louisiana sticks close to the Mississippi River, and goes no farther west, no farther "inland" than a few miles. The great river is not only the transportation system for goods, it is the escape route in time of trouble.

And that is the problem that Pike poses to the Spanish. Whether he actually impinges on the legal border or even has the gall to press on to Santa Fe is not the issue. The greatest damage he can do is to make it seem possible to cross the prairie. It is that vast space that is the border, the barrier, that protects New Mexico and the country to the south where the legendary gold and silver mines of Mexico still produce wealth.

The dragoon and militia force from Santa Fe arrives in the Pawnee village (in far eastern Colorado) without surprising the chiefs. It is huge: 100 dragoons and 500 mounted militia and a *remuda* of some 2,500 spare horses and pack mules. It is visible for miles. Even at a walk, 10,000 hooves raise an enormous dust cloud from the sunburnt short-grass prairie of late summer.

And from our distance that may seem like a huge force to send out after a single American lieutenant and a squad of soldiers—flyswatting with a rifle butt. It is not an army needed to cope with the Americans; it is just a comfortable number of men to enter the country of Pawnee and Comanche horsemen.

The Pawnee head chief, according to what he tells Pike a few weeks later, listens to the Spanish explain what they are doing. When they tell him that they plan on riding east, through Pawnee country to find this Pike, the chief objects.

His real motive, which Pike may not understand fully, is simple; it is not to protect Pike, but to maintain the status quo. It is in a sense the business of the Pawnee (and the Comanche and Kiowa) to interpose themselves between New Mexico and Louisiana, between Spain and the United States. The Indians will live in the vast plains, the white men will stick to their farms and houses in the settlements by the Rio Grande of the west and the Great River of the east. The Spanish listen to the Pawnee, and do not move east toward the Mississippi.

Whether the chief, Sharitarish—White Wolf—is as convincing as he believes he is, the Spanish move north and west, toward the headwaters of the Platte and Arkansas Rivers. They will catch Lieutenant Pike there, as he tries to penetrate the mountains and cross over to New Mexico. And so, all 2,500 or more animals and 100 dragoons and 500 militia move on in a column, raising another great cloud as they trample the dry grass of August into a powdery lane the width of, and somewhat resembling, a county fair racetrack.

109

September 4, 1806, Floyd's Grave

NOT ALL THE SIOUX along the Missouri are as unsociable as the Teton Brule bands. The captains remember their amicable dealings with the Yankton Sioux in the summer of 1804. Just before arriving at the Yankton camps in that first summer, the expedition was saddened by the death of Sergeant Charles Floyd, a painful dying, most likely from appendicitis. His major symptoms, as Lewis noted them in the journals, included a complete stoppage of the bowels, a common effect of appendicitis. Lewis's treatment was a violent chemical purge, standard practice at the time, and the best way to rupture an infected appendix.

Floyd is the only man of the Corps of Discovery to die on the trip, felled not by Indians or grizzly bears or drowning, but by a microbe that invaded his useless appendage. They buried him with ceremony that summer, naming the nearest river Floyd's River and his resting place Floyd's Bluff.

On their descent, within a week of the second anniversary of Floyd's death, the company stops and ascends the steep bank to the top of Floyd's Bluff. The surface of the grave is disturbed, dug up as if to disinter the sergeant. The men rearrange the sod, straighten the marker, and, apparently without a prayer or a speech, return to the boats. Perhaps it should be noted here that the journals of Lewis and Clark must be the longest and fullest narrative of four years of human activity in the nineteenth century that make no reference at all to organized Christian religion or communal prayer.

A few days after stopping at the grave, they encounter a small band of Yankton Sioux, and Clark learns why the grave is disturbed. One of the Yankton Sioux chiefs, Clark relates more than a year later to a questioner in Philadelphia, was camped near Floyd's grave in 1805 and is responsible for digging it up. The Yanktons, already decimated by European diseases, cut off from the upper Missouri by their altogether unfriendly cousins, the Teton Brules, were a sad lot when Lewis and Clark visited them in 1804. That is part of the reason why they find Floyd's grave disarranged in 1806.

Clark explains it thus: "A chief of one of the Sioux bands encamped near it lost one of his sons. He had Floyd's grave opened and his son put in with Floyd for the purpose of accompanying him to the other world, believing the white man's future state was happier than that of the Savages."

Floyd's grave is moved twice in the next century, as the restless Missouri undercuts its bluffs. Now much tamed by dams (one of them makes a Lake Sacagawea), its banks are stable, and Floyd will not be moved again in our lifetimes. No one remembers if they moved the Sioux boy, too. That is the trouble with trying to plan the future or recapture the past. The living do not know and the dead do not remember.

110

❦

September 23, 1806,

The Corps Returns, Amazing All in St. Louis

DRIVEN BY an increasing desire for many things—clean clothes, whisky, tobacco, decent food, sex, a bed to sleep in—the members of the party row and paddle vigorously down the Missouri. They are in such a rush (and also they have passed south of the great herds of game) that instead of wasting time hunting and cooking, the men unanimously agree to press on, subsisting on a diet of papaw fruit from the timbered bottomlands of the river. The papaw, with the very descriptive name of custard apple, grows on shrubs or small trees, and has an irritating outer skin concealing a gelatinous pulp. For the last two weeks of their trip, the men complain of sore eyes, perhaps from handling so much of the fruit, and also, as the equinox approaches, from looking all day to the south, the lower sun glinting on the river, shining into their eyes. And, of course, they have not had a bath for some months, not since leaving the Lolo Creek hot springs in early July.

What keeps them from arriving in St. Louis red-eyed, leather-clad, and bone filthy is a new army post, Fort Bellefontaine, lying just upstream on the Missouri from its junction with the Mississippi. General Wilkinson is inadvertently their benefactor. After notifying the Spanish of the corps' activities in 1804, and encouraging the Spaniards to capture the party, Wilkinson extended American power slightly upstream into the Louisiana Purchase. What it did provide was a stranglehold on upstream traffic on the Missouri, should Wilkinson complete his scheme of licensing traders through his military posts.

At the fort, the men acquire clean skins, new clothes, and a night's rest. Sheheke, the Mandan chief, is taken to the public stores and given trade goods and tobacco.

Their arrival in St. Louis on September 23 is the occasion for a celebration, and time for Lewis, whose buttocks are finally healed, to sit down and write a long letter to Jefferson. It is not the letter he wants to write—that letter would describe the easy passage from the waters of the Missouri to the great central lake of the west and down the Columbia. That letter would describe the long-sought height of land in the western half of the continent where all the great rivers rose, flowing to the Gulf of Mexico and the Pacific Ocean. Instead, he must amend and forward the summary judgments he made a year previously while hunkered in the winter rains of Oregon. He will put the best possible face on it:

> The passage by land of 340 miles from the Missouri to the KoosKooske [the headwaters of the Snake/Columbia system] is the most formidable part of the tract proposed across the Continent; of this distance 200 miles is along a good road, and 140 over tremendous mountains which for 60 miles are covered with eternal snows; however a passage over these mountains is practicable from the latter part of June to the last of September, and the cheap rate at which horses are to be obtained from the Indians of the Rocky Mountains and west of them, reduces the expenses of transportation over this portage to a mere trifle.

Lewis acknowledges that for serious transportation, his route is no alternative to sailing around the Cape of Good Hope. But he continues whistling in the twilight: "Still we believe that many articles not bulky, brittle nor of a very perishable nature may be conveyed to the United States by this route with more facility and at less expense than by that at present practiced."

This means furs, the only valuable goods that are portable, unbreakable, and won't rot on the way. The only problem is that the Columbia side of the Rockies is deficient in beaver, the gold standard of fur bearers. Lewis hopes that "there might be collected the skins of three species of bear affording a great variety of colors and of superior delicacy, those also of the tiger cat, several species of fox, marten . . . besides the valuable sea otter of the coast." His "tiger cat" remains a mystery. Lewis is a reasonably good field biologist (although it takes him several weeks to realize that grizzly bears are not ordinary black bears and several months to understand that both species of bears come in different colors of fur), and there is nothing in the Columbia basin remotely resembling a tiger. He remembers seeing one. It is, and it was, at best a dream, at worst a hallucination.

He closes with a warning against the British (he fears the pesky North West Company is moving west and south) and a promise to provide a more detailed report and a complete map when time allows. He has work to do, not least paying off the men. In at least one instance, by the time he is ready to pay in cash, it goes to a saloonkeeper who holds the soldier's note for two years' salary owed. It is not possible that the man drank it all up in cheap whisky in a week and survived to sign the IOU, but even in frontier St. Louis, there are many other downtown delights for the appetite, all available for the promise of cash money on payday.

111

September 26, 1806,

Pike Arrives at the Pawnees, to No One's Surprise

THE SMALL EXPEDITION led by Pike moves north from the Osage country on horseback, looking for the Pawnees. There are just nineteen enlisted men, plus Pike and Lieutenant James Wilkinson, son of the General of the Army. A civilian acquaintance of General Wilkinson, a "Dr. Robinson," is along as a volunteer. Robinson claims some murky business draws him to Santa Fe, and he is accompanying Pike merely to approach that New Mexico capital. He is probably spying for Wilkinson. Until his death in a half-dozen years, Robinson is involved in one frontier scheme after another. The Americans move north across what is now Kansas, and just north of what becomes the Kansas-Nebraska border they find the great Pawnee village at Red Cloud, Nebraska, a town later named for that famous Sioux war chief.

White Wolf (Sharitarish), the Pawnee chief, immediately tells Pike that a squadron of New Mexican dragoons and militia are looking for him. This is not for Pike's benefit. The point White Wolf makes is this: He controls the plains, and he has convinced the Spanish to stay out; if they must look for Pike, look for him up in the front range of the Rocky Mountains, on the headwaters of the Arkansas and Platte Rivers. And Pike should have as much sense and respect. The Americans are not particularly impressive; the Spaniards from New Mexico came 500 strong, rode good horses, and the 100 dragoons wore light armor. Pike's platoon looks like Boy Scouts by comparison.

"We were given to understand," Pike says, after a night of parleying with the Pawnees, "that our requests could not be complied with"—the Pawnees would not lend him an interpreter, sell him horses he desperately needs, nor would any chiefs travel east to meet the Great Father. "And [we] were strongly urged by the head chief to return the way we came and not prosecute our voyage any further; this brought on an explanation as to our views towards the Spanish settlements," that is, Pike's intention to go all the way to Santa Fe. White Wolf again tells Pike that the Spanish wanted to ride to the Missouri valley (Pike ascended the Missouri and then the Osage River in southern Kansas before setting out for the Pawnee country on horseback) and capture him there. The chief says he stopped the Spanish. And now he wants Pike to be as reasonable as the Spanish, and desist from approaching their borders and especially from crossing Indian country.

"He told me in plain terms (if the interpreter erred not) that it was the will of the Spanish that we should not proceed," Pike writes. White Wolf outlined all the many obstacles between Pike and Santa Fe, "and finding all his arguments had *no effect* [Pike has a habit of emphasizing all phrases that reflect his self-image as a courageous man of steel nerves, undaunted will, &c., &c.] he said, 'It is a pity.' "

Fortunately (and rarely) we have another more detailed version of the meeting. Joaquin de Real Alencaster, governor of New Mexico, writes to the governor general of all New Spain, Nemesio Salcedo, the following spring, after he has had a chance to interview some of Pike's enlisted men. One of them "declares that Pike asked that they show him the road by which the Spanish troops had gone away, and Salitari [White Wolf] answered that he ought not to go near the Spaniards because it would go ill with him." White Wolf also tells Pike that the Spanish may think he is helping Pike, which would go very badly for the Pawnee. Then comes one of those moments of independent perspective on Lieutenant Pike that are all too rare:

"Pike answered him," Alencaster writes, "insisting that they show him whatever way they had gone; but that Salitari repeated to him that he was not going to show him, and Pike would have to use diligence and seek it out himself." Then White Wolf, aware how easy it would be for anyone to find the trail of 2,500 shod horses and mules in the dead and dying prairie grasses of autumn, counsels Pike thus: "If he wanted someone to show him, he should look in the village for some crazy kid [*mozo loco*], or someone of no reputation, to show him." In short, all Pike would need is the help of the village idiot. It should be said that Pike will find the trail of 10,000 hooves, although he will not be able to tell in which direction the squadron was moving.

Alencaster adds a second enlisted man's account. This man had made friends with an American émigré to Santa Fe. The soldier told his new friend that the reason Pike wanted to know about the military strength of New Mexico and northern New Spain was because this "General Wilkinson . . . had forty thousand men ready to enter these provinces in order to conquer them." Alencaster has no more to add, and closes: "This is all I have been able to find out, using the most exquisite methods."

112

September 30, 1806, A Banquet in Nashville

MERIWETHER LEWIS AND WILLIAM CLARK, and the rest of the residents of St. Louis, are blissfully ignorant of events on the Ohio River, the lower Mississippi, and New Orleans. A great conspiracy, the movement of nearly a thousand armed men, the building of a small fleet of riverboats, all this and more goes on without their notice. Burr is afoot, and St. Louis is unaware.

This is a simple function of geography. The lightly settled valley of the Ohio River and the Mississippi from where the Ohio enters at Cape Girardeau downstream to New Orleans is territory all of a piece. St. Louis, hidden across the width of Indiana and Ohio from Cincinnati, well upstream on the Mississippi from Cape Girardeau, is out of touch.

Burr, with his characteristic energy, crisscrosses the Ohio River valley, raising funds, enlisting young men, gathering supplies for a march to Mexico. His agents even carry forged letters from the Secretary of War, Henry Dearborn, and enlist young men who believe they are joining in a patriotic war against the "hated Dons." (It is, in the prose of 1806, impossible to write "Dons" without the adjective "hated," just as today all survivors of tropical maritime disasters are never rescued from mere waters, but must be plucked from "shark-infested waters.")

Burr reaches his apogee in Nashville at the end of September. His powers of persuasion have not been dimmed by time. He convinces General Andrew Jackson (soon to be the victor at the Battle of New

Orleans in the War of 1812 with Britain, a feat that will make him
president in 1820) that war with Mexico is under way, and Jackson
puts the Kentucky militia on alert, and builds and provisions a half-
dozen large keelboats to carry Burr's army to New Orleans, whence
they will march on toward Mexico. Jackson sponsors a banquet in
Nashville, and when Burr offers a toast to the imminent defeat of
Spanish Mexico, a round of cheering begins which effectively ends the
spoken program and carries on until the party is over.

The following morning, perhaps still buoyed by the adulation of
the young men of Kentucky, Burr writes a most remarkable letter to
General Wilkinson. As will happen with celebrities, men gone mad on
their own reputations (think movie stars, think professional basketball
players), Burr, after the first sentence, refers to himself in the third person. Here are samples extracted from the letter to Wilkinson:

> I, Aaron Burr, have obtained funds and have actually com-
> menced the enterprise. Detachments from different points and
> under various pretensions will rendezvous on the Ohio, 1st of
> November. [So far, so true.]

> Naval protection of England is assured. [A simple lie; Merry
> is recalled, nothing will happen.] Truxton [admiral-in-chief of the
> American Navy] is going to Jamaica to arrange with the [British]
> admiral on that station. It will meet us at the Mississippi. [More
> lies.]

> It will be a host of choice spirits. Wilkinson shall be second
> to Burr only. The object is brought to the point so long desired.
> Burr guarantees the result with his life and honor, with the lives
> and honor and fortunes of hundreds of the best blood of the coun-
> try.

> The people of the country to which we are going are prepared
> to receive us; their agents, now with Burr, say that if we will pro-

*tect their religion, and not subject them to a foreign power, that
in three weeks all will be settled.*

There are no Spanish (or Mexican) agents within a thousand miles
of Burr. In case Wilkinson is not sufficiently enthusiastic, Burr closes
with an appeal to Wilkinson's prideful nature:

> *He [Samuel Swarthout, a conspirator and bearer of the letter]
> has imbibed a reverence for your character, and may be embar-
> rassed in your presence, put him at ease, and he will satisfy you."*

Swarthout, the reader will not be surprised to learn, has never met
Wilkinson, and his professed admiration for the general resides entirely
in the imagination of Burr.

The oddest note, and the one that will have the greatest repercus-
sion is in the first sentence of the letter: "I . . . have actually commenced the enterprise." That thought will pierce the soul of General
Wilkinson.

113

October 8–10, 1806, Wilkinson at Natchitoches

THE GENERAL OF THE ARMY and the civil governor of the Territory of
Louisiana, James Wilkinson, finally, after a half-dozen direct orders to
move, obeys his commander-in-chief and leaves Natchez. He marches
on the border at Natchitoches to confront the Spaniards, who are con-
testing the border between what are now the states of Louisiana and
Texas. This takes him into Orleans Territory, virtually contiguous with

the modern state of Louisiana. Orleans Territory has a civil government of its own, and Wilkinson, acting governor of Louisiana Territory (everything from modern Louisiana north) is supposed to be a purely military authority once he passes south of the Orleans-Louisiana border (which persists as the boundary between the states of Louisiana and Arkansas). This is not important at the beginning, but it will be. The governor of Louisiana should have absolutely no civil authority in the city or the surrounding territory. But Wilkinson is never bothered by legal niceties.

Burr's letter catches up with Wilkinson in the field on the eighth of October, by the morning of the ninth he has decoded it. The messenger bearing the letter is an old political crony of Aaron Burr from the state of New York, that ingenuous fellow Samuel Swarthout.

It is difficult to imagine just what emotions overcome General Wilkinson when Swarthout gives him the letter. The awful thing in the Burr letter is the simplest fact: Burr is really going to attempt what has been, up to that moment, a grandiose scheme, almost a game, an entertainment. Even Burr seems to understand that something new is under way: "[I] have actually commenced the enterprise" seems written in some surprise. It may be an even greater surprise to Wilkinson.

Wilkinson, a man who can spend six months getting around to obeying an order, is transformed into a dervish of decisiveness. Historians tend to account for Wilkinson's activities on the Sabine in one of two ways: Either he panics at the thought of Burr actually starting a revolution or more likely he realizes Burr doesn't have a prayer. In either case, he will betray Burr. Wilkinson knows there is no British fleet or American Navy on the way. You cannot, in the vulgar but accurate phrase, bullshit a bullshitter. Wilkinson can get everything he needs without Burr. All Wilkinson wants is the pomp and glorification of a general's life and enough cash to purchase all the luxuries available on the frontier. Burr says he will make Wilkinson "second only to Burr" in Mexico. So what? Wilkinson is already only second to Jefferson (and Jefferson's secretary of war) in the United States, without dodging a single bullet or spending a single night on a hard bed.

Is this an astonishing, inexplicable change of heart by Wilkinson? Not entirely. He is hardly the only man in history to wish to back out of a dangerous situation. Most soldiers are afraid; it is nothing to be ashamed of. Wilkinson's situation is different. He has a choice, and he makes it.

The first order of business is for Wilkinson to establish an alibi and create a witness to his probity. Wilkinson brings the hapless Swarthout to meet with the army unit's second-in-command, a Colonel Cushing. This is the plot that Swarthout explains to Cushing in Wilkinson's tent on the morning of October 9:

Burr will take control of the government of New Orleans, seize control of all the ships in port, "borrow" all the gold in the city's banks, and sail for Veracruz and march on Mexico City. Burr will be the emperor of all of Mexico, the New Orleans and Louisiana Territories, and as many of the trans-Appalachian states as will join him.

Wilkinson's next task is to do something about those pesky Spanish troops on the other side of the Sabine. It makes a nice scene: the portly Wilkinson in his dress uniform, riding under a flag of truce, meeting the Spanish commander at some halfway point and agreeing to separate their troops, creating a broad no-man's-land along the Sabine River, an unoccupied zone 100 miles in width between Natchitoches in New Orleans Territory and Nacogdoches in Texas. This buffer zone, negotiated on the spot, merely confirms the secret understanding Wilkinson already has with his Spanish paymasters, an agreement to an unofficial cease-fire.

Wilkinson has two more chores—writing letters to the government of Spain and to the president of the United States. To the viceroy of all the New World, in Mexico City, Wilkinson offers to explain the details of a monstrous plot against Spain and her colonies. It will only cost the government a reasonable price, $150,000 in gold. To Jefferson in Washington City, he writes a short, fairly accurate account of Burr's plot. He assures Jefferson that he, Wilkinson, is taking all necessary steps to thwart this scheme and protect the United States.

There are very odd things about the letters. Wilkinson never explains how he came by this knowledge. Even odder, he does not name Aaron Burr as the arch-conspirator. He cannot seriously imagine that he can hide that fact from Jefferson. Worse, his only alibi in case of troubles will be Colonel Cushing, who knows it is Burr. And everyone in western North America knows it is Burr. A half-dozen men have already written Jefferson that it is Burr. The Spanish, English, and French ambassadors to Washington all know it is Burr.

The simplest explanation is this: Wilkinson is constitutionally incapable of telling the truth. Even when the truth serves his purposes, he simply cannot finish the job. He must have a secret; he must, so to speak, lie about the truth.

114

October 10, 1806, Martial Music on the Ohio

WHILE GENERAL WILKINSON is betraying Burr, the little colonel is in Cincinnati. This is a patriotic settlement, named for the quasi-Masonic, semi-royalist clique Society of Cincinnati. The Cincinnatis, to shorten their name, are former officers of the Revolutionary War dedicated to the almost obscene adulation of George Washington, the "Cincinnatus of America." (The original is a Roman general who, like Washington, stopped farming a slave-labor plantation and led an army, and then, without ceremony, retired to his farm.)

This is not a raw frontier settlement full of adventurous young men, nor is it a slaveocracy, another fertile recruiting ground for glorious military feats against Mexico. The entire town is perfectly aware of the Burr conspiracy and is firmly decided against it. Ohio is really an extension of the settled east coast; it is not a wilderness outpost. Separation is unthinkable. There is talk in the city of raising a mob and hounding Burr, driving him away.

On the evening of the tenth, a crowd gathers and surrounds the tavern where Burr has taken rooms. A fifer appears and plays the "Rogue's March" as Burr dines inside. This is a tune the colonel would know, one played universally in the armies of the United States and Great Britain whenever a soldier or an officer is being expelled from the ranks. The sound would accompany a ceremonial ripping of the insignia from the miscreant's uniform; it would be played as he is kicked out of the barracks and onto the streets to fend for himself. It is a cheerful little tune with a brief, mocking coda: "dee dah, doo dah" in slow time. Being kicked out of the army in those times was sometimes a blessing.

Burr is nothing if he is not amusing. To a companion at dinner, as the sound of the fife and the rumble of the snare drums penetrates the walls of his tavern, Burr merely remarks that he enjoys martial music.

The night that Wilkinson betrays Burr and the citizens of Cincinnati scorn and threaten Burr, Lieutenant Pike marches west along the banks of the Arkansas River headed for the "Mexican Mountains." He has sent young Wilkinson home, as was always planned, building some rough boats so that Wilkinson and four enlisted men can float down to the Mississippi. It was never General Wilkinson's intention that his son would accompany Pike to the end, wherever that end is supposed to be.

There are no mails between New Orleans and the plains of Colorado. Whatever Pike set out to do at General Wilkinson's orders he will continue to do without knowing that, at home, Wilkinson has changed his mind. If the general has his way, there is to be no war with Mexico along the border and no invasion of Mexico by Aaron Burr. General Wilkinson is settling those matters, and Pike is just a loose cannon on the deck, rolling toward the front range of the Rocky Mountains. The rules of the game have changed, and he doesn't know it.

115

October 22–25, 1806, Jefferson Waffles

MEETING IN WASHINGTON CITY, Jefferson and his cabinet finally take up the question of exactly what to do about Aaron Burr. The pressure to do something, anything, is at last too much for Jefferson. The eastern papers reprint articles from the western papers naming Burr, Wilkinson, and some minor players in the plot. Jefferson is receiving letters almost weekly from one or another correspondent, including government officials, outlining the details of the plot, naming the conspirators, describing the conspiracy's timetable. Nothing specifically precipitates this cabinet meeting, nothing but the accumulation of months and months of warnings.

Even if it is the intent of Aaron Burr to separate the trans-Appalachian west from the United States, Jefferson has a problem. He is the man who suggested that liberty might require regular revolutions. He is well known to have said that the departure of the western territories and states would be no more wrong than a brother leaving home and striking out on his own. Moreover, it is not really against the law to foment a rebellion. In America, to this day, "treason" is an overt act, not an idea or a desire. At the first cabinet meeting, the decision is to send secret instructions to the governors of Ohio, Indiana, Mississippi, and the territory of New Orleans as well as to the district attorneys of Kentucky, Tennessee, and the territory of Louisiana. Burr is to be arrested if found to be "committing any overt act." The authorities are ordered "unequivocally to have him tried for treason, misdemeanor."

There is that peculiar word, as in the grounds for impeachment, "high crimes and misdemeanors." Today misdemeanor is a category of trivial offenses: parking tickets, littering. At the turn of the nineteenth century, a misdemeanor can be a crime against all of society, an upsetting of the right order of things.

On October 24, the cabinet gathers again. They agree to send a naval force to protect New Orleans, but only if Mr. Gallatin, the secretary of the Treasury after whom the third fork of the Missouri has just been named, can find the money. That is, find the money without getting Congress involved. That is, do it quietly. Burr is not so much a threat, one gathers, as an embarrassment.

And on October 25, Jefferson convenes the cabinet again. He has second thoughts. The most recent mails from the west, he explains, have no news about Burr. This "total silence," he tells them, proves that Burr "is committing no overt act against law." No naval forces will go to New Orleans. The emphasis on "overtness" is more than a legal nicety. The charge of treason was a favorite of British monarchs, a catch-all, roughly equivalent to "antisocial behavior" in modern Communist dictatorships. Nothing but the clearest evidence would convince a jury of men who still remembered the Revolutionary War.

On the one hand, Jefferson looks weak, indecisive, faltering. But wait until the game plays out. Jefferson is right to wait until Burr commits an "overt" act. What exactly that means will be decided later.

116

❧

October 26, 1806, Better News from the West

ALTHOUGH THE MAILS bring Jefferson no news of Burr, a letter written in St. Louis on September 23 arrives in Washington City the day between the first and second cabinet meeting concerning the threatened separation of the west. Only after the third meeting in the Burr matter can Jefferson take time to reply.

As is his habit, Jefferson writes his own letters, and makes a copy on his "polygraph." This is not the lie-detector of the same name we know today. It is the double-writing device he has been using for two years. A similar device, when it is adjustable as to scale, is used to enlarge or diminish drawings and is called a pantograph.

The reason for mentioning this machine is to remind us that Jefferson is not "dashing off a note." It is more than the delay between the letter's arrival and his reply; it is a matter of the method of writing. A letter written on the polygraph requires a steady hand and a deliberate thought process; one cannot tap one's polygraph pen on the table or against one's teeth. One cannot doodle on a scrap of paper beside the letter being written. So, calmly and steadily, the second president of the United States responds to his correspondent in St. Louis, Meriwether Lewis, on October 26, 1806:

> I received, my dear Sir, with unspeakable joy your letter of Sep. 23 announcing the return of yourself, Capt. Clark & your party in good health to St. Louis. The unknown scenes in which you were engaged & the length of time without hearing of you had begun to be felt awfully.

If this sounds a bit chiding, Jefferson in fact has suffered for the past year without even a rumor as to the corps' whereabouts. The letters promised from the Great Falls of the Missouri never arrive. In case Lewis misunderstands, Jefferson continues a bit later by saying the purpose of his letter is not to complain:

> Its only object is to assure you of what you already know, my constant affection for you & the joy with which all your friends here will receive you. Tell my friend of Mandane also that I have already opened my arms to receive him. Perhaps, while in our neighborhood, it may be gratifying to him, & not otherwise to

*yourself to take a ride to Monticello and see in what manner I
have arranged the tokens of friendship I have received from his
country particularly as well as from other Indian friends: that I
am in fact preparing a kind of Indian hall.*

Not much is left of the Indian hall. The visitor to Monticello will
see a few artifacts, a tanned buffalo robe among them, scattered among
elk antlers and mountain sheep horns. Sheheke, the Mandan, never
sees Monticello.

117

❧

October 28, 1806, Like Father, Like Son

ON THIS DATE, the separation of Lieutenant Wilkinson from Pike's
party takes place. It is of more than passing interest.

The reasons for young Wilkinson being on the expedition in the
first instance are unclear. It is apparently intended as a field trip, a practice session, a little hands-on experience. He is not expected to stay
with Pike, but at some point, as winter descends, to return by boat
down the Arkansas River. Unfortunately, it is an extremely cold winter and the low and slow-flowing Arkansas is already icing in from its
edges by the end of October. The party cobbles together a little cottonwood canoe and a second boat made of buffalo hides stretched over
branches, and young Wilkinson with four men is set off to fend for
himself and float the ice-plagued Arkansas.

He finds time to write a despairing letter to his father, apparently
giving it to a passing trader. Somehow, even from the plains of
Colorado, the letter is delivered. Wilkinson begins by pointing out that

he is essentially being abandoned by Pike, left with little food, not even tools to repair the boats or axes to cut firewood, and with insufficient armed men should they encounter even a handful of hostile Indians. It is a sort of last will and testament and a remonstrance to the uncaring gods, officers, and parents who are offering him up to the elements and the Pawnees. It does have one interesting note, however. Young Wilkinson writes that if the Arkansas, as it threatens, does become too ice-bound to navigate, he and his party will simply head south by the compass until they reach the larger Red River and return to the Mississippi by that route.

Here is the point raised by young Wilkinson: Pike, when the time comes, will claim that he is in New Mexico, and on the Rio Grande, entirely by mistake. He is merely looking in a reasonable, logical way for the headwaters of the Red River. Lieutenant Wilkinson, who has no previous experience with life on the plains, is perfectly sure (and perfectly correct) about how to find the Red River, about how to stay within the bounds of the Louisiana Purchase. The Red River is in exactly the right place. It is on the east side of the Rocky Mountains, and flows east to the Mississippi. If you are on the Arkansas (as Pike will be) and you want to go home via the Red, you just march south until you get to the next sizable river. Everything Lieutenant Pike will have to say about the location of the Red River must be chalked up to an almost infinite capacity for misrepresentation.

As seems to happen so often on the plains, the gods smile upon, and the Indians are indifferent to and ignorant of, anyone traveling by water. The same luck that held for Lewis and Clark on the rivers of the west will hold for young Wilkinson. He arrives at little Fort Arkansas, near the Mississippi, without even seeing a Pawnee. His escort of enlisted men have had quite enough of young Wilkinson by the time they reach Fort Arkansas, and three of them will desert, immediately upon arrival.

118

꧁꧂

November 14–15, 1806, Repeating the Obvious:
Pike in Colorado, Jefferson in Washington City

BY PURE COINCIDENCE, a certain consensus is reached on the boundary between the Louisiana Purchase and New Spain, and within a 24-hour period at that. Two very different groups of men will define "Spain," or as we would say, "Mexico."

Jefferson, meeting with his cabinet on November 14, outlines a bargaining position for the current negotiations with Spain over the southern and western boundary of the Louisiana Purchase as it impinges on the northern boundary of New Spain, that is, modern Texas and New Mexico. As leaders always will when outlining a bargaining position, Jefferson tells the cabinet what will be the most the government hopes to gain.

Here are the new borders that Jefferson hopes to achieve:

> *The boundary between the territories of Orleans and Louisiana on the one side and the dominions of Spain on the other shall be the river Colorado from its mouth to its source thence due N. to the highlands inclosing the waters which run directly or indirectly into the Missouri or Mississippi rivers, and along those highlands as far as they border on the Spanish dominions.*

This requires some translation. The "river Colorado" is not the modern Colorado that runs from north to south on the western side of the Continental Divide. Jefferson means, using the Spanish adjective, the "red" river. (In Spanish, *colorado,* literally "colored," always means "reddish" unless further modified.) The Red River is in fact the first border between Mexican Texas and the Louisiana Purchase. If you look at a map of Texas today, the Red is the wiggled line that makes up the entire northeastern boundary of the state. (The anomaly of the north-thrusting rectangular Texas Panhandle ignores the old Red River boundary and crosses it.)

The boundary running north from the Red River's headwaters is not entirely specific, in part because no one has any idea where the Red's waters rise. So, Jefferson opts for a simple due north line to the "highlands inclosing the waters" that flow into the Mississippi and Missouri. This line is also visible on a modern map; it is the due north/south line that marks the boundary between New Mexico and Colorado and the western edge of the Texas Panhandle. In an addendum to the negotiating position, Jefferson suggests that all the territory between that northerly line drawn from the headwaters of the Red River toward the eastern limit of New Mexico should remain unsettled for thirty years after agreement on the Red River boundary is reached with Spain. Jefferson is making no claim even to the headwaters of other rivers that run into the Mississippi or Missouri. He is only suggesting that a buffer should be created.

The day after Jefferson and his cabinet agree on the negotiating position, the advancing party of Lieutenant Pike spies a small, blue landmass on the western horizon. Here is Lieutenant Pike's own description of what happens when his men spy the Rockies, when the men realize they are in sight of their supposed goal, when the men understand that their final destination, the headwaters of the Arkansas River, is within reach:

> At two o'clock in the afternoon I thought I could distinguish a mountain to our right, which appeared like a small blue cloud; viewed it with the spyglass, and was still more confirmed in my conjecture, yet only communicated it to doctor Robinson, who was in front with me, but in half an hour, they appeared in full

view before us. When our small party arrived on the hill they with one accord gave three cheers to the Mexican mountains.

OK. Everyone in Pike's party knows that those mountains are in Mexico, which is part of New Spain, which is a dominion of Spain.

119

November 27 – 28, 1806, Pike's Pique

PIKE AND HIS PARTY move steadily but slowly toward the Rockies. When the Pawnee chief refused to help Pike move west through Indian country, denying him the additional horses he needed, or a guide, Pike proceeded on, the men taking turns riding, walking in the meantime. Some fifty miles west of the place where they first spied the Rockies (that was near modern Rocky Ford, Colorado) Pike finds himself suddenly surrounded by sixty Pawnee braves. Armed with rifles and bows and arrows, the Pawnee are apparently returning from a marauding expedition. They maul and harass Pike and his men, but it stops short of murderous violence. Pike's party departs the mob of surly Indians minus several small items—hand axes, a sword (probably Pike's, but he does not admit to it), a broad ax, a few canteens, and other personal possessions. As Pike's men are breaking free of the mob, wrestling and protesting like schoolboys being pantsed at recess, Pike complains to the war chief, who remarks, cryptically, "They are pitiful." He may have meant all the young men involved in the melee.

Besides fourteen enlisted men, Pike is accompanied by the mysterious Dr. John Robinson, who may be tagging along on his own, or who may be carrying messages from General Wilkinson to the Spanish com-

manders in Santa Fe. The evening after Pike and his men squirm away
from the offensive Pawnee, Pike leaves his men leaderless on the prairie
and, accompanied by Robinson, backtracks. As he explains it:

> *I felt myself sincerely mortified, that the smallness of my num-
> ber obliged me thus to submit to the insults of a lawless banditti,
> it being the first time ever a savage took anything from me, with
> the least appearance of force. . . .*
>
> *After encamping at night the doctor and myself went about
> one mile back, and waylaid the road, determined in case we dis-
> covered any of the rascals pursuing us to steal our horses, to kill
> two at least; but after waiting behind some logs until some time
> in the night, and discovering no person, we returned to camp.*

It is difficult, reading along in Pike's journal, to remember that he
is seriously talking about two men (and Pike is an indifferent rifle shot)
waylaying as many as sixty armed, well-mounted Plains Indians. There
are some men with an almost limitless capacity for exposing themselves
to danger for a purpose—an officer calmly rallying his troops by ignoring bullets whistling about his head is an example from modern war.
And then there are men with a completely limitless ability to project
themselves into danger without considering the consequences for the
men they lead. Such a man is our Pike.

A few days after the incident with the Pawnees, Pike finds another
attractive adventure. They are at the foothills of the front range of the
Rocky Mountains, and Pike singles out what appears to be the highest
of the snow-covered peaks and decides to climb it. What exactly this
has to do with exploration is not clear. He takes Dr. Robinson and two
enlisted men, leaving a dozen men to fend for themselves on the now
snow-covered foothills. This is an abridged version of Pike's own
account, which begins on November 26:

> *Expecting to return to our camp that evening, we left all our
> blankets and provisions at the foot of the mountain. Killed a deer*

of a new species, and hung his skin on a tree with some meat. We commenced ascending, found it very difficult, being obliged to climb up rocks, sometimes almost perpendicular; and after marching all day, we encamped in a cave, without blankets, victuals or water. We had a fine clear sky, whilst it was snowing at the bottom.

27 Nov. Thurs.

Arose hungry, dry, and extremely sore, from the inequality of the rocks on which we had lain all night, but were amply compensated for toil by the sublimity of the prospects below. The unbounded prairie was overhung with clouds, which appeared like the ocean in a storm; wave piled on wave and foaming, while the sky was perfectly clear where we were. Commenced our march up the mountain, and in about one hour arrived at the summit of this chain.

The summit of the Grand Peak, which was entirely bare of vegetation and covered with snow, now appeared at the distance of 15 or 16 miles from us, and as high again as what we had ascended, and would have taken a whole day's march to have arrived at its base, when I believe no human being could have ascended to its pinnacle. This with the condition of my soldiers who had only light overalls on, and no stockings, and every way ill provided to endure the inclemency of the region; the bad prospect of killing any thing to subsist on, with the further detention of two or three days, which must occasion, determined us to return.

Found all our baggage safe but the provisions all destroyed. It began to snow, and we sought shelter under the side of projecting rock where we, all four, made a meal on one partridge, and piece of deer's ribs the ravens had left us, being the first we had eaten in that 48 hours.

It would be amusing. He climbs a foothill, not a mountain. The one he sees is not even Pike's Peak, but a lesser object called Almagre Mountain. But there is an evil foreshadowed: The men are wearing the uniforms he gave them back in Louisiana Territory—cotton shirts and pants, boots, but no stockings. He might have added, no caps, no extra blankets, no tents, and no salt, sugar, or flour.

120

November 8 and 25–29, 1806,

Almost Everyone Declares Peace with Spain

IN THE SECOND WEEK of November, Jefferson concludes that the Burr plot might well lead to a war with Spain over Mexico, although he continues to pretend that the Burr conspiracy is confined to separating the western trans-Appalachian states and territories from the United States. Without notifying Congress, and in order to placate the Spanish government, Jefferson sends orders to Wilkinson to withdraw from the Sabine, create a neutral ground, and retire to New Orleans to defend the city against Burrites and like-minded adventurers. If this command to Wilkinson sounds familiar, it is because as you know Wilkinson on his own hook, after deciding that the better part of valor is to remain superficially loyal to Jefferson, has already negotiated a truce on the Sabine and is in New Orleans. On the surface, this looks like some vibrant mental telepathy. In fact, a peace-loving president and a cowardly general have simply found the same answer to their very separate questions.

On November 25, Jefferson is given a letter from Wilkinson delivered by a young lieutenant who pretends to be traveling from Orleans

Territory in order to resign his commission. It is the letter (already described in our entry for October 21, 1806) warning the president of a huge conspiracy to attack New Orleans and Mexico. This is the same letter in which Wilkinson pretends not to know who the arch-conspirator is. Wilkinson relates that he has negotiated a truce at the Sabine in order to return with all his forces to New Orleans, there to defend the city.

Two days later, Jefferson issues a proclamation against any and all "sundry persons," in the language of 1806, who might conspire to wage war upon Mexico and thus upon Spain. Private citizens are warned not to participate or cooperate in any actions supporting the expedition. All civil and military officers are ordered to seize materials, weapons, boats, and provisions related to the enterprise and to arrest and bring to a proper place for trial any and all of the conspirators. The specific crime (a "high misdemeanor") enjoined here is that of making war upon a nation with which the United States is at peace—Spain. Jefferson does not say a word about the plot to separate the west. This is understandable. It may not amount to an insurrection; it may be a natural division, like a dividing protozoan, creating two nations out of one. As for the modern idea (as it says in the Pledge of Allegiance) of "one nation, indivisible," it will take all the blood of the Civil War to make that a reality.

Stopping Burr depends on peace with Spain and quiet along the Mexican border. Burr knows that without at least a Mexican escapade, if not a full-scale war, he cannot continue to pretend that he is leading an army of liberation into Mexico. There is only one military officer out of the reach of Jefferson's proclamation. There is only one military officer who still has the capacity to create some kind of inflammatory incident on the border with Spain's Mexico. Zebulon Montgomery Pike, in between episodes of mountain climbing and buffalo hunting, is out there in the foothills of the Rocky Mountains looking for two things: the headwaters of the Arkansas River and the five hundred horsemen of the New Mexico militia and dragoons. He has found their trail once or twice.

It is hard to believe, but he is apparently following the trail backward in November; he is going along the trail the New Mexicans made on their return to Santa Fe, but he is headed, for the moment, northwest and away from Santa Fe. If only he had that *mozo loco,* that village idiot, with him, he would recognize that the closed end of the horseshoe print points in the direction of travel. By the time he figures this out, the snows of late November are covering all the trails.

Wilkinson is in New Orleans, protecting it from Burr. Jefferson is in Washington City, mobilizing the country against Burr. And Pike is lost in Colorado, but intent, somehow or other, to pick a fight with the Mexican Dons.

121

❧

December 1–6, 1806,

Pike's Men Try to Shorten the Expedition

BEGINNING ON THE FIRST of December, and continuing through the night and most of the following day, Pike and his men struggle up the south bank of the Arkansas River, seeking shelter from the first blizzard of the winter. This is Plains country, treeless, except for the occasional stand of cottonwoods in the river bottom, and the wind is relentless, undeterred. They are forced to cross the Arkansas when the southerly bank becomes a sheer cliff running straight down to the water. The river is running high, and floes of ice batter their legs as the men and the few horses stagger across the stream.

"The ford was a good one," Pike writes in his journal, "but the ice ran very bad, and two of the men got their feet froze before we could accommodate [them] with fire, etc." Worse, a packhorse disappears, as Pike explains, because it "took a freak in his head." Three men, trying to catch the horse, are caught by darkness in the dying hours of the blizzard and do not return to camp. "I was very apprehensive," Pike says, that "they might perish on the open prairie."

When the men limp into camp on the third of December, one of them has frozen feet and the horse is still away; they had not the strength to drag back the unwilling beast. Now there are three totally disabled among the twelve enlisted men. Pike takes comfort in the thought that at least it is not quite as cold in Colorado as it was on the Mississippi the winter before: "The hardships of [this] voyage had now begun, and had the climate only been as severe as the climate" on the first expedition, "some of the men must have perished, for they had no winter clothing."

Now the narrative gets tricky (and murky). This is what Pike says after he has spent most of November looking for the Spanish soldiers (and a week off for recreational mountain climbing) when he is theoretically heading up the Arkansas to its headwaters and then right back home, via the Red River:

"I wore, myself, cotton overalls, for I had not calculated on being out in that inclement season of the year."

The men understand (or think they understand) that the purpose of the expedition is to map the headwaters of the Arkansas (which will be the western boundary of Louisiana in that latitude). The following day, they grasp the opportunity. Showing much more enthusiasm and initiative than ever before on either expedition (most of his men on this trip are veterans of the Mississippi ascent), several volunteers leave the camp and ascend the Arkansas to the gorge that today gives Canyon City, Colorado, its name. Like many Colorado locations (Garden of the Gods, for example), the canyon has acquired a sobriquet: "Royal Gorge." The men report back in the afternoon and Pike takes them at their word: The volunteers, he writes, "have ascended until the river was merely a brook, bounded on both sides with perpendicular rocks, impracticable for horse ever to pass them." On his manuscript map, Pike writes, at this location, "Last of ye Arkensaw."

The men, expecting Pike to turn south now, to head for the Red River and follow it back to civilization, are soon disappointed. Pike orders a march to the northwest. He believes that he perceives another trail left by the New Mexican dragoons, and this is his chance to confront them, to find them within the Louisiana Territory and create an incident, if not a whole war. It is not certain what this trail is; some historians think it is an old Indian track. If it is the mounted militia from Santa Fe, Pike is going the wrong way, against the direction of travel of the dragoons and cavalry. Like many things in history, it is very likely both. Indian trails have a way of becoming the preferred track for everyone else.

The front range of the Rocky Mountains is confusing, even to a modern traveler with a road map. Pike moves west up what is now called Oil Creek, finds his way into South Park, and then heads south, traveling between the front range and the higher "Collegiate" Rockies along the Continental Divide (Mount Harvard, Mount Cornell, etc.). As he moves south, Pike finds an east-running river, tells himself and the men that it is the long-desired Red River. Pike assumes that he has circled around and behind the headwaters of the Arkansas. The men can only assume that they are headed home. There is only one compass with the party, and Pike has it.

122

December 3–11, 1806, Burr Becomes Notorious

A VERY STRANGE PROBLEM faces the federal government in the matter of Aaron Burr. If he is raising an army to invade a country (Spain's Mexican colonies) with which the United States is at peace, what Burr is doing on that matter is illegal. All that is required to prove the illegality of the Burr plot is for war to break out between the United States and Spain. Wilkinson could have forced that weeks ago, down on the Sabine, but he had no stomach for it, and he had no stomach at all for continuing his part in the Burr conspiracy. Seldom has a fault, cowardice, meshed so perfectly with the nation's need. A Wilkinson unable to fight becomes the savior of New Orleans. Lieutenant Pike, on the other hand, is still rattling across the foothills of the Rocky Mountains, trying to find some Spanish Mexicans to attack.

If Burr is merely raising an insurrection against the United States itself, it is extremely questionable whether that is illegal, and even if it is, what force might be used to put it down. This is a country, after all, that raised an insurrection against its government (Great Britain) not thirty years earlier. The use of federal troops to put down insurrection is, almost certainly, illegal. A militia—that is, a collection of citizen soldiers—may properly undertake to defend the commonwealth. The attorney general of Kentucky, following Jefferson's orders, brings a charge of fomenting war against Spain, rather than the more problematic charge of treason by way of rebellion. Burr agrees to appear in court and defend himself.

Because of the distrust of federal authority, the first armed men who set out to stop Burr in his tracks are not federal law officers or United States army troops but militia companies from both banks of the Ohio River. The citizen-soldiers out to stop the Burr conspirators include a truly democratic mob from Virginia (now West Virginia) called the Wood County Militia. While Burr is getting ready to go to court in Kentucky on charges of inciting a war with Spain, his co-conspirators and his young recruits are outfitting themselves to descend to New Orleans. Their rendezvous camp is on Blennerhassett Island, that sylvan retreat of the Irishman with that most non-Celtic name. It is hardly a secret camp, and it is well known to the Wood County Militia who arrive just as Burr's co-conspirators, including Harman Blennerhassett, flee south by boat. The militia help themselves to the Blennerhassett wine cellar before taking off downstream along the Virginia shore. The Burr conspirators, covered both by a cloak of darkness and the fact that many of the militia are literally blind drunk, escape.

That same week, Aaron Burr goes on trial in Frankfort, Kentucky, for the only crime of which he can be accused: organizing an invasion of Mexico. Burr's defense attorney is the young Henry Clay, newly appointed senator from Kentucky. Kentuckians are, to put it simply, great haters of Mexico and Mexicans, of whom they know nothing directly, but whom they despise for their religion, culture, language, and the economic fact that when Spain controls the mouth of the Mississippi, Spain controls Kentucky's trade with the outside world. Any man setting out to thrash the Spanish Dons is Kentucky's hero. It takes the grand jury just a day to turn Burr loose, concluding that "no violent disturbance of the public tranquility or breach of the laws has come to their knowledge."

For now, the plot goes forward. Men, some greedy, some patriotic, some merely itching for adventure, are gathering along the Ohio, ready to descend on New Orleans like wolves on the sheep fold. Unbeknownst to any of them, their presumptive co-conspirator, General of the Army James Wilkinson, is putting New Orleans under martial law and building defenses against Burr's army along the river, manned by commandeered sailors and militia and slave laborers and his own professional army. And Pike staggers on toward Santa Fe.

123

December 25, 1806–January 7, 1807,

Pike Catches Up with Himself

CHRISTMAS DAY usually provokes explorers to examine their condition, and Pike is no exception. "I must take the liberty," he writes, "of

observing that in this situation, the hardships and privations we under-
went, were on this day brought more fully to our mind. . . . Here 800
miles from the frontiers of our country, in the most inclement season
of the year, not one person clothed for the winter, many without blankets (having been obliged to cut them up for socks, etc.) and now lay-
ing down at night on the snow or wet ground. . . ."

As usual, Pike regards these privations as imposed on him, as though
he had no particular responsibility for his situation and his men's condition. Still, whatever else he is, or is not, Pike is admirably hardy. "I will
not speak of diet," he remarks, "as I conceive that is to be beneath the
serious consideration of a man on a voyage of such a nature."

He says he believes (and he certainly tells his men) that the party is
descending the Red River, which, followed to its bottom, will put them
back in "civilization." It is perhaps just as well that he is the only person in the party with a compass, and even better that they are circling
about through the defiles and confusing geography of the land between
the Front Range and the Rocky Mountains proper. Even the men know
that the source of the Red River is south and east of the Arkansas. Yet
for almost a month, Pike leads them to the north and west of the "last
of ye Arkensaw."

There are a few ways to explain Pike's movements. Surely he has
lost all hope of confronting the New Mexican cavalry—nothing moves
in this weather of its own accord. But he is by no means sure where
the divide lies between the Mississippi drainage (the Arkansas and Red
Rivers) and the Rio Grande. Given that ignorance it is even possible
that he doesn't believe that he is on the Red (as he tells the men and
writes in his journal), but that he hopes he is on the headwaters of the
Rio Grande. If he is, heading downstream will take him to Santa Fe.
Perhaps he is merely confused by the weather and thoroughly lost. In
any case, he is lying to the troops.

On New Year's Day, 1807, they spy a prairie ahead some several
miles. Pike believes it is about eight miles off; twenty is more like it. The
news of the prairie ahead, he writes, "gave great joy to the party." The
Plains are two causes of joy: they are on the way home, and they promise

buffalo meat to a band barely surviving on the occasional lean mule deer. In fact, he is on some level ground between the Front Range and the Rockies. For five days, they struggle down the "red" river. Pike sends men ahead to hunt and leave meat by the stream for the following party, now broken into half a dozen groups of two men each, making way as best they can. His leadership, at this point, consists entirely in pairing the men up in buddy groups and making them responsible for their own survival. The hunters leave deer carcasses. Magpies and ravens make off with most of the meat before the staggering pairs of men arrive.

On the fourth of January, he recognizes at last where they are. They are at the same gorge of the Arkansas his men said held the river's source. They are at Royal Gorge above Canyon City. He has spent three weeks wandering and now finds himself at his own campsite of the tenth of December past. "This was my birthday [his twenty-eighth]," he notes, "and most fervently did I hope not to pass another so miserably." For the next four days, his men straggle into their old camp. Surely now they can go home. The Arkansas is known to them now; they are returning from its true headwaters, from where it is nothing but a trickle in the valley between the ranges. Their mission is accomplished. The voyage, as Pike styles it, is complete.

124

January 14, 1807, A Testimonial Feast for the Lewis (and Clark) Expedition, Washington City

THOMAS JEFFERSON, Washington's best host, provides a huge celebration for Meriwether Lewis. The guests include members of the cabinet,

Philadelphia scientists, and the nation's unofficial poet laureate, Joel Barlow. The most important foreign dignitary is Sheheke, the Mandan chief. William Clark never makes it to Washington City. The event becomes a party for Lewis. So much adulation is not necessarily healthy for a man given to mood swings, but for the night, Lewis is happy. As the evening wears on, toasts—or "volunteers" in the argot of the time—are given, including this one from Lewis that is exactly what one might expect from a man educated by Presbyterian ministers:

"May works be a test of patriotism, as they ought of right to be that of religion." Cheers and applause, according to the newspapers, followed this remark.

The entertainment for the evening, between the meal and the "volunteers," is a poetry reading by Barlow, titled, as unfairly as usual, "On the Discoveries of Captain Lewis":

> Let the Nile cloak his head in the clouds, and defy
> The researches of science and time;
> Let the Niger escape the keen traveler's eye,
> By plunging, or changing his clime.
>
> Columbus not so shall thy boundless domain
> Defraud thy brave sons of their right;
> Streams, midlands, and shorelands elude us in vain,
> We shall drag their dark regions to light.

And so forth, for the better part of an hour.

Instead of footnotes or afterwords, let us look at some obscurities in the poem. The references to two African rivers, the Nile and the Niger, remind us that those rivers are, in 1807, unexplored by Europeans. Barlow's reference to "Columbus" in the second stanza reflects his penchant for renaming America for the explorer, rather than for the otherwise obscure mapmaker Amerigo Vespucci. Barlow's epic doggerel poem about the United States is for that reason titled "The Columbiad."

All things Jeffersonian are hateful to the New England Federalists, and within the month, a parody of the Barlow epic appears in the press, written, though not signed, by John Quincy Adams:

> *Good people, listen to my tale,*
> *'Tis nothing but what true is;*
> *I'll tell you of the mighty deeds*
> *Achieved by Captain Lewis—*
> *How starting from the Atlantic shore*
> *By fair and easy motion,*
> *He journeyed all the way by land,*
> *Until he met the ocean.*

And this doggerel, too, goes on and on and on and . . .

Two men present at the dinner are two persons who will play a large and inadvertently unpleasant part in Lewis's career. His friend and business associate, the St. Louis trader Pierre Choteau, is in Washington City for the celebration. He is there specifically to accompany Sheheke, who is the second ogre in an upcoming nightmare. In the spring, Sheheke is supposed to return to his people, and Choteau is supposed to outfit the return party. And Lewis's world will start to unravel when the Mandan cannot go home again.

125

January 15, 1807, Lewis Makes Amends

THE MORNING after the testimonial dinner, Meriwether Lewis takes time to write a letter to Secretary of the Army Henry Dearborn. One can, one should, assume that since the exploration of the Missouri and the Columbia went so well that Lewis is a leader of men. But actual evidence of something so intangible is really scarce in the journals— both he and Clark are extremely modest about their own contributions. The morning's letter to Dearborn is worth reading, particularly since the subject, mutinous expression, is something that Lieutenant Pike is going to deal with in just nine days, out there in the foothills of the Rocky Mountains.

You may recall Private Newman, who was almost forcibly taken away from the Cheyenne camp on the Missouri, on the expedition's first summer. It was a camp with any number of maidens interested in trading sex for food and shelter, and Newman had something of a breakdown. Lewis fairly summarizes the Newman case for Dearborn:

In the course of the expedition, or shortly before we arrived at the Mandan Villages he committed himself by using certain mutinous expressions which caused me to arrest him and to have him tried by a Court Martial formed of his peers; they finding him guilty sentenced him to receive seventy-five lashes and to be discharged from the permanent party, this sentence was enforced by me, and the punishment took place. The conduct of this man previous to this period had been generally correct, and the zeal he afterwards displayed for the benefit of the service was highly meritorious. . . . [Newman] exerted himself on every occasion to become useful. This disposition induced him to expose himself too much to the intense cold of that climate, and on a hunting excursion he had his hands and feet severely frozen with which he suffered extreme pain for some weeks. Having recovered from this accident by the 1st of April 1805, he asked forgiveness for what had passed, and begged that I would permit him to continue with me through the voyage, but deeming it impolitic to relax from the sentence, altho' he stood acquitted in my mind, I determined to send him back, which was accordingly done. Since my return I have been informed that he was extremely serviceable as a hunter on the voyage to St. Louis and that the boat on several occasions owed her safety in a great measure to his personal exertions, being a man of uncommon activity and bodily strength. If under these circumstances it should be thought proper to give Newman the remaining third which will be deducted from the gratuity awarded Paptiest La Page who occupied his station in the after part of the voyage I should feel myself much gratified.

When Newman snapped on the upper Missouri, it was not the first time in the party's history. While Clark was in charge at Wood River, during the winter that they built the pirogues and fitted Lewis's keelboat, discipline was much looser.

Clark is always more tolerant than Lewis, whether it is young men misbehaving or Indians being too fond of long speeches and excessive hugging. This is Clark's brief summary of a single week's troubles at Wood River in the late winter of 1804:

> *Shields threatened Ordway's life in March, Warfington and Potts fought. Newman and Colter fought, Colter loaded his gun to shoot Sergeant Ordway and disobeyed orders. Reubin Field made a mistake and repents. Gibson lost his tomahawk. Whitehouse wishes to return [to the expedition's roster]. Frazer wishes to return and says he "has done bad."*

Clearly, something had to happen with discipline, and Lewis is probably responsible for the general elevation of behavior. That does not make him a better man than Clark, who might well have become a sterner officer once the expedition entered Indian country. But one does admire Lewis for even thinking of Newman.

John Newman would live a long life, surviving as a trapper on the Missouri for another twenty-four years until the Yankton Sioux, mildest of all that confederated tribe, kill him.

126

❧

January 17, 1807, Burr Surrenders, Temporarily

THE GREAT CONSPIRACY is beginning to unwind in the dreary darkness of a Mississippi River winter. Burr's volunteer army is scattered among dozens of boats, and the boats are disorganized, descending the river in groups of two or three. Some men are openly armed, other boats carry hidden stores of arms, and many boats are entirely innocent of any means of deadly force or self-defense. The river is miles wide, dark, roily. The army of Aaron Burr, floating south in the long winter nights, amounts to no more than winter flood debris. It is an elusive army, and easily escapes halfhearted pursuit, less from its military ingenuity than from the vastness of the Mississippi.

By the middle of January, Aaron Burr understands at last that there is not going to be a march on Mobile, Baton Rouge, or New Orleans, much less an invasion of Mexico. Even in the small and distant settlements of Mississippi and Louisiana, newspapers bring word of President Jefferson's proclamation asking citizens and soldiers to capture Burr. The arrival of Wilkinson in New Orleans to protect the country against the anticipated flotilla of Burr's volunteer army is common knowledge.

Burr maintains a cheerful demeanor. He claims to have no designs on New Orleans. He is not going to Mexico. He and a few adventurous young men are headed west toward Texas to claim some land in the western part of Orleans Territory. No one believes him, and some, especially in the territory of Mississippi, are more disappointed than relieved. Spanish West Florida cuts them off from the Gulf of Mexico; anyone intending to make war on the Spanish Dons is welcome in Mississippi.

So it is, with federal troops stirring and state and territorial militias pursuing him and his scattered, vagrant band of supporters, that Burr surrenders. He insists on giving himself over to the *civil* authorities of Mississippi. His greatest fear is falling into the military and federal authority of his one-time ally, General Wilkinson. There is martial law in Orleans Territory, and Burr could be hanged for treason after a brief military trial.

So, on January 17, Burr arrives at Natchez, Mississippi, and offers himself up for trial. The hearing in Tennessee did not conclude his innocence; he was merely released for lack of witnesses and evidence. Jefferson's orders to arrest him are binding on both state and federal officers of the law. Burr, now fearful of Wilkinson, is safer in court than he would be on the river. After giving his word as a gentleman, he moves freely about the small society of Natchez, eating dinner on his reputation as a veteran of the American revolution against Britain and as a champion of a new revolution against Spain.

Meanwhile, along the Mississippi and Ohio Rivers, his few armed allies are being picked up, one boatload after another, by the militias and the United States Army. Some melt away into the oak forests along the rivers. A few sell their stores of arms at fire-sale prices. A few go to jail, waiting trial for something, a kind of treason, a form of sedition. They are, by and large, middle- and upper-class young men, most with at least an elementary education. It will be the common wisdom about the Burr Conspiracy that it provided the territories with a surplus of dancing masters and penmanship instructors. Within days, the conspiracy is gone out like a campfire in the rain. Burr waits for his trial and spends the evenings charming his hosts in Natchez.

127

January 22–24, 1807, Pike's Men Have Had Enough

IN THE SECOND and third weeks of January, Pike leads his men south and west from their canyon camp on the Arkansas. They are the archetypal ragtag lost platoon—without winter clothes, without blankets, without boots in most cases, stumbling along with rags wrapped around their feet, wearing roughly made shoepacs of untanned buffalo hide. They have no food except what they can forage. Even the buffalo have left the foothills, and the snow is piling up, two feet deep on the level, blowing into drifts that cannot be traversed. There is ice in the brooks.

By January 22, the weak are falling. Two privates, a John Sparks and a Thomas Dougherty, have frozen feet and cannot march. Pike leaves them. He notes that he gives them some ammunition, whether to defend themselves or shoot themselves is not clear. Certainly, they cannot hunt; they cannot even move.

On the next day, Pike marches the remaining men due west, toward the treeline on the foothills. It is not a foolish idea. There would be firewood, and perhaps some deer in the forest. Unfortunately, they have to cross a creek. "Here we all got our feet wet," he writes. "The night commenced extremely cold. When we halted at the woods, at eight o'clock . . . we discovered that the feet of nine of our men were frozen, and to add to the misfortune, of both of those whom we called hunters among the number."

There is nothing to eat. The temperature drops to 9 degrees below zero Fahrenheit. Colorado is beginning to sort out the men by mere metabolism. Pike is unfazed, and, remarkably, four of the ill-clad enlisted men do not yet have frozen feet. This is the second night without food.

On the morning of the twenty-fourth, Pike strikes west by south, directly toward the "Great White Mountains." These are the Sangre de Cristos, these are the ones he and all the men call the "Mexican Mountains," these are the peaks he says are the "natural boundary" between Spain and the United States. If it is always a question—what Pike is up to—it is answered. His men now realize that they are not going home. "I heard," Pike writes, "a man express himself in a seditious manner." Pike relates the man's insubordinate remarks: "He exclaimed that 'It was more than human nature could bear, to march three days without sustenance, through snows three feet deep, and carry burdens only fit for horses,' and so forth.

"It was in my power to chastise him when I thought proper," Pike writes. "I passed it unnoticed for the moment, determined to notice it at a more auspicious time."

As the men build fires, Pike manages to shoot a buffalo, a lone beast, separated from the herd. He brings the meat to camp "to the great joy of our brave lads who immediately feasted sumptuously."

After dinner, Pike calls the men together and singles out Private John Brown, the one who spoke of this being more than human nature could spare. This is Pike's account of his speech. Of course he prepares it for publication long after the event, but that does not matter. This is how Lieutenant Zebulon Montgomery Pike believes an officer should behave; whether he manages, at the time, to be so eloquent is less important than the man's self-image.

Brown, you this day presumed to make use of language which was seditious and mutinous. I then passed it over, pitying your situation and attributing it to your distress, rather than your inclination, to sow discontent amongst the party. Had I reserved provisions for ourselves whilst you were starving, had we been marching along light and at our ease whilst you were weighed down with your burden, then you would have had some pretext for your observations.

But when we were equally hungry, weary, emaciated and

charged with burden (which I believe my natural strength is less able to bear than any man's in the party), when we are always foremost in breaking the road, reconnoitering and the fatigues of the chase, it was the height of ingratitude in you to let an expression escape which was indicative of discontent. Your ready compliance and firm perseverance I had reason to expect as the leader of men and my companion in miseries and dangers.

Your duty as a soldier called on your obedience to your officer and a prohibition of such language, which for this time, I will pardon. But I assure you, should it ever be repeated, by instant death I will revenge your ingratitude and punish your disobedience.

Whatever the men think, this is the end of complaining. There is nothing to do but follow Pike. He has the compass and the map. And even if one wishes to desert, toward the Mississippi, toward the rising sun in the east, there is nothing on the way home but five hundred miles of snow-covered prairie and untold numbers of Pawnee and Comanche Indians.

128

January 22, 1807, Jefferson Writes History

WEST OF THE APPALACHIANS, General of the Army James Wilkinson has a commonly used nickname. So many are aware of his years of serving as an informer for the Spanish government that men of more patriotic feelings can refer to him, with the sure knowledge that their correspondent will understand, as simply "The Pensioner." East of the mountains, Wilkinson has a less specific reputation. He is regarded by many who meet him as a blowhard. In spite of his sudden burst of patriotic energy at New Orleans, some think he certainly conspired with Aaron Burr. A New England Federalist, Senator William Plumer of New Hampshire, writes in his journal shortly after the New Year that he is astonished that someone as clever as Burr would make a conspiracy with such a "hasty, imprudent, unguarded" man as Wilkinson. A few weeks later Plumer remarks that Wilkinson is so disreputable that even his "friends distrust him . . . they hope his [self-] interest will restrain him from committing treason."

To such an audience of skeptics, Jefferson writes his message to Congress on January 22. The message is in response to demands that he explain exactly what the Executive plans to do about Aaron Burr, whose schemes are widely discussed from New Orleans to Bangor, Maine.

Jefferson acknowledges that he has been aware of something rotten in the western territories since September, but "it was not until the latter part of October that the objects of the [Burr] conspiracy began to be perceived, but still so blended and involved in mystery that nothing distinct could be singled out for pursuit."

What Jefferson will not admit is that he has had every evidence for months in 1806, but resolutely ignored it, no doubt because the information has come to him from Federalist agents and appointees. It is not until he hears from that loyal Democratic-Republican James Wilkinson, he tells Congress, that he understands that Burr "contemplated two distinct objects, which might be carried on either jointly or separately, and either the one or the other first, as circumstances should direct. "One of these," Jefferson continues, "was the severance of the union of these states by the Allegheny mountains, the other, an attack on Mexico." What has made him sure of his facts, Jefferson relates, is that Wilkinson reported in November that "a confidential agent of Aaron Burr had been deputed to him, with communications partly written in cipher and partly oral, explaining his designs."

This is, of course, the letter and messenger that reached Wilkinson on the Sabine, the message that frightened Wilkinson, concentrated his mind and caused him, following his natural path of self-preservation, to make a quick truce with the Spanish army and return to New Orleans to denounce Burr, declare martial law, and pose as the defender of the Union. To a largely astonished Congress (and remember, this is a printed message, not a speech, so the third president is spared guffaws), Jefferson describes Wilkinson's actions, and Wilkinson's motives: "The general, with the honor of a soldier and fidelity of a good citizen, immediately dispatched a trusty officer to me with information of what had passed."

Jefferson has a last difficult bit of explaining to do. While Burr is still on the loose, Wilkinson arrests and sends to Washington City for trial several accomplices of Burr's. These arrests pose two legal problems: the defendants were seized under an unauthorized and certainly illegal state of martial law, and even if the arrests had been legal, the defendants have every right to a speedy trial before their peers in the territory or state where the alleged crime was committed.

Jefferson, in convoluted legalese, expresses a wish that the conspirators be rearrested, legally, when they arrive in the east. The Senate, on the following day, January 23, goes even further and passes a law suspending the writ of habeas corpus for three months—thus legalizing any arrests, including that of Burr, no matter by what authority or in which territory. Burr may be a failure as a revolutionary, but he is a great success at frightening the Senate, whose members suspend the constitution of the United States (and all the majesty of British law) with but a single dissenting vote.

Just three days later, with the calm that even a few hours' thought and a good night's sleep can bring, the House of Representatives defeats the Senate bill with vigor, 119 to 13.

The results are predictable now. Jefferson, the Congress, the conspirators themselves, know that they will all be released as soon as they appear before a magistrate. The only question is whether the arch-conspirator, Aaron Burr, will pay a penalty.

129

❧

January 28–February 7, 1807, Pike Invades Mexico

IT IS TIME to recall to mind a member of Pike's small party. Dr. Robinson is one of those drifting adventurers common to all frontiers, men who find themselves involved in dubious undertakings. He lives and dies a mystery man, but in the winter of 1806–1807 he is in the employ of General Wilkinson. His pretext for being with Pike is that he needs to reach Santa Fe in order to collect a debt. This is not much of a pretext if Pike is actually just exploring the headwaters of the Arkansas and Red Rivers.

There are two possible reasons (and both may be true) that Wilkinson sends Robinson along with the lieutenant's squad. As a civilian, Robinson may escape imprisonment when, and if, Pike's unit is taken into custody. In that sense he is a deliberate redundancy, a backup if Pike is on a spying mission and cannot complete it. And Robinson, who does practice medicine and has some formal education, may be a better observer than Pike, who for all his enthusiasm, sometimes neglects to examine his surroundings with much care or insight.

Robinson's informal role on the expedition is as Pike's companion and comrade-in-arms. He and Pike slay the buffalo that are keeping the party alive. Robinson is one of the small group that goes mountain climbing. Pike and Robinson are the pair who attempt to waylay the Pawnee braves. On the seventh of February, Robinson's actions provide the best understanding of what Pike is up to.

The day after Pike lectures Private Brown, the healthy members of the party cross the Sangre de Cristo Mountains, a grueling march of some 3,000 feet of vertical climb and more than twenty miles of trail through, as Pike's journal says, "snows, some three feet deep." He

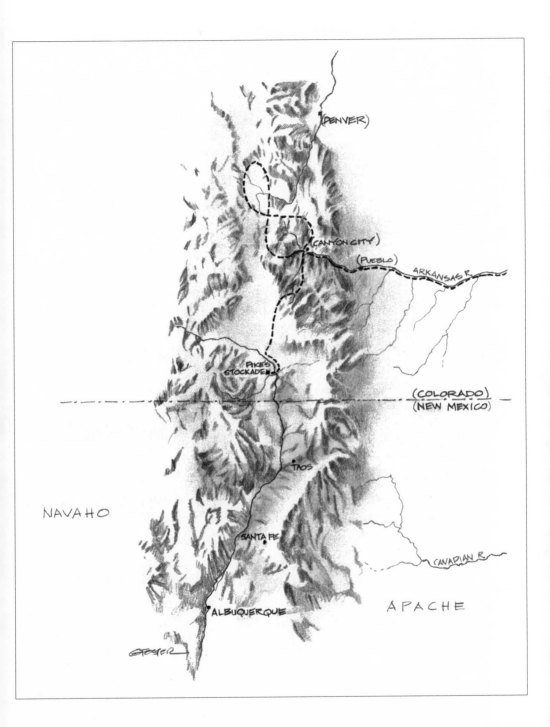

PIKE TRESPASSES INTO NEW MEXICO,
FEBRUARY 1807

crosses the watershed of the Sangres and descends into the Rio Grande valley along "a brook which led west, which I followed down, and shortly came to a small run, running west, which we hailed with fervency as the waters of the Red River." There is no way of telling whether the men believe it is the Red; the mutinous remarks suggest that at least Private Brown knew the realities. It is conceivable, barely, that Pike believes it is the Red. You will recall that in December he leaves the Arkansas, scrambles along the Front Range of the Rockies (and goes on his mountain-climbing detour) for more than a month, heading generally west, and then follows a river that turns out to be the same old Arkansas. If the Arkansas can hide behind a mountain range before running east to the Mississippi, perhaps the Red can do the same.

More likely, and Pike will lie in his journals as easily as the next man, he manages to convince the men that this river, like the Arkansas they know too well, will cut back east through the "Spanish Mountains" and be the Red River, and lead them home.

Assume for a moment that everyone agrees that this Rio Grande is really the Red, or the "Rio Colorado" of Texas, as it is known then. Pike takes the final step. He crosses the Rio Grande and ascends a tributary that enters the river from the southwest. In short, even if it is the Red, he has crossed into undoubted, undisputed Spanish territory. If it is the Rio Grande, of course, he has long since trespassed.

On the sixth of February, he and eight of his men construct a small wooden fort, surrounded with pointed logs facing outward, a *"frisee"* he writes in his journal, using his newly acquired French to good effect. "Thus fortified," he claims, "I should not have had the least hesitation of putting the 100 Spanish horse at defiance until the first or second night, and then to have made our escape under cover of the darkness— or made a sally and dispersed them when [they were] resting under a full confidence of our being panic struck by their numbers and force." In other words, on the sixth, he expects to be attacked by the Spanish dragoons for invading their country, the province of New Mexico of the Empire of Spain.

On Saturday, the seventh of February, Pike sends a detachment back across the Sangres to collect the "baggage left with the frozen lads, and to see if they were yet able to come on. This detachment left me with four men only, two of which had their feet frozen." If you are wondering how an officer and four men are going to hold off 100 dragoons, you are doing what Pike wants. He is beginning to make an excuse for his future behavior, to make you forget the boasts of the day before, the willingness to "put the 100 Spanish horse at defiance." History is not always written by the victors; mere survivors can do the same.

And it is on this day that he cuts his military strength to four men (including the "two of which had their feet frozen"). He bids adieu to Dr. Robinson, who sets off for Santa Fe. Pike has a map of Mexico. It shows the Red River east of the Sangres and the Rio Grande west, where it is, and it shows Santa Fe accurately on the Rio Grande. Dr. Robinson sets off for Santa Fe by walking straight down the bank of the stream "which we hailed with fervency as the waters of the Red River" on January 28. It is purely and simply the case, given the departure of Dr. Robinson down the river, that both he and Pike are quite sure they are camped on a tributary of the Rio Grande and that their stockade, by anyone's definition, is in the Spanish province of New Mexico. Dr. Robinson is a hardy soul, but only a madman could set out for Santa Fe, without food or a map, if that hardy soul doesn't know full well he is on the Rio Grande.

Lies, as police detectives know, are so much more difficult to tell than the truth. Pike writes that he and Robinson cooked up the debt-collection story "when on the frontier . . . making this claim a pretext for Robinson to visit Santa Fe." This does not account for the fact that Robinson is really carrying papers related to the debt; he brought them from St. Louis, weeks before Pike's "pretext." Pike is presumably being more honest when he writes: "Our views were to gain a knowledge of the country, the prospect of trade, force, etc., whilst, at the same time, our treaties with Spain guaranteed [Robinson] the right to pursue his claim."

The bottom line, as it were, will be written in a few months by the governor general of all New Spain to the Spanish ambassador to Washington, the Marquis de Casa y Yrujo: "In everything about which Pike gave information (both by word of mouth and in writing)," writes the honorable Nemesio Salcedo, "he has contradicted himself, not telling the truth about anything."

As a footnote to Salcedo's remarks, which you may regard as biased, attention must be paid to the map Pike published of his "voyage" to Santa Fe. It is in large part a copy of a map drawn by the great explorer of the Americas, the Baron von Humboldt. Pike's copying is overt in the smallest details, including his marking the area near the Colorado-Kansas border as "Immense Plains used as Pasturage by the Cibolas," which is a bad translation of the same mark on the same place on Humboldt's map: *"Plaines immense ou paissent les Bisons."* Where the buffalo graze makes more sense than where the Cibolas graze, as the Cibolas are the mythical Indians of the Seven Cities of Gold long sought by Spanish explorers. Humboldt's map does have the word *Cibolas* near the comment on the bison (or buffalo).

Baron von Humboldt had loaned a hand-drawn copy of his map to Thomas Jefferson, asking the president to keep it confidential until Humboldt could publish it (which he did in 1810, in Paris). This is the same manuscript map that General Wilkinson "borrowed" before a meeting with Aaron Burr to discuss the march on Mexico. Wilkinson obviously had a copy made and gave that to Pike.

Pike uses the map, by the way, to make a boast that he never had the gall to make in his printed journals. At the very top of the map, in tiny print, it says "Territory explored by a detachment of troops commanded by Captain Pike." The little dotted line of the detachment's route reaches a river, right at the top margin of the map, called "Rio del Piedro Amarillo del Missoure."

Pike is claiming that *he* explored the Yellowstone headwaters. To paraphrase Salcedo, in everything that Pike claims, by word of mouth or in writing or in drawing a map, he is not telling the truth about anything.

130

❧

February 10, 1807, The Mandan Chief in Philadelphia

JEFFERSON'S LINKS with Philadelphia are many and strong. The American Philosophical Society is there, and a member, the painter Charles Willson Peale, runs the small museum and zoo that displays some of the curiosities of the Philosophical Society alongside Peale's personal collection.

But the subject of Peale's letter of February 10 to Jefferson is more delicate. Sheheke, the Mandan chief, and others sent by Lewis to the Great Father are setting out for St. Louis at the conclusion of their tour of the eastern cities. This letter is the first sign of trouble with Sheheke, who will be a great burden to Meriwether Lewis before the year is out.

"In a conversation with a *friend* this morning," Peale writes, "as the Indians were leaving this city, he said they were sadly diseased; they had been with the women of bad fame in the lower part of the town and contracted the venereal disease.

"I have had no opportunity to enquire for the facts of this report," Peale continues, "however, I think it my duty to give you this notice, with the idea that you will give orders for their cure before their departure."

It is understandable that Jefferson, with the Burr conspiracy still unchecked (as far as he is aware) pays no attention (as far as we can tell from the historical record) to the medical needs of Sheheke and the other chiefs. Peale, of course, cannot anticipate Jefferson's lack of interest, and he closes his letter with a postscript:

"If it is known to those who have had the care of these Indians that I have given you this notice, they may be offended with me, and my situation requires me to make friends."

The problem with Sheheke is not curing him of whichever venereal disease he has, it is getting him home in any condition. The Teton Sioux control the banks of the Missouri just downstream from the Mandan villages, and as everyone in the party remembers, when the Corps of Discovery passed by them in the fall of 1806, oaths and curses and imprecations and threats of violence filled the air between the boats and mounted Sioux on the bluffs above the river. By the end of April, Meriwether Lewis will be worrying about how to get Sheheke and his family past the Sioux.

131

February 17, 1807, Pike Is Merciful

AT HIS DIMINUTIVE FORT on the Conejos River, Pike is visited by two Spanish-speaking men, a European, and a "civilized Indian." They profess some curiosity about the small round fort he is building, all set about with pointed tree trunks. Pike lies to them, saying he is on his way down the Red River to Natchitoches near the Texas-Louisiana border. They depart bemused, after accepting "a few trifling presents, with which," Pike writes, "they seemed highly delighted."

What follows now is Pike's account of his own emotions, and it is difficult to believe. As Pike's journals are full of half-truths, the reader may wonder if this memory of his is even remotely accurate. Don't worry. The point is not whether what he writes is true. What matters is that he thinks it *ought* to be true; it is the way an officer and a gentleman should behave.

> *After their departure, we commenced working at our little fort, as I thought it probable the governor might dispute my right*

to descend the Red river, and send out Indians, or some light party to attack us. I therefore determined to be as much prepared to receive them as possible.

This evening the corporal and three of the men arrived, who had been sent back to the camp of the frozen lads. They informed me that two men would arrive the next day; one of which was Menaugh, who had been left alone on the 27th January, but that the other two, Dougherty and Sparks, were unable to come.

They said that they [the first two men with frozen feet were left behind more than three weeks earlier] had hailed them with tears of joy, and were in despair when they again left them, with the chance of never seeing them more. They sent on to me some of the bones taken out of their feet, and conjured me by all that was sacred, not to leave them to perish far from the civilized world.

Ah! little did they know my heart, if they could suspect me of conduct so ungenerous. No! Before they should be left, I would for months have carried the end of a litter, in order to secure them the happiness of once more seeing their native homes and being received in the bosom of a grateful country.

What they suspect him of, most certainly, is continuing to behave with the same cavalier disregard that he has shown for the entire journey. They are proof themselves that he is capable of stranding the entire party on the Plains in the middle of winter. They recall that he is wont to go mountain climbing on a lark and spend more than a month looking for a superior Spanish force in order to start a conflict. He has brought them into a high plains winter without food, transportation, or adequate clothing. And just before leaving the cripples behind, Pike tells his men that the Red River is on the other side of the "Spanish Mountains." They know better, and these aspects of Pike's character make Dougherty and Sparks understandably nervous.

They are rescued, still picking at the mortifying flesh of their feet, in a week's time. Two men travel from the Conejos back to the

Arkansas River to pick up the horses which, too lame to travel, are recovering there. Tied to their mounts' backs, the crippled men cross the Sangre de Cristos on February 27 or 28. By the time they get to the fort on the Conejos, Pike's war with Spain is over.

132

❧

February 20, 1807, Burr in Captivity

CONTEMPORARIES OF BURR often remark on the compelling nature of his gaze. It certainly convinced untold numbers of women to open their hearts to him, to put it politely. It is a piercing and hypnotic pair of eyes, perfect for not only the seduction of women but for the traducing of a jury's best judgment or a patriot's better instincts. It is felt by the object of Burr's intense focus, but that bifocal aspect is not caught in his more youthful portraits. They are done either in profile or in the style of the heroic portrait, with Burr looking off toward some unseen object out of the frame of the painting. We have only a single full-frontal picture of him, one where his eyes bore into the viewer. Unfortunately, he is an old man in that painting. The seductiveness of his more youthful gaze is imaginable, but now marred by a droopiness of both the upper and lower lids.

Burr, released by the grand jury in Mississippi just as he was in Kentucky and for the same reason, lack of witnesses, is still not safe. He can be charged again, and perhaps a new jury will see that he is, in fact, an agent of sedition at least, and probably worthy of a trial for treason. And that is only the threat of a civil court. Burr knows that General Wilkinson, who has betrayed and abandoned him, is perfectly capable of sending a military unit to find him, bring him to trial at a military court in New Orleans, and hang him. Indeed, although Burr does not know it at the time, Wilkinson has sent a half-dozen chosen soldiers, dressed in civilian clothes, to seize Burr and drag him to New Orleans.

Although Burr merely suspects that Wilkinson's agents are out to capture him, the day he is released by the Natchez grand jury he disappears, not to be seen again by the authorities for two weeks. In that fortnight, the governor of Mississippi decides, after months of tolerating Burr and believing his protestations of innocence, that the colonel must be taken into custody. By the second week in February, every man's hand is against him.

With a few friends, Burr travels south, into the part of Mississippi territory which will become Alabama; that is, he travels toward present Mobile, then in the disputed Spanish province of West Florida. He is up to one of two things, escaping to Europe, or, more romantically, leading an army against Mobile, capturing West Florida, and retrieving some part of his great scheme to take all Mexico. This is unlikely. He is just fleeing; he is not dressed for the part of a conquering hero. The talk of taking the Floridas is just talk, a way of ingratiating himself with the settlers of the Tombigbee River valley, men who hate the Spanish who control their access to one sea.

Burr is wearing a long coat that goes down to the stirrups of his horse. He is playing the part of a poor wanderer. His two travel essentials, a tin cup and a large knife, are carried visibly, one tied to each end of a tattered piece of cord he wears around his neck like a shawl. (Inns in the rural south do not provide guests with drinking glasses or silverware.) Burr wears a large, wide-brimmed dirty hat that was once white. It is pulled down over his considerable forehead all the way to his eyebrows.

On the eighteenth of February, while passing through the village of Wakefield, in what is today Alabama, Burr and his companion stop and ask for directions to a gentleman's house. A lawyer, one Nicholas Perkins, wonders why such disreputable-looking men would be seeking the house of a wealthy local landowner. He stoops a little, and

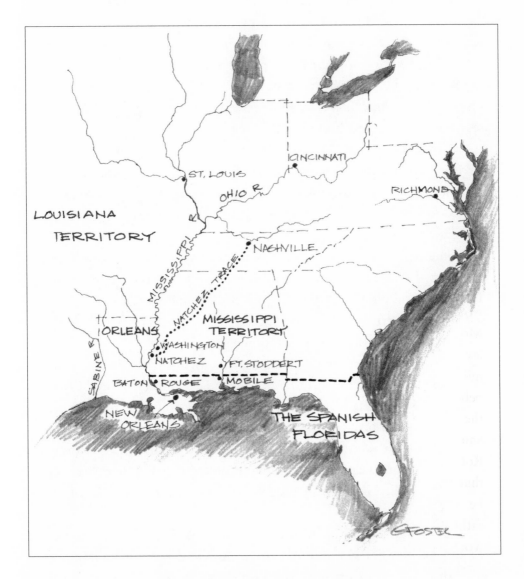

THE END OF THE BURR CONSPIRACY,
OCTOBER 1806 TO JANUARY 1807

peers under the floppy brim of the white hat, and is caught short by an astonishing piercing gaze. He has never seen Aaron Burr, but he has heard about the eyes. Within a few days, at Nicholas Perkins's behest, the United States Army takes Aaron Burr into custody. Burr is still wearing the hat, the long coat, and the knife and cup about his neck. He is easily identified.

133

February 26–March 6, 1807,

Pike Pretends He Is Lost

WHERE PIKE builds his little fort on the Conejos River, just upstream from its confluence with the Rio Grande, the Sangre de Cristo Mountains loom up on the eastern horizon. To the west, the flat valley of the Rio Grande stretches out to a distant horizon, seventy or so miles to the snowcapped peaks of the San Juans. If Pike sincerely believes that he is on the Red River, then the Rio Grande must be on the other side of those faraway mountains to the west, and so Taos and Santa Fe must be beyond those peaks we call the San Juans. Dr. Robinson, when he left Pike's fort, walked due south, down the river that truly is the Rio Grande, heading straight for Taos and on to Santa Fe. Robinson and Pike both know that it is a reasonable march on rather level ground to Santa Fe. Not even Pike, foolhardy as he is, would start out for a Santa Fe on the far side of those distant, shimmering peaks. The joke is getting stale.

On February 26, fifty Spanish dragoons and fifty mounted New Mexican militiamen ride up to the polygonal fort on the Conejos. They bring two French-speaking citizens with them. The men who found Pike and his half-built fort back in the first week of February have reported that Pike does not speak Spanish. None of the New Mexican soldiers speak English. They very sensibly decide to try French as a medium.

Pike does have a schoolbook command of French (he carries a grammar and dictionary with him), and somehow, in an apparently friendly discussion with pauses for looking up words, it is agreed that he will go down to Santa Fe, the capital of New Mexico, with the Spanish troops. He explains that some of his men are being brought over the mountains, and that they are lame from frostbite. The Spanish leave a detail at the fort to escort the stragglers to Santa Fe when they arrive. The march to Santa Fe passes a few pueblos, probably including Taos, and perhaps the San Juan and Nambe pueblos if the party keeps to the eastern, Santa Fe side of the river. The Pueblo Indians, Pike recalls, are extremely curious about the white men, who seem to have very bad clothing, no proper shoes, and no hats. Pike says they ask if he comes from a place with towns, or do they live in the wild, like those uncivilized Plains Indians? He is mortified at his appearance; it is not befitting his rank and stature, and one of the first requests he makes of his captors is a loan of cash to buy some respectable clothing.

On the third of March, Pike is brought before the governor of New Mexico, Joaquin de Real Alencaster, and this dialogue takes place:

> You come to reconnoiter our country, do you?
> *I marched to reconnoiter our own.*
>
> In what character are you?
> *In my proper character, as an officer of the United States Army.*

Alencaster is a provincial governor but no fool. He allows Pike's men the freedom of Santa Fe, has them followed, and then interrogates anyone with whom they speak. There are a few American English-speakers in Santa Fe, and one of them reports that Pike has come all this way to expedite an invasion of Mexico by General Wilkinson. One of the men, speaking directly to the governor, says that Pike expects to be liberated by force if he is captured. Alencaster reports all this to the governor general of New Spain in Chihuahua, Nemesio Salcedo.

It is Alencaster's report that provokes, as we have noted, Salcedo to write that "in everything about which Pike gave information (both by word of mouth and in writing) he has contradicted himself, not telling the truth about anything."

For someone who has invaded Mexico (putting the little fort on the western side of the Rio Grande is a way of ensuring that he cannot be anywhere but in Spanish territory) and continues to lie about it, and lie clumsily, Pike is treated with remarkable consideration by the Spanish. He is loaned money, his men are fed and clothed. He is allowed to leave Santa Fe for Chihuahua under guard, but still carrying his (unloaded) arms. He is an escorted guest, not a prisoner. There are two possibilities that can explain this excess of courtesy. Both may be operative. He is Wilkinson's man, and Wilkinson is in good repute with the Spanish, back on their payroll and behaving peacefully. They may take the possibility of a forceful liberation of Pike seriously. The last thing they want is another American military force crossing the no-man's-land of the high prairie now occupied by no one but the Indians. That grassy wilderness is an important buffer for New Mexico. For either or both reasons, Pike can have no complaints about his voyage home. It is a long journey, straight south to Chihuahua, and then northeast to Nacogdoches. The Mexicans are not delaying Pike's return; it is just that the country between the Santa Fe to Chihuahua road and the Chihuahua to Nacogdoches road is a howling wilderness.

134

❧

March 14, 1807, Lewis Defends His Turf

THE LAST SOLDIER to actually join the Lewis and Clark expedition, Robert Frazier, accompanies Lewis to Washington City and Philadelphia. He may have been invited to the celebratory dinner; we know not. Frazier's enlistment in the Corps of Discovery came in the winter of 1804–1805, when he replaced a deserter, Moses Reed, on the company's roster.

Reed had attempted to desert before the party reached the Mandan villages in the fall of 1804. He was punished, assigned to laboring duties, and sent back to St. Louis in the spring, along with the mildly mutinous private Newman, the one who wanted to bring one of the willing Sioux women along for the ride. That same boat, in the spring of 1805, also carried the magpie and the prairie dog.

Frazier arrives in Washington with a journal he has kept from the journey and believes that he has the captains' permission to publish it. When Lewis hears of the project, he is nearly distraught, and writes a letter to the newspapers, addressed "To the Public." He warns of "spurious publications now preparing for the press on the subject of *my* late tour to the Pacific Ocean." He wishes to "teach the public to be on guard" against these works. Lewis is nothing if not revealing of his motives. The unauthorized journal would, he writes,

> *depreciate the worth of the work which I am myself preparing for publication before it can possibly appear, as much time, labor, and expense are absolutely necessary in order to do justice. . . . I think it is my duty to declare that Robert Frazier, who was only a pri-*

vate on this expedition, is entirely unacquainted with celestial observations, mineralogy, botany, or zoology, and therefore cannot possibly give any accurate information on those subjects. . . . The whole which can be expected from his journal is merely a limited detail of our daily transactions.

Frazier's journal disappears from view. Even the manuscript evaporates. However, Sergeant Patrick Gass also has a journal and has a contract with a certain David M'Keehan to have his account published. It is not surprising that Gass would have a journal. He was a respected noncommissioned officer when Lewis chose him for the expedition and a classic "top kick," capable of writing his own reports. Gass's journal is published in this year, but not without M'Keehan taking the opportunity to make perfectly horrid fun of Lewis. This sort of rhetoric, which is about to be quoted, is by the way entirely normal for the era. Freedom of the press is so valued, and the morals of the country so unsettled, that the worst sort of things can be said in print, things that would result in a thrashing if said to anyone's face. M'Keehan takes Lewis's letter referring to Frazier's journal and returns the favor at considerable length, here greatly reduced, but with most of the bile intact:

Who would have thought that after so much liberality shown by the country, your Excellency would have been found contending with the poor fellows, who for their small pittance were equally exposed with yourself to the toils and dangers attending the expedition.

The publication of the journal of Mr. Gass I expect will have the following good effects; first, it may save many the trouble of purchasing your three volumes and map, by affording them at a cheap rate, a plain and satisfactory account of the tour; in the second place, it will so depreciate the worth of your work that there may be a chance of getting it at a reasonable price; and in the third place, as it will contain plain matter of fact, it may deter you from swelling your work with such tales of wonder as have sometimes issued from the Ten-Mile-Square. [That would be Washington City, now the District of Columbia.]

I must pass over the unhappy affair with the Indians on the plains of Maria's River, and all that affecting one of your own posteriors, and conclude with congratulating you that Mr. Gass's Journal did not fall into the hands of some wag, who might have insinuated that your wound was not accidental, but that it was the consequence of design—that the young hero might not return without more scars (if not honorable, near the place of honor) to excite the curiosity and compassion of some favorite widow Wadman, who might have been languishing during his absence. In what a ludicrous situation he might have placed the young hero with his point of honor just past the point of a rock with Crusatte taking aim! Perhaps there will be a representation in the plates embellishing your second volume!

The "widow Wadman" is a character in Laurence Sterne's *Tristram Shandy*. She's after a second husband and has her eye on Tristram's Uncle Toby. It is a cruel, pointed joke. Uncle Toby suffers from a mysterious war wound and is almost completely unintelligible when he speaks. The suggestion that Lewis deliberately took a slug in his buttocks is ludicrous, but typical of the journalism of the day. Meriwether Lewis, unfortunately, does not have an easy manner or a sense of humor, and a letter like this hurts him to the core.

135

⚜

March 5, 1807, Pike Buys a Souvenir

THE ONE THING Lieutenant Pike has neglected on his voyage is acquiring some kind of present for the president. He is jealously aware of the Lewis and Clark Expedition's materials, brought down from the Mandans in the spring of 1805, including the animal skins, and particularly the live animals—the prairie dog and the magpie. On the march from Santa Fe to Albuquerque, an opportunity presents itself, and Pike, always quick to react, realizes he is looking at a remarkable gift for Jefferson.

Somewhere along the way, probably at San Juan pueblo, Pike spies an Indian with two baby animals. They are siblings, two grizzly bear cubs taken, he understands, on the Continental Divide, that is, in the San Juan Mountains.

Recalling the moment in a letter to Jefferson, Pike says "I conceived the idea of bringing them to the United States for the Excellency, although then more than 1,600 miles from our frontier post. I purchased them of the Savage, and for three or four days made my men carry them on horseback."

In a rare moment of biological insight, Pike realizes these are not ordinary black bears but a new species; they must be grizzlies. In a less rare moment of puffery, he claims to be familiar with the animal: "Whilst in the mountains we sometimes discovered them at a distance, but in no instance was ever able to come up with one . . . [this] induces me to believe they seldom or ever attack a man unprovoked."

How odd, you may think, recalling the experience of Lewis and Clark with more than a dozen vicious grizzly bears. One of the differences is that Pike is talking about a few weeks in the mountains at a time when grizzly bears, if that indeed is what he saw (and he makes no mention of them in his journals), are beginning to hibernate. Operating with little information, but with his usual blithe confidence, Pike instructs the president on the proper rearing of a grizzly bear.

The cubs, small and weaned by necessity "became extremely docile when at liberty, following my men like dogs through our camps, small villages, and the forts where we halted, and when well supplied with sustenance would play like young puppies with each other and the soldiers." On the trek, however, when bounced about in their cages on horseback and going without food or water in the Mexican sun, "they would worry and tear each other until nature was exhausted, and they could neither fight nor hallo any longer." Pike advises Jefferson to give them a large space and keep them well fed: "I am nearly convinced that they will harmonize and become much more docile than if chained and confined asunder."

Jefferson takes his advice when the bears arrive, and shares his opinion about the prospect of raising a friendly grizzly bear with Charles Willson Peale:

> *I put them together while here [in Washington] in a place 10 feet square. For the first day they worried one another very much with play, but after that they played at times, but were extremely happy together. When separated & put into their small cage again, one became almost furious. Indeed one is much crosser than the other, but I do not think they have any idea of hurting anyone. They know no benefactor but man.*

That is an interesting idea, a faith that nurture, in the modern dichotomy, will prevail over nature. The Great Father is indeed the all-loving, all-encouraging parent, not only to the Indian but to the bear. And the phrase "no benefactor but man" is more than a statement about captive bears. The Negro, or the Indian, is a perpetual child to Jefferson (and to every known author, politician, or preacher of his time), destined never to grow into, literally, manhood. Of course, if you are a very bad child (or a very bad bear), there is the simple solution, as Jefferson said to the assembled chiefs, that the superior white men are also "all *gun-men.*"

136

March 5–25, 1807, The Transit of Burr

BURR, in captivity at Fort Stoddert, Mississippi Territory, may be the most popular man in town. This military post on the Tombigbee River is on the way to Spanish West Florida. It is recently built in that part of Mississippi Territory that will be set off—after West Florida is grabbed from Spain during the War of 1812—as the state of Alabama. In 1807, the Spanish in Florida stand between the eastern Mississippi settlers and the sea, a choke point to imagined yet unrealized wealth from trade in agricultural staples. If Burr were a free man asking the population of southeastern Mississippi to join him in attacking Florida, it is altogether likely he could raise a small army overnight. Edmund Gaines, the young lieutenant in charge of the fort, has already had one prisoner escape, a confederate of Burr's, Colonel Robert Ashley, who is known to be staying in town and talking up Burr's character and good intentions. Burr is playing chess with the local judge's daughter, another bad sign. She visits him in the stockade. It is all very decorous, but Burr's animal charm on women is undiminished by his incarceration. Gaines also knows that Burr is trying to bribe his guards, an even worse sign. And some local layabouts are talking about storming the brig and setting Colonel Burr free.

On the fifth of March, without waiting for specific orders, Lieutenant Gaines hires Nicholas Perkins, the lawyer who identified

Burr, to take Burr to the nearest eastern town, Fredericksburg, Virginia, which is just across the Potomac River and downstream from the Ten-Mile-Square of the nation's capital. With the help of a military guard of eight picked men, Perkins takes Burr east, through Indian country as wild and unpredictable (the Cherokees and Creeks are still unsubdued) as anything seen by Pike on his way to Santa Fe. When they reach civilization, in the shape of the hamlet of Chester, South Carolina, Burr makes his bid for freedom.

Given the wildness of the territory they traverse, Burr has been allowed to carry his pistols and the same large knife he wore on a rope around his neck when disguised as a traveling sailor. In Chester, he leaps from his horse and, brandishing those pistols, tells some surprised young loiterers that he is the famous patriot Colonel Burr and pleads with them to take him before a civil magistrate for he is wrongfully charged and he is unlawfully held. While the rubes gape, the soldiers disarm Burr, pick him up bodily (not difficult, given his size), sit him back on his horse and tell him to shut up.

It is not a foolish request that Burr makes, in all truth. Burr is being transported from Mississippi, where, if he is an accused criminal, he ought to be tried in court. A magistrate might very well release him. After all, Burr is the survivor of two indictments, released by grand juries in Kentucky and Mississippi without a trial. Why not again?

137

May 1807, The Mandan Can't Go Home

ENSIGN NATHANIEL PRYOR, a newly minted officer (he is the Sergeant Pryor of the Lewis and Clark expedition), is charged with returning

Sheheke, the Mandan chief, to his village. This is, of course, the mildly diseased Sheheke, victim of the ladies of the night in Philadelphia. It seems simple enough, a couple of dozen soldiers and boatmen in two keelboats will sail and pole up the Missouri, drop off Sheheke and his family, and slide back down the river.

Unfortunately, there are unfriendly Indians along the way. Pryor might expect trouble from the nomadic Brule Sioux, given the shouting match between the party and the tribe on their way down the river in 1806. He discovers, in the summer of 1807, that it is the Arikaras, who live on the river year-round, that are the problem. The Sioux may be meaner when they visit the Missouri, but the Arikaras live there. The reader will remember them as the tribe that did not drink, the ones who chided Lewis for offering them whisky, a substance that only made men stupid. The Arikaras always demanded a payment, a bribe or a toll, of the few traders who went up the Missouri to the Mandans. The Corps of Discovery, with its cannon and heavily armed men, was not shaken down in the summer of 1804, and the expedition was still cheerfully giving presents to the Indians they encountered. But Pryor's little fleet carrying Sheheke home is attacked when it tries to pass the Arikara's territory without paying tribute. After a gunfight, with a few dead and a man about to lose a leg, Pryor turns around. It will be years before Sheheke goes home.

Oddly, the best thing that comes out of the first attempt to return Sheheke is the amputation of that leg. It is the limb of Private George Shannon, another veteran of the Lewis and Clark expedition. Shannon is one of the wild young men from Kentucky who became the stalwart adventurers of the expedition. Losing his leg, however, turns him from adventuring to the study of law. Living on a government disability pension, he becomes a lawyer, and before his peaceful death in 1836, serves as U.S. senator from Missouri. He is the single enlisted member of the Corps of Discovery to find success in civilian, and civilized, life.

The worst thing about the failure of Lieutenant Pryor's foray is that Meriwether Lewis, when he returns to St. Louis in the summer of 1808, will make a serious attempt to do two things—raise a small army of volunteers and fur traders to return the Mandan to his people and use that trip as the beginning of a fur-trapping and fur-trading venture on the upper Missouri. The biggest mistake of that mission will be that Governor Lewis will spend territorial funds on presents with which to bribe the Indians who live along the river between St. Louis and the Mandan villages. He will buy the presents from his partner in the fur-trading venture, Pierre Choteau. It will look like a conflict of interest, and from the summer of 1808 until Lewis's death, various bean-counting bureaucrats will hound him for his mistakes.

But this is the summer of 1807, and all is right with the world in general and the Louisiana Purchase in particular. Lewis is in Washington and Philadelphia, garnering praise wherever he goes. William Clark is in Virginia, wooing, wedding, and impregnating his cousin Julia (known to him familiarly as Judith) Hancock, namesake of Judith River, a tributary of the Missouri in Montana. Lieutenant Pike is in custody in Mexico, marching circuitously home from Santa Fe. Aaron Burr is in custody, and the conspiracy is reduced from a threat to a curiosity.

138

August 31 and September 14, 1807,

Burr Wins One, and Burr Walks

THE FEDERAL COURT SYSTEM in 1807 is so small it isn't even a system. When a judge is needed to try Aaron Burr, the only available candidates are members of the Supreme Court. The Chief Justice, the much-esteemed-by-history John Marshall, chooses himself to hear the case.

The trial of Burr ends up in two parts. The first charge considered is the high crime of treason (attempting by arms to separate the west, amounting to levying war against the United States). The second indictment is for the high misdemeanor of beginning, on American soil, a war against a "sovereign nation" with which the United States is a peace, that is, marching on Spain's Mexico.

What Burr has going for him is a pervasive sentiment in the United States that has nothing particularly to do with his case. At the turn of the nineteenth century, Americans still have an enormous distaste for Britain's history of using treason as a kind of catch-all capital crime to remove political opponents permanently. Even wishing the king dead was treason in Britain. Treason, of course, is what the British accused the Americans of doing when the War of Independence began. That is what lies directly behind Benjamin Franklin's admonition to the signers of the Declaration of Independence: "If we do not hang together, we will all hang separately." Mr. Franklin was not joking or exaggerating.

To prevent the charge of treason from being liberally applied to political dissidents, the Constitution defines making war on the United States as an overt act. Conspiring is not illegal, planning is not illegal, even assembling to make war may not be illegal. The prosecution must prove two separate actions to constitute the crime. First, they must prove the defendant's intent to overthrow the government. Second, they must prove an overt act that follows upon the intent. Making war means marching, to put it simply, against some post or office or official of the United States. The Constitution also requires that the intent, as manifested in speech or written word, and the overt act itself must be witnessed by, and testified to by, two citizens. The distaste of the founders for treason in the British tradition is so profound that this is the only criminal act defined in the Constitution, and the purpose of the framers in being this specific was to limit the state's power to convict. The closest the government can come to an overt act by Aaron Burr is the assembling, and sailing, of the armed gunboats from Blennerhasset Island on the Ohio River. And Burr was not present.

Now, he can be convicted if the principals and participants at

Blennerhasset Island are convicted first. Then he would be an accessory. But no act of war is proven or even alleged against the men on the armed boats. And there aren't two witnesses to claim Burr intended to make war upon the nation.

The problem is that everyone knows that Burr intended to make war upon his country. So, to move from that reality (guilty as hell) to the legal reality (not provably guilty) troubles the mind of Chief Justice Marshall. He writes an impenetrable decision that takes over three hours to read and essentially, finally, says that Burr cannot be *proved* a traitor. On September 1, the next day, the government abandons its case on treason. This leaves the high misdemeanor of starting a war with Spain.

That trial begins on September 9, and on September 14, Justice Marshall makes a ruling on evidence that simply cuts the trial off at the knees. It came down to the basic problem: Burr is entitled to a trial in the district where the alleged crime occurred, but he is on trial in Virginia, not Kentucky or Ohio or Mississippi. Marshall rules that the court would hear "any testimony showing that the accused performed within the district [that is, the district of the trial] any one of the acts charged in the indictment." On the following day, September 15, the prosecution gives up, the jury meets, and Burr is declared not guilty.

Burr and the court think that is the end of it, but the administration has one last attempt at jailing, if not hanging, the colonel. They move to have him shipped back to the west, to stand trial in Ohio, near where the armada assembled. Justice Marshall hears two weeks of testimony on that petition, and on October 20, rules once again that Burr is innocent of treason. Counting territorial and state courts (Mississippi and Ohio), this is the third time Burr beats the treason rap. Marshall does agree to send him and his alleged co-conspirators back to Ohio on the misdemeanor count. The allegation to be tried, in Marshall's words, is "preparing and providing the means for a military expedition against the territories of a foreign prince, with whom the United States were at peace." That is not a grammatical error. In Marshall's Federalist mind, the United States are not so united as to take the singular verb.

The bottom line? Burr, freed by the court pending his appearance in Ohio (not even bail was posted), goes into hiding, and around the time that his trial opens in Ohio he is on his way to England under an assumed name, but better dressed this time, not wearing a knife and a tin cup around his neck. He will eventually return to the United States and make a small living practicing law in New York City and in 1836 will die peacefully in what we would call today a "single residential occupancy hotel."

His tombstone in the college chapel grounds at Princeton only mentions his service in the Army of the Revolution and as vice president of the United States, 1801–1805. What else could it say? "Rascal" would be the kindest word one could use if an adjective is needed.

139

St. Louis, Summer of 1808

IT DOES INDEED appear that all is well with the world, and that still seems true in the summer of 1808. Meriwether Lewis is the governor of Missouri, William Clark is the Indian agent for the United States. Little Jean Baptiste Charbonneau, Clark's "Pompey," is living with Charbonneau and Sacagawea in St. Louis where Clark can see him. Clark arranges some make-work jobs for Charbonneau and continues to press his real desire for the boy, to adopt him, raise him as his own, white, child.

Pike is home safe, and well regarded by the public for his escapades in New Mexico. He is so popular that on more than one occasion, when General Wilkinson's reputation is sullied for his presumed role in the Burr conspiracy or for his illegal declaration of martial law in

New Orleans, Pike testifies to the excellent character of Wilkinson. By the summer of 1808, he is Captain Pike, and his military career is in the ascendant.

But here are some of the problems: the Mandan Sheheke is still in St. Louis; Meriwether Lewis hasn't even opened the journals, let alone started on the task of rewriting them for publication. York is getting "uppity"; he has the notion that loyalty and heroism on the expedition give him some special standing and he asks permission to marry. Clark has to thrash him soundly to get that idea out of his head.

And one more problem. Lewis is starting to drink and take drugs. The drink is whisky, the drug is opium. He's taking daily doses of opium-laced medicine for chills, fevers, and the blahs. At night, he puts himself to sleep with a double dose.

As anyone familiar with the symptoms of alcoholism can tell you, there are some subtle derangements of the mind that are not so visible as the blind staggers or as audible as a slurred tongue. One of them is grandiosity, or megalomania, or unrealistic expectations. Take your pick—it's all the same thing. Lewis puts almost all of his money in land speculations, essentially gambling, not investing. And then he imagines a truly grand scheme. It begins with the problem of returning Sheheke to his village. Lewis, reflecting on the failure of Ensign Pryor's attempt the previous summer, decides to go up the Missouri with overwhelming force. In addition to taking a few dozen soldiers up the river, Lewis will raise a small army of volunteers, as many as 150 gun-men, and break through the Arikara blockade. As soon as the Mandan is home, the regular army men will return to St. Louis and the volunteers will turn into a fur-trapping and trading company and continue on up the Missouri to the Rockies. Lewis knows that public funds will gratefully pay for the return of the Mandan (even President Jefferson finds time to fret about the delay), and it is Lewis's grand scheme to use the Mandan as an excuse to establish a great upper Missouri trading company. Pierre Choteau, a friend of Lewis's since he was organizing the expedition in the winter of 1803–1804, will run the trading company. William Clark will be a partner. Lewis seems incapable of recognizing the conflict of interest, but back in Washington at the War Department, this scheme only encourages the accountants to a greater scrutiny of Lewis's expenditures.

Nothing comes of the plan to return the Mandan in the summer of 1808. Lewis is having trouble organizing his life. The journals of the expedition remain unedited. He is losing receipts for his expenditures of public funds. He is ignoring letters from Washington. He seems not to be doing much more than getting through the day and sleeping all too soundly at night.

140

June 8, 1809,

Madness, All Madness: The Mandan and Lewis

THE SUMMER OF 1809 is surely the most difficult season in Meriwether Lewis's young life. The authorities in Washington City are disputing his bills to the government. If his extra expenses to return the Mandan are flat-out disapproved and he must pay the bills himself, he is ruined. Fellow bureaucrats in St. Louis are no help. Perhaps jealous of the governor, perhaps merely disliking Lewis for his increasingly unpleasant demeanor (there are few happy drunks outside of fiction), they seem to spread any bad news, any reprimands from Washington City, almost before Lewis reads the correspondence.

And then there is Sheheke, the hapless, clapped-up, homesick Mandan chief. He is to be returned at any cost, particularly if it is the cheap cost of Indian lives. Lewis's instructions to Pierre Choteau, the trader who is supposed to take Sheheke home, are bizarre to biographers of Lewis. They regard the plans as a sign of madness in Lewis, a prelude to his subsequent suicide.

Perhaps. Lewis is not at all fond of Indians. A reader can slog through several hundred pages of the journals of the expedition without finding many affectionate, understanding, or even tolerant remarks about most Indian tribes. Certainly Lewis is in a rage about the Arikaras stopping the return of Sheheke in 1808, and what he proposes to have done in the summer of 1809 is perfectly reasonable by Virginia planter standards. Lewis's father was a great Indian-killer; it came with the territory.

Lewis tells Choteau that, in addition to his 250 armed white civilians, he should engage at least 300 Sioux (always at some low level of war with the Arikaras). When they reach the Arikaras, Choteau will demand the delivery of any Arikara involved in the killing and wounding of the men in Ensign Pryor's party in the summer of 1808. If the Arikaras cannot supply the actual perpetrators, Choteau will take a number of Arikara equivalent to the number of men killed in 1808 and, in full view of the tribe, shoot them. If that doesn't do it, Choteau will make it clear to all the neighboring tribes that it is the desire of the Great Father that the Arikaras be wiped off the face of the prairie.

Choteau is a dutiful deputy. A few months later, ascending the river, he falls in with some of the Sioux. Their chiefs are acquaintances of Choteau from a visit to St. Louis, and they allow him safe passage up the Missouri. But that is all they allow. This is part of Choteau's account:

> Agreeably to my instructions, I attempted to avail myself of an auxiliary force of three hundred Sioux, to cooperate with the detachment against the [Arikaras] and was refused. They said one tribe ought not to countenance any attempt to destroy another, and if I still persisted in that resolution, myself and my party might be destroyed before we reached the Ricaras.

Choteau agrees, and bribes some Sioux war chiefs to accompany him to the Arikaras and help him persuade them to let the Mandan pass. Choteau's style of persuasion is fairly blunt: "I told them that their Great Father the President of the United States had sent me to conduct the Mandan chief to his village a second time." Reminding the Arikaras of their sins in the summer of 1808, Choteau adds that he has "orders to destroy your nation, but the chiefs of the Sioux and Mandan nations have united together and interceded for your pardon. At their particular request, I shall ground my arms, until new orders can be received from your Great Father who alone can pardon or destroy."

A considerable distribution of tobacco, powder, lead, and war paint among all the Indians, fully using up all the extra trade goods purchased by Meriwether Lewis for just such an emergency, resolves the several conflicts among the various tribes. Choteau tries to get the Mandan chief to distribute some of his considerable pile of goods, but Sheheke refuses. Those presents, he tells Choteau, are "all his own." Leaving the Arikaras unpunished, Choteau's party sails peacefully upriver to the Mandan-Hidatsa villages. So, after three years, and a trip to Washington City and the steamy docksides of Philadelphia, freighted down with tobacco, vermilion paint, and gunpowder, the Mandan is home.

141

October 11, 1809, Lewis Is Dead

BY THE TIME Governor Lewis departs St. Louis for the nation's capital on September 8, he is already taking leave of his senses. Not without some cause: He feels the crush of personal debt, compounded by the government's questioning of his public accounts; he has an extraordinary sense of failure in regard to the journals of the expedition, which he carries with him, still unopened. And there is the demon whisky, the devil opium, and his own mercurial nature, all conspiring to destroy him. He plans to descend the Mississippi to Natchez, and then travel overland, first along the Natchez Trace to Knoxville, Tennessee, and then up the Great Trading Road and the Shenandoah Valley Road to Baltimore and Washington City. These are "federal roads," and although ill-maintained, they are relatively safe, free of bandits, scalawags, and renegade Indians.

Lewis is in appalling condition when he leaves St. Louis, at once morose, angry, defensive, and outraged. William Clark is one of the last people he speaks to, although it is a few days after his last conversation that Lewis actually gathers up his belongings and starts downriver. These are probably days of drink, some opium for his malaria, and some more for his insomnia. William Clark writes his brother to this effect:

> *I have not spent such a day as yesterday for many years. . . . I took my leave of Governor Lewis who set out to Philadelphia to write our book (but more particularly to explain some matter between him and the government). Several of his bills have been protested, and his creditors all flocking in near the time of setting out distressed him much, which he expressed to me in such terms as to cause a sympathy which is not yet off. . . . If his mind had been at ease I should have parted cheerfully.*

According to sketchy reports, Lewis attempts suicide twice on the river, by what means we know not. On reaching Fort Pickering (now Memphis, Tennessee) he is taken into protective custody by the commandant, Captain Gilbert Russell. Lewis spends two weeks at Fort Pickering. He is deprived of his store of whisky but not, apparently, of his stash of opium pills. Seemingly recuperated and fit, he is allowed to leave, escorted by the Indian agent to the Chickasaw Nation, a Major James Neelly. They descend the river to Mississippi, pick up the Natchez Trace, and start overland toward Washington City. The party is separated on the Trace (some horses stray, and Neelly stays behind to recapture them). Lewis is allowed to go ahead alone, promising Neelly that he will stop and stay at the first house he meets. And Lewis does keep his word.

He stops at the house of a Mrs. Grinder, engages a place to stay (the floor of her log cabin), drinks a little whisky, eats a little food, and spends the afternoon and evening alternating—fugueing—between silence and barely comprehensible ranting. Mrs. Grinder will testify that she did not understand what he was talking about. Sometime in the night, he takes out two single-shot dueling pistols he is carrying and shoots himself in the head with one (a glancing blow that does not pierce his skull) and in the body with the other. Neither wound is immediately mortal.

Mrs. Grinder is too frightened to go to him until dawn, when she finds him busily engaged in bloodletting with his razor, slashing at his arms and legs. She recalls he said this: "I am no coward. But I am so strong [it is] so hard to die." But not impossible. When full morning light comes, Lewis is dead.

The odd circumstances of Lewis's death are grist for speculation, then and now: Mrs. Grinder not coming to his aid at the first shots in the night; someone evidently stealing some of his possessions, his watch turning up in New Orleans years later. To this day, conspiracy theorists imagine Lewis's death is a murder, and the silliest of these theorists are the ones who believe the contemporary Federalist papers, which hint darkly at some Republican plot. The very silliest accuse Jefferson.

Better it is to remember that no one who knew him was surprised. Clark famously writes to his brother Jonathan as soon as he hears the news: "I fear, O! I fear the weight of his mind has overcome him."

Thomas Jefferson, a private citizen when Lewis dies (succeeded by the fourth president, his Monticello neighbor, James Madison) will write a brief biography of Lewis intended for the first edition of *The Journals of Lewis and Clark*, published in 1814. The War of 1812 is raging when Jefferson pens his memorial, which accounts for some emphasis on Lewis as a military man in Jefferson's essay. It is fair to say that there is a certain coldness in the prose. But then, Jefferson lives and dies without much visible emotion. His biographical note concludes:

> *Governor Lewis had from early life been subject to hypochondriac affections. It was a constitutional disposition in all the nearer branches of the family of his name, and was more immediately inherited by him from his father. They had not however been so strong as to give uneasiness to his family. While he lived with me in Washington, I observed at times sensible depressions of mind, but knowing their constitutional source, I estimated their course by what I had seen in the family. During his western expedition the constant exertion which that required . . . suspended these distressing affections [or so Jefferson believed]; but after his establishment at St. Louis in sedentary occupations they returned upon him with redoubled vigor, and began seriously to alarm his friends. He was in a paroxysm of one of these when his affairs rendered it necessary for him to go to Washington. . . . About 3 o'clock in the night he did the deed which plunged his friends into affliction and deprived his country of one of her most valued citizens whose valor and intelligence would have been now employed in avenging the wrongs of his country and in emulating by land the splendid deeds which have honored her at sea.*

At about the time that Jefferson is writing these words, the War Department finally settles the accounts that caused so much of Lewis's "affliction." The government acknowledges that it owes Lewis's estate six hundred and thirty-six dollars and twenty-five cents and it accepts all his bills for the extra expense to return Sheheke to the Mandan villages.

Shortly after Lewis's accounts with the government are settled, Jefferson pens a note to William D. Meriwether, a cousin and the executor of Lewis's small estate: "I have some claim on Governor

Lewis's estate for monies furnished him some time before he set out on his Western expedition. . . . I mention it at present merely for information, and leave it to the convenience of the estate." The amount Jefferson so genteelly requests is not large: one hundred dollars and four cents, to be exact.

142

October 1808 (?), Night of the Grizzly Bear, Philadelphia

WITH LEWIS IN HIS GRAVE, there are just a few loose ends to be wrapped up. These include two grizzly bears, Zebulon Montgomery Pike, and a few members of the Corps of Discovery.

Sometime in the fall of 1808—the record is maddeningly incomplete in that particular detail—Lieutenant Pike's two grizzly bears come to a predictable and bad end. From the first, in spite of Jefferson's (and Pike's) assumption that all the grizzly bears need to become tame is a little human kindness, the bears are insufferable. As Jefferson writes to his daughter, Anne Randolph, within weeks of the bears arriving at Monticello: "These are too dangerous and troublesome for me to keep."

Within the month, certainly before Christmas 1807, the bears take up residence at the private museum and zoological park operated by Jefferson's good friend, Charles Willson Peale. They are not the first grizzlies in captivity. In 1803, a French-Canadian frontiersman gave a juvenile grizzly to Peale. By 1804, it was large enough to break out of its cage in the Pennsylvania statehouse. Peale, a gunman as well as an artist, shot it. You would think Peale could guess what would happen this time, but this is the Age of Reason, and these are the first bears to be raised by philosophers.

The Peale Museum, one of Philadelphia's premier tourist attractions, is situated within the confines of Philosophical Hall, the home of the American Philosophical Society, and within an adjoining wing of the Pennsylvania statehouse. The bears are a premium attraction, housed in a cage in the interior courtyard between Philosophical Hall and the statehouse.

This is the brief account of history, in regard to two animals now verging on three hundred pounds in weight and looking much like the bears of one's worst dreams:

> *One night the creature broke loose from his cage and stalked into the cellar of Philosophical Hall. The family was in terror . . . Peale closed the cellar door and window, and in the morning entered and shot the creature. The survivor was killed in its cage and mounted with its mate.*

When the Peale museum closed in the 1840s, Harvard University bought most of the natural history and Indian materials. The bears went to Harvard, along with a leather shirt worn by Meriwether Lewis, and that solitary specimen of Lewis's woodpecker *(Melanerpes lewis)*, among the cartloads of specimens. The shirt is displayed occasionally, and no doubt will be again during the bicentennial of the expedition of Lewis and Clark. The stuffed woodpecker will probably stay where it has been for more than a century—lying on its back in a drawer on the fifth floor of the Peabody Museum of Comparative Zoology. No one has the foggiest notion what happened to the stuffed bears.

143

April 23, 1813, Pike's End

PIKE REMAINS in the army after his return from Mexico. General Wilkinson, whom all men of reasonable intelligence know to be a traitor, survives the Burr fiasco simply by being the first officer to denounce his own co-conspirator. He is required to face a court-martial, but he is also allowed to pick the jury, all officers friendly to him or obligated to him, and he is unsurprisingly exonerated.

Wilkinson remains General of the Army, and his protégé, young Pike, is well taken care of. He is Captain Pike by 1808, Major Pike by 1810, and on the outbreak of the War of 1812 in the summer of that year is promoted to the temporary rank of brigadier general.

Pike's only setback is his inability to gain a special payment from Congress for his two expeditions. He is frustrated that Lewis and Clark gained the thanks of Congress and a special payment. They, he petulantly emphasizes in his own writings, made only *one* voyage, compared to his *two*. On the first mention of Pike's request for special compensation in the House of Representatives, speakers arise to announce that if Lieutenant Pike persists in this petition, they will open a full investigation of his expedition to Santa Fe. And that is the end of that.

Pike, though bound by the limits of activity imposed by a long period of peace, manages to keep himself fully occupied. His most unique effort, prior to the War of 1812, is his creation of a special corps of soldiers hitherto unknown in the United States. He decides that the most powerful weapon on the battlefield is not the musket, nor the bayonet, nor is it the sword. He creates a company of—one cannot make up things like this—pike-men. The pike is a stabbing blade on the end of a long pole. His men are derisively called "Pike's Pikers." Not until he has armed them, drilled them in pike tactics (basically shoulder-to-shoulder advances with the pikes bristling) and failed to excite the interest of any superior officers does Pike desist and disband his pike-men.

In the spring of 1813, an army of invasion is mounted on Lake Ontario, with General Pike in charge of the brigade meant to capture the capital of Upper Canada, a city then known as York, now Toronto. After a safe crossing of Lake Ontario, he lands with his men and meets only token resistance from a small force of Canadian volunteers, who flee without inflicting, or taking, any casualties.

What happens then is not entirely clear. Witnesses agree that, with the Canadians disappearing in the distance, Pike is attracted to a small rise in the otherwise flat plain fronting the capital city. He stands on it, the better to watch the irregular Canadian troops disperse. What he is standing on is the half-cellared powder magazine of the defending army.

The stored gunpowder explodes, hurling Brigadier General Pike through the air and mortally wounding him with fragments of rock from the walls of the magazine. There are two versions of why this happens. The slightly less likely story is that Pike, who is very fond of tobacco, tosses away a smoldering cigar butt, which, falling through the roof of the small and hastily constructed battlefield magazine, ignites the gunpowder. The more reasonable if perhaps the less Greek-tragic and fateful explanation is that the fleeing Canadians, unwilling to see the ammunition stores fall into American hands, set a slow fuse to detonate the powder after their hasty retreat. The first explanation only requires that Pike show the same disregard for his safety so characteristic of his explorations. The second does assume that the dispirited rabble in front of the capital are capable of such foresight.

It is part of the story, or part of the myth, that General Pike on his deathbed asks to be covered with Old Glory, and dies underneath the flag of the United States. That, too, is possible. The only account is from Mrs. Pike, who is at his side, having accompanied him on this expedition. It is mentioned in her petition for an increase in her widow's benefits.

There is a small footnote. The invading Americans decide to burn the archives and government offices in the capital of Upper Canada. It is to revenge that specific insult that, in the early summer of 1814, a British raiding party invades Washington City and burns our capitol building.

144

Death Notices

FOR THE MOST PART, the men of the Corps of Discovery departed this life without further adventures or sufficient notoriety to have anyone notice their passing. George Drouillard, the inestimably valuable hunter and translator, did die sufficiently horribly to be remarked upon at the time. Along with a few other men, Drouillard was trading with the Indians and trapping beaver near the three forks of the Missouri. This is exactly the spot where Meriwether Lewis, in his unfortunate interview with the Indians on the Marias River, promised to build a trading post. The Blackfeet attacked the trappers in the spring of 1810, killing two and wounding several. The remaining men stayed close to the fortified trading post until, in early May, George Drouillard grew bored with inactivity and went out trapping. He made one successful foray, and on the second was surprised by the Blackfeet, killed, dismembered, and left for the coyotes.

John Colter, a woodsman personally recruited by Meriwether Lewis while his keelboat was being built in Pittsburgh, was so enamored of the frontier that he left the returning corps at the Mandan villages and went directly back up the Missouri with some fur trappers who passed the villages in the summer of 1806. Lewis and Clark gave him a supply of powder and lead, and let him keep his Model 1803 rifle. The other enlisted men gave him "useful articles" of their own and all wished him good fortune. Colter, while trading and trapping on the Yellowstone River, may have been the first white to see the volcanic basin of Yellowstone Park. That is highly problematic, but he did see the sulfur springs in what is now called the Sunlight Basin, just east of Yellowstone National Park on the scenic highway to Cody, Wyoming. Colter's most famous exploit, which occurred not far from where George Drouillard was killed, was his run from the Blackfeet. Colter said they had captured him, and while deciding just how to kill him, their war chief suggested letting Colter run for his life, after stripping him naked and taking his moccasins. Colter claimed to have outrun the pursuers (and killed one with the man's own spear), making his way from the Jefferson River to the Madison, and then over the Bozeman Trail to safety on the Yellowstone, among the much more amicable Crow Indians. Some authorities credit Colter with traveling up the Madison into the present-day national park (which would have brought him to the great geyser and mudpot basins). In any case, whatever he saw, Colter's advice after 1810 was that anyone in his right mind would stay out of the country. He died, probably of yellow fever, near his home in Tennessee in 1813.

And then, of course, the Charbonneaus: Pierre lived into the 1840s, last heard of from the Missouri River country; Sacagawea, shortly after giving birth to a second child, a girl, Lisette, died on December 12, 1812. She was living at Fort Manuel, a trading post funded by Manuel Lisa, the St. Louis trader so despised by Lewis and so amicably tolerated by Clark. The cause listed in the fort's daybook was a "putrid fever," probably the result of childbirth and her persistent pelvic infection, the same one treated by Clark at Great Falls in 1805. Lisette and Jean Baptiste became wards of William Clark. Lisette simply disappeared, on an unknown date from unknown causes and is buried God knows where. Pompey really was a gifted child; William Clark was an excellent judge of character. After finishing a modest education in St. Louis, Jean Baptiste went out west, trading and trapping for a few years.

In 1823, at the age of eighteen, he came to the notice of a German prince, Wilhelm of Württemberg, who was traveling the frontier on a recreational shooting and amateur scientific expedition. Jean Baptiste was so remarkable (being three-quarters Indian and able to read and write would be enough to set him apart) that Wilhelm took him home to Germany for more than six years, where Jean Baptiste added French and German to his English. He returned to the west in 1829, and made a living guiding and trapping. He was noticed again by history when he guided the Mormon Battalion from New Mexico to San Diego, California, in the Mexican War of 1848–1849. He must have been a good pathfinder, for they safely crossed the Sonora and Borrego deserts on the march west. He had odd jobs in California, tried his hand at gold mining, and in 1866, at the advanced age of sixty-one, set out for the new gold strikes in Montana. He died of pneumonia in Oregon, on May 16, 1866. He is buried near Danner, Oregon, in the bleak high desert of the Great Basin.

145

Epilogue

DID IT MATTER? All that rowing and poling and walking and riding? The western line of the border between the United States and Canada was not finally fixed until 1846. Our claim to the Oregon country (now, approximately, the states of Washington and Oregon) was so tenuous that a kind of joint occupancy with the British was agreed upon after the War of 1812. The Forty-ninth parallel, that perfectly straight line separating Canada and the United States from Minnesota to Washington (the one that on a Mercator projection map makes a gentle curve) is well north of Lieutenant Pike's headwaters of the Mississippi and Meriwether Lewis's Marias River. It is a line of convenience, not possession. We acquired New Mexico (and the breakaway New Mexican territory of the Texas Republic) after a brief, bloody war of occupation in 1848.

Lewis and Clark's route over the Rockies remained so difficult and remote that a through highway wasn't completed along the Lochsa River until after World War II. The South Pass, the route of the Oregon Trail, was the true way west, and railroads and highways preferred that gentler high desert route, south of the Shoshones' Wind Mountains, and hundreds of miles south of the Corps of Discovery's route.

Pike's expedition to New Mexico produced nothing except bad feelings between Spain and the United States. His last desperate move, crossing the Sangre de Cristos in the dead of winter, was on a trail that remains almost impassable today. Pike's Peak? He never even saw it. His circuitous route to New Mexico, going as far north as the Kansas-Nebraska border and working south along the Front Range of the Rockies, never brought him within a hundred miles of the Santa Fe Trail. Yet, he was a hero in the nineteenth century, as one of the men who opened the west. The last biographies printed of him are two juvenile books, both written at the turn of this century. He has slipped beneath the notice of professional historians.

In fairness, Lewis and Clark were destined never to find the way west, for their charge was to ascend the Missouri to its headwaters, and they were very lucky to have those orders. On the rare occasions when they tried crossing the Great Plains on horseback, they failed utterly. Lewis's exploration of the Marias on horseback resulted in the death of two Blackfeet, and very nearly his own. When that small party detached from Clark's group on the Yellowstone in 1807 to ride cross-country to the Sioux villages, they hadn't been out of the river for twenty-four hours before all their horses were stolen. It was no country for tenderfeet, and for all their resourcefulness, all their tenacity, all their understated bravery, Lewis and Clark were no match for the prairie and the horsemen who controlled it.

Burr continues to fascinate, more for his passionate behaviors (shooting Hamilton and carrying on amorously far beyond any American of his era) than for his wild scheme to become the emperor of the west. He is a likable rogue, endlessly entertaining, ultimately irrelevant.

You could remove all of them from history, and things would turn out very much the same. America would still reach from sea to sea, from Canada to Mexico. The ground was taken first for mines and then for cattle and then for farms. It was crossed, as the Indians receded, by rough wagon tracks and then by railroads. It is sadly unromantic, but true, that in the long run picks and plows far outweigh guns and glory. Work defeats adventure, every time.

Index

About the Author

M.R. MONTGOMERY has been a journalist for thirty years and is the author of five other books. He graduated from Stanford University and the University of Oregon with degrees in American history. A native of Montana, he has returned often in search of the landscape and community that make up the last remnants of the days of bison and longhorns, cowboys and schoolmarms. He lives near Boston with his wife, Florence.